Family, Population and Development in Africa

Family, Population and Development in Africa

Edited by Aderanti Adepoju

Zed Books Ltd
LONDON & NEW JERSEY

Family, Population and Development in Africa was first published
by Zed Books Ltd, 7 Cynthia Street, London N1 9JF, UK,
and 165 First Avenue, Atlantic Highlands, New Jersey 07716,
USA in 1997.

Cover designed by Andrew Corbett
Set in Monotype Garamond by Ewan Smith
Printed and bound in the United Kingdom
by Biddles Ltd, Guildford and King's Lynn

A catalogue record for this book is available from the British
Library

Library of Congress Cataloging-in-Publication Data

Family, population and development in Africa / edited by
    Aderanti Adepoju.
        p.   cm.
    Includes bibliographical references and index.
    ISBN 1-85649-465-9. — ISBN 1-85649-466-7 (pbk.)
    1. Africa—Population.   2. Family—Economic
aspects—Africa.   3. Households—Africa.   4. Africa
Economic conditions—1960–   I. Adepoju. Aderanti.
HB3661.A3P637 1997
304.6'096—dc20

                                        96-22286
                                        CIP

ISBN 1 85649 465 9 cased
ISBN 1 85649 466 7 limp

Contents

Acknowledgements

The preparation for this volume involved several actors at various levels. I was encouraged to raise the theme by my family, both as a contribution to the International Year of the Family (1994) and to reflect on Africa's dramatically changing situation.

The contributing authors have been most cooperative, as was Mrs Diouf, who processed the documents, often several times. Mr Fred Murphy edited the draft chapters, often under pressure.

The publication of this volume is made possible within the context of the 'Population, Human Resources and Development in Africa' project, funded by the United Nations Population Fund (UNFPA). However, the content reflects the individual views of the contributing authors rather than those of UNFPA or the several other UN organizations the authors, myself included, are associated with.

Aderanti Adepoju

Preface

This volume clearly reminds us that the African family indeed has a wide-ranging set of functions and responsibilities that vary with culture, political setting and economic conditions. The African family is still the most crucial socializing agent: it moulds the formative stages of the child whose future is to a large extent conditioned by the socio-economic conditions of the family.

However, the age-long cooperation which nurtured and sustained the coherence of members of the family is now seriously threatened by modernization, urbanization, the disintegration of its members through migration and the effects of the vacillating economic situation in Africa.

The chapters included in this volume vividly illustrate how the dramatic changes in Africa's economic fortunes have adversely undermined the ability of families adequately to meet the basic needs of their members. Concurrently, the deteriorating socio-economic situation has rendered large family size a crushing burden.

Attention is drawn to the wide variety of different marriage forms and types of conjugal relationships in various parts of the region. In spite of changing circumstances, it is also made clear that the extended family by and large has been sustained. Directly or indirectly, decisions on child-bearing are largely family decisions.

Differences in culture, religion, traditions, ecology, political systems, historical evolution and economic structures are indicated in the role and status of women within the family and society.

The reproductive and productive roles of the family are circumvented by a unique set of cultural, institutional and sociological imperatives – an understanding of which should guide relevant policies and programmes designed to improve the condition of life of the family members, bearing in mind the centrality of the African family in both social, economic and political regimes.

All told, it is imperative that macro population and development policies are responsive to the needs of families and their constituent members who are caught in a web of crises – poverty, economic insecurity, political instability and social upheaval.

Lamine Ndiaye
Director, Africa Division
UNFPA, New York

Notes on contributors

Oluwole Adegboyega PhD Demography/Statistics, London School of Economics. Nigerian; UN expert and CTA adviser on censuses, Central Office of Statistics, Gaborone, Botswana.

Aderanti Adepoju A Nigerian economist–demographer, professor and head of the Department of Demography, University of Ife; research professor and dean, Faculty of Business Administration, University of Lagos (Nigeria); UNFPA training coordinator, population, human resources and development in Africa, Dakar (Senegal). Recent publications: editor of *Swaziland, Population, Economy, Society*, UNFPA New York, 1991; editor of *The Impact of Structural Adjustment on the Population of Africa*, James Currey, London, 1993; co-editor with C. Oppong of *Gender, Work and Population in Sub-Saharan Africa*, James Currey, London 1994. Has published several articles and contributed chapters of books on migration, population policy and development issues.

Alice Armstrong PhD Law, University of Copenhagen. Dutch; regional coordinator women and law in Southern Africa (WLSA) Research Project, Harare, Zimbabwe; former lecturer in law, University of Swaziland, Kwaluseni, Swaziland. Expert in law and women's issues.

A. F. Aryee Ghanaian sociologist; research fellow at the Regional Institute of Population Studies, University of Ghana. Specialist on nuptiality.

Sally E. Findley American associate clinical professor of public health, Center for Population and Family Health, Columbia University. Specialist on Migration; co-researcher with CERPOD, Bamako, Mali.

P. K. Makinwa-Adebusoye DSc. Harvard; Nigerian; professor, population scientist and head, Population Unit, Nigerian Institute of Social and Economic Research, Ibadan, Nigeria.

Wariara Mbugua BA Princeton, MA, PhD, Pennsylvania, USA. A Kenyan sociologist-demographer, she was head of research, Centre for African Family Studies, Nairobi; former lecturer, Population Research and Studies Institute, University of Nairobi, now regional adviser, women and development, UNFPA, Harare.

James P. M. Ntozi PhD Demography, London School of Hygiene and

Tropical Medicine. Ugandan demographer, associate professor and head, Institute of Applied Statistics and Economics, University of Kampala, Uganda.

A. B. C. Ocholla-Ayayo Kenyan anthropologist; associate professor, Population Studies and Research Institute, University of Nairobi, Kenya.

Christine Oppong PhD, Cambridge. British (Ghanaian by marriage). Senior anthropologist with ILO Geneva. Lectured at the University of Ghana. Specialist on gender issues, published extensively on the subject.

John B. Ssekamatte-Ssebuliba Ugandan; social demographer; lecturer and head, Department of Population Studies, Makerere University.

CHAPTER I

Introduction

Aderanti Adepoju

In recent years questions about the efficacy and the appropriateness of development strategies and models in Africa have arisen as a result of overwhelming evidence that important indicators of well-being are showing a downward trend instead of the expected secular upward trend (UNDP, 1994). Indicators such as per capita income, infant mortality, literacy rates and so forth in many African countries have either stagnated or declined to levels observed 10 years ago or earlier. This has happened despite development interventions purported to lead to an increase in food production, to provide accessible health services to all and to ensure that new cohorts of children are better educated than their predecessors.

In response to this, leaders and planners in Africa have endeavoured to grapple with the difficult problem of trying to arrive at a workable solution to the variety of crises precipitated by the continued impoverishment of a large proportion of Africa's population. An important breakthrough has been the emerging consensus that development efforts in Africa must reflect not just the gravity of the problems but their complexity as well. In this respect one of the principles that has been adopted is the need to establish linkages in thus far disparate development efforts in order to achieve sustainable development (OAU, 1981). This has been informed by the observed complex interactions between population trends, development and the environment. Thus a reconsideration of how the management of population and of the environment can effectively be linked together in order to achieve the elusive goal of sustainable development has occupied the attention of a wide spectrum of Africans, including planners, researchers, intellectuals, activists, leaders and many more over the past decade (UNECA, 1992a).

For a long time population was treated as an endogenous variable in the development equation. Population was seen to be a factor that was influenced by various development parameters, but not vice versa. Misgivings about the inappropriateness of such an equation for Africa led to its restatement when African governments convened for the second African Conference on Population in Arusha in 1984. They adopted the Kilimanjaro Plan of Action which focused governments' attention on the crucial need to acknowledge the causal linkage between population and development efforts, and consequently to integrate population variables in the planning process. The urgency of formulating comprehensive population policies was underscored as a framework within which such linkages can best be understood and tackled (UNECA, 1984).

The Earth Summit in Rio de Janeiro further crystallized the perception that the rational management of the environment is critical to the achievement of development which can be sustained for generations to come. In Rio, therefore, the triangular relationship between population, environment and sustainable development was consolidated.

While strongly reinforcing this perception, the third African Conference on Population in Dakar, Senegal in 1992, introduced an additional specificity to the African context, that of the centrality of the family as the vital but missing link in the interdependent population–development–environment interrelationship. Conceptually the inclusion of the family in this scenario was informed by the fact that the family in Africa has been and still remains the basic unit of reproduction (population growth), production (development) and consumption (environmental resources) (UNECA, 1994a).

The context of population policies

As a means of addressing the undesirable consequences of population growth, African governments have taken bold steps to ameliorate perceived population problems such as high rates of population growth, unprecedented levels of teenage childbearing, unfettered growth of cities consequent upon rural–urban migration, and so on. Thus far 18 countries in Africa have adopted comprehensive population policies, and almost 25 are in various stages of doing so. Yet a review of these policies indicates that progress has been slow, primarily because of misconceived or inappropriately packaged programmes (Adepoju, 1994a).

Not surprisingly, therefore, the cultural and economic justifications for high fertility in Africa persist (Sadik, 1989). Early marriages continue to take place despite legislation to the contrary. The onset of childbearing is also early leading to a variety of problems, not least of which is that it denies many women the opportunity of enacting alternative roles to that of maternity. Infant and child mortality remain unacceptably high as does maternal mortality, currently the highest in any part of the world. The incidence of abandoned babies has reached alarming proportions and the practice of unsafe abortion and its sequelae are straining the meagre and already overstretched health services and resources. Polygyny, in its various forms, remains a norm in most African societies and has recently surfaced in the cities and urban areas, posing a challenge to residential arrangements and introducing unknown but potentially complicating factors to the already crowded urban dwellings (Mbugua, 1992; Marindo-Ranganai, 1994).

Attempts to address these issues, however, have met with limited success because interventions have been misconceived and the centrality of the family in determining observed behaviour has not been taken into account. In all matters pertaining to reproduction, the family in Africa remains the fundamental unit on which all decisions are based. Therefore policies to effect changes in various population parameters, such as fertility, mortality and migration, need to contend with the pressures exerted by the family on the individual members of the family – pressures that may appear irrational but which in fact are based on sound social expectations.

Persistence of traditional mores

In the traditional setting, marriage as the basis of procreation was a prolonged process between two families and not between individual members of those families. Even the selection of mates was in the hands of the family. This process reflected the fundamental role of the family as the basis of all life-cycle events, a role reinforced by the entire socialization process being entrusted to the family. Thus a marriage was not a discrete event in the life of a family but part of a continuum of responsibilities, not simply activities, that included births, namings, initiations, funerals and other rituals. Today, despite the changes that have occurred, family norms and values governing procreation have not yet been eroded, as is witnessed by the persistence of such practices as the payment – and the expectation of such payment – of bridewealth or dowry by Africans from all walks of life (Brown, 1950; Ngondo, 1992; Locoh, 1991; Adepoju, 1994b).

Such values, norms and responsibilities also justify the family's need, and the strategies it adopts, to perpetuate its own lineage. These factors have sometimes reinforced large family sizes and a preference for male children, because male children alone carry the responsibility for the survival of the lineage. Since inheritance is tied up with lineage perpetuation, women will hedge against being disinherited by bearing many children so that the sex composition, as well as the children's survival probabilities, guarantees that they have at least one or two sons who will obtain a portion of the family fortune. In many African cultures today women without surviving sons are condemned to destitution upon the death of their spouse because they cannot inherit his property in their own right. The survival of male children also acts as a deterrent to divorce and desertion, for similar reasons.

Although for a long time demographers and other social scientists anticipated the demise of polygyny as a result of westernization and urbanization, its resistance to change as an institution has been a symptom of its continuing utility as a family form. In the traditional context polygyny served as a source of power and prestige because it epitomized the self-sufficiency of labour in the predominantly rural economies (Marindo-Ranganai, 1994). In modern times the survival of polygyny is still attributable to its continuing relevance to family-based entrepreneurial initiatives, where the imperative to keep family resources in the hands of the family is achieved by letting co-wives manage different sectors. A new coping mechanism for the polygynous family in modern times has been the introduction of separate and distant residences of co-wives, sometimes in different towns, as a way of optimizing family-controlled resource generation and management (Ngondo, 1992).

In spite of these types of evidence of how the family continues to exert its influence on the majority of Africans, policies to regulate population growth in African countries have been translated into narrowly focused family planning programmes with messages targeted solely at women. However, if such messages are effectively to change fertility behaviour, they have to take account of the complex nature of fertility decision making within the African family context (Adepoju and Mbugua, 1994). Such decisions are made within an intricate power structure which takes account of gender relations as well as age differentials, and the privileges within each socio-cultural set-up that accrue to each.

The characteristic feature of African families as multi-generational units means that each generation brings to bear on all important decisions different experiences, expectations and exposure to events that have shaped its perceptions. Fertility decision making is as influenced by all these multi-generational norms, values and beliefs as are decisions, for example, on how land under the care of the family is to be utilized (Findley et al., 1995). Moreover the co-residential arrangements of multi-generational families put relentless daily pressure on the younger generation to conform to the expected reproductive behaviour, in a manner which is far more concentrated than when such generations are living apart. Consequently family planning messages must be segmented and targeted at each locus of power within the family, to cater to the different stakeholders within the family who have a capacity to influence the overall sequence of the fertility decision-making process. In most cases today, simply because the manifestation of fertility is portrayed by women, policy tends to target and focus on them in isolation, in attempts to reduce fertility for example. Whereas this has an intrinsic value because women bear the brunt of ill-health as a result of a high tempo of childbearing, the fertility decision-making process is much more complex, and does not rest with women alone.

The current slow uptake of family planning practices in Africa can in fact be partially explained by the strong resistance of the older generations who are in constant ideological conflict with the younger generations. However, the former often have the resources, both tangible and intangible, to impose their wishes regarding reproductive issues on the latter. It is also because the older generations, who are the custodians of family land and can decide how it is used, are left out of important aspects of population policies that efforts to improve the nutritional status of various segments of the population can and often do fail. To a very significant extent access to land, and even the form that access takes, is controlled by the older generations on behalf of the family. Land adjudication systems, in many instances, have not succeeded in breaking this pattern. So what crops are to be planted, what proportion is to be sold and even which portions of land are to be used and for how long, are decisions that are often made in response to changes in the family structure rather than in response to food prices or the perceived need to cater for the nutritional well-being of members of the family. It is therefore common in Africa to see malnutrition of children and women in the midst of a surplus of certain types of crops or alongside vast tracts of seemingly under-utilized land.

By the same token the success of health policies is frustrated because the health-seeking behaviour of mothers and their children is controlled by someone else, usually an older relative. In several African societies, men take decisions on such 'women's issues' as prenatal care, postnatal care, child care and family planning.

Research in Africa has also revealed that the pronatalistic nature of African men which discourages the small family norm and promotes a preference for marrying very young girls is not only a phenomenon of uneducated men but also, and increasingly, of well-educated men (Oppong, 1994; Ngondo, 1992). The reasons for this are imbedded more in the nature and structure of the family than in individual men's pursuits. Consequently the opposition to male attitudes in matters pertaining to the family formation process, be it marrying very young girls or discoursing the adoption of family planning, is seen as challenging and undermining men's authority and decision-making responsibilities on behalf of and in the interests of the family. Such responsibilities are perceived to override the preferences and desires of the individual man or woman, or even couple. So, as long as there is a failure to recognize the interconnection between the family's productive and reproductive activities, and how these in turn are manifested by different members of the family, population policies will continue to be out of step with the reality of the lives of the people.

Development strategies

The paradigms of development used in Africa have to a large extent paid scant regard to the family as a dynamic source of change as well as a recipient of change. Yet structural adjustment programmes have provided unequivocal demonstration that in Africa it is the family as an entity – rather than the individual members of the family – which defines the types of adaptation mechanisms as well as the boundaries of adaptation parameters employed by each member of the family (Adepoju, 1994a). That there are exceptions to the rule is not in doubt; however, the pervasiveness of the influence of the family in the everyday lives of Africans of vitually all social and economic standings has created a challenge that requires the centrality of the family to be acknowledged in development planning.

An often-heard criticism of development planning and its failure to attain its intended objectives in Africa in the 1960s and the 1970s is that it was not people centred, being mainly focused on growth in the economy. The 1980s have come to be known as the lost decade because development planning failed to improve the living conditions of the majority of Africans (UNDP, 1993). If anything, certain key indicators of development have deteriorated.

Given this dismal track record, the International Labour Offiice (ILO) refocused attention on the importance of adopting a basic needs strategy the essence of which is to ensure that people obtain remunerative employment, a minimum level of good health and sanitation, adequate shelter and that poverty alleviation becomes central to development efforts (ILO, 1976). Such a strategy was based on experience which indicated that it is possible to have economic growth both without distribution and without development. So for development to be meaningful it has also to be egalitarian.

More recently the UNDP has adopted the concept of human development which brings to the fore issues such as human capacity building, literacy, access to infrastructure, reduction of infant mortality rates and enhancing life expectancy as measures of development. This is in contrast to measures of abstract economic growth which formerly passed as indicators of development (UNDP, 1993).

In the midst of this process of rethinking development it is crucial to recognize that, in the African situation in particular, the family is the pivot around which development indicators radiate. Their measurement therefore needs to be linked to the family because they share the same fate. In spite of changes that have occurred to the African family, it still remains fundamentally the primary unit of production and consumption. It supplies all the factors of production – land, labour and technology, no matter how rudimentary. Within it a gender division of labour obtains, with women as the specialists in almost all aspects of food production, both for consumption as well as for supplementing the family income.

In traditional settings the family has also been the basis of informal sector activities. These have now metamorphosized into the modern informal sector activities incorporating the apprentice system. In most

African countries today the informal sector has become the 'sponge' absorbing the rapidly growing labour force, and often serves as the springboard to entering the market economy (ILO, 1991). Another coping strategy adopted by the family in the face of economic crises is migration (see below 'Spatial mobility and labour migration').

An important and enduring function of the family that has not been taken into account in development planning is its role as the provider of social security for all its members, regardless of whether they have worked in the formal sector and have some form of pension or not. In any case even pensions (if and when they are obtained) are considered part and parcel of the family resources and are usually invested in one family enterprise or another. In the industrialized countries social security payments take a rather significant proportion of government spending. In Africa this burden is largely borne, and in some countries almost entirely so, by the family. Development planning should therefore focus on how to ensure that the family performs better in this role, which given the current trends is likely to continue to exist for a considerable time.

Environmental degradation

The physical environment of the African continent is very heterogeneous. It consists of fragile arid and semi-arid ecosystems which coexist with the more stable rainforests and coastal lowlands. Resource endowments are, therefore, largely determined by the ecological patterns prevailing. The stable ecologies support the more lucrative cash crops, while the more arid areas are stretched to their limits by subsistence farming and the rearing of livestock. The seasonality and the precariousness of the weather complete the picture of Africa's varied environmental system (UAPS, 1992).

Given the rudimentary nature of the technology available to the majority of Africans, a continuous battle is fought against environmental degradation in the context of high population growth rates and increasing demand by families for fertile agricultural land. Because of environmental degradation, women and children have been saddled with an increased workload associated with the search for water and fuelwood. For women the task of managing an increasingly deteriorating environment, worsened by hazards such as constant floods, droughts, locust invasions and so forth, and making it yield some sustenance for the family is fast becoming a dauntingly complex affair; it is challenging their ingenuity and all the resources at their disposal, periodically occasioning massive losses of resources and displacing whole families and communities (Findley and Ouedraogo, 1993).

However, natural calamities are not the only cause of environmental problems. Developments paradigms which have focused exclusively on taxes, trade and related economic issues have failed dismally to embrace the issue of environmental protection, and particularly how it can be linked more closely with the everyday lives of those most affected by environmental degradation. Questions of nature conservation and renewable natural resource sustainability were evidently omitted altogether from development 'mega-projects' such as hydro-electric dams, which have contributed significantly to the displacement of thousands of families and the destruction of natural resources, rather than structuring a harvestable village-based yield. Various large bilateral and multilateral endeavours were taken to promote a vision of economic and social progress that had no apparent comprehension of ecology or conservation – attempting to use economic solutions to resolve non-economic problems. The consequential aftermath has largely been left to families to contend with as best as they can.

Family transformation

The family, globally, has been undergoing rapid transformation as a result of social changes, modernization, development and the recent economic crisis (UN, 1991b). The family in Africa is no exception. It is perhaps for this reason that it has been argued there is no such thing as *the* African family; and quite rightly so, if such a concept implies homogeneity of form.

In fact, due to a variety of interlocking factors, the family in Africa is still in a state of flux; it is sandwiched between tradition and modernity, between tyrannical regimes and democratic reforms. But although it may have taken many diverse forms, it is the African family rather than some other institution(s) that primarily continues to bear the burden of the various stresses being experienced in the different sectors of society, be they economic, social, political or of a different kind. In that respect, therefore, the significance of the African family in terms of functions and responsibilities has probably increased rather than decreased. So even in the different forms that it has assumed, the family remains the most fundamental and basic social unit.

So what changes have been experienced by the African family? Perhaps the most obvious are the structural changes. Today, although the traditional extended family survives, in some cultures it is neither residential, nor does it consist of kith and kin only because natural or man-made catastrophes have reinforced the family as the safe haven of first resort. Additionally dual families with a singular head, which are bi-residential rather than co-residential, have emerged as a new version of the traditional polygamous family. They are based largely on the need to maximize income through the participation in economic activities of all the spouses, as well as other adult family members – including children when they come of age. Families without adult male kin have also proliferated. These consist of female-headed households, where the males have migrated, died or simply deserted (Adepoju and Mbugua, 1994). Africa is also witnessing the spectacle of families being headed by children as a result of very early pregnancy, demise of the parental generation through armed conflict, as well as the scourge of AIDS. None the less, despite these intense problems, familial obligations to siblings, children, in-laws and other relatives remain strong.

Gender concerns in the family

Interest in how development has impacted on women has focused attention on their role within the family. Although the variations are wide, there has been a surprising tenacity displayed in the maintenance of some of the traditional roles of women, often reinforced by development concepts that are based on an unclear understanding of how the family exerts control over the functions of African women. By the same token, however, faced with the need to adapt itself in the face of new crises the family has also innovated new roles for women. The coexistence of the traditional and the emergent new roles of women within the family is often glossed over, leading to a rather simplistic interpretation of women's lives.

Within the traditional African society, the family was the major source of social status for women. Even in the midst of the evolution of gender roles this remains the case for the large majority of African women. Thus women's status is largely a derived status – she is someone's wife, the mother of a son and to a lesser extent someone's daughter. Logically it follows that any woman who is married enjoys – or is seen to attain – higher status than an unmarried one. Having children confers still additional status. In many Africa cultures, therefore, the value of the bride price to some extent symbolizes the status of the woman: this varies from 20 head of cattle in Swaziland up to 200 cattle among the Dinkas of Southern Sudan. Failure to stay within a marriage, often persevering in difficult circumstances, or to bear children, is enough reason to recall the bride price or bridewealth. In fact the persistence of the bride price, albeit in increasingly different forms, in the face of the increasing modernity of conjugal relationships is a good example of how the family still retains its grip on individuals – even in respect of the most intimate of matters.

Likewise in the past, polygyny was a practical response to the generally low sex ratios – there being more females than males – as well as a solution to the demand for labour. However, this practice was reinforced by tradition, with marriage being a major preoccupation for women, and indeed their parents, primarily because only through marriage could women gain access to any means of production. Hence parents eagerly awaited the occasion to marry off their daughter(s) soon after they reached puberty, which in several societies can be as early as 14 years or even less. So for many African men wealth is still manifested by marrying the next wife: traditionally wives are status symbols. The elder wife plays a visible role in the process: she is to be consulted, and in most cases chooses the next wife and acts as her mother, socializing and supervising her in the new setting.

That polygyny continues to thrive in many parts of Africa, with marriage still being almost universal and age at marriage persisting at under 18 years for 90 per cent of the women in Africa (Mbugua, 1992) attests to the relevance of cultural supports to such behaviour: behaviour which, from an African perspective, is based on sound economic sense. Such behaviour finds sufficient rationale in the fact that in the low technology production systems which are the mainstay of Africa's rural majority, the labour of women and children is largely controlled by the family and remains an indispensable lifeline, vital to the very existence of the family. Child labour is widespread and unlikely to be affected by laws and regulations imposing child labour restrictions because it is not of an organized commercial nature, but is rather perceived as a legitimate role for children. The assistance that children provide – in child caring, herding and fetching water or fuelwood – releases the adults, especially women, to undertake more urgent and major tasks. Thus in seasons when extra hands are needed to pitch in, families perceive no contradiction in withdrawing girls from school so that they can help, because all children are considered a family resource at all times.

The fact that such behaviour perpetuates the cycle of poverty, particularly among women who lose opportunities for skill development and to enter the job market, can only be understood if one examines the broader picture of how the family functions. There is, for example, a clear rationale on how the prerogative of investment in different family members, which is held by the family though culturally determined, is exercised. In turn differentiated investment in family members, particularly by gender, tends to be made according to who is perceived to be most likely to bring the highest returns on that investment. In most cases this boosts biased family investment in education in favour of boys.

But as the family in Africa is forced to adapt to changes emanating from without, it is having to redefine some of the roles assigned to different members of the family. This process of adaptation is one of the prime causes of the stresses being experienced and is responsible for the different family permutations that have been observed to be taking shape. These include female-headed families, dual households, families with non-kin dependants, children assuming familial responsibilities over their siblings and so forth (Mbugua, 1992). In all cases women are having to assume or are assigned new roles that sometimes deviate considerably from traditional ones, because the exigencies of the family demand it. In contrast the African man is losing some important traditional roles, without adopting new ones. This represents one of the crucial mismatches between current policies, which more often than not are based on outmoded notions of a normative type of family structure, and the prevailing situation.

None of the changes that are emerging have eroded the African families' hold and control over African women, and it is therefore important that policies to improve the situation of women take this into account. Moreover, while it appears evident that women operate under a lot of constraints, it should be kept in mind that the family imposes constraints of various kinds on all its members, whether on the basis of gender, age or marital status. Therefore the lot of women is intricately tied up with the family and addressing one issue means also addressing the others. This needs to be constantly kept in mind since attempts to transplant concepts of gender equality and equity which have worked elsewhere, without a thorough critique of their relevance, appropriateness and suitability to Africa, are bound to fail – or, at worst, confound the lot of African women. Such models, while clearly seeking to emancipate women from the burden of subordination, must be first adapted to the context of African women's lives within the family. For example, studies have shown that in some countries women would rather forego autonomy, in terms of economic empowerment, if it means that they become socially alienated from members of their extended family (Armstrong et al., 1993).

Spatial mobility and labour migration

One strategy that the family uses to recover its investment in selected members of the family is migration. Propelled by the economic crisis, migration today has become an increasingly important coping mechanism for the very survival of the family (Adepoju, 1991c). Decisions about who should migrate, where and for how long are therefore still sanctioned, if not completely controlled, by the family. This promotes the inter-generational flow of resources within the context of the family through migrant remittances.

Since until recently migration was sanctioned only for the male members of the family, investment in education was also overwhelmingly in their favour. Some of the changes being observed involved rising levels of female migration, a large proportion of which comprises autonomous female migration. To the extent that this is a relatively new phenomenon, it constitutes important changes in gender roles in Africa. This search for better economic opportunities results not only in new forms of family but also creates new challenges for policy.

At the same time, however, labour migration, mostly of males, is resulting in the assumption of new roles among women who are left behind. They become the resource managers and decision makers, particularly within the agricultural sector. How such women, who head families with a high proportion of other women and children, can be effectively reached and assisted by policy becomes another area of concern.

Civil strife and its effect on the family

The presence of conflict in Africa has had a profound impact on the family which is likely to have far-reaching effects. At the time of writing there are no less than 16 conflicts in Africa, ranging from the sporadic urban violence of South Africa to the decades-old wars of Angola, Mozambique and Sudan. One of the immediate consequences of the strife in Africa is the burden of the maimed and the disabled that is placed on the family, since rehabilitation of such people by governments is far from adequate.

The maiming continues even in those countries where the fighting has abated because of the types of weapon used during the conflict, the most dangerous being land mines and similar anti-personnel devices. It is estimated that in Africa there are currently between 5 and 10 million land mines planted all over the countryside in such states as Angola, Mozambique and even parts of Zimbabwe. These pose major threats to civilians years after hostilities have ceased and complicate the task of providing aid to war victims. It also hinders the return of refugees to their traditional occupation – farming. The situation is seriously aggravated by the fact that land mines were laid without maps, and made to instil fear in civilians (*International Herald Tribune*, 17 December 1993, p. 3). Even though, in countries such as Zimbabwe, large tracts of arable farmland where it is thought that land mines were laid have been cordoned off, the danger still exists. So many innocent victims such as children, women and the elderly continue to suffer the indiscriminate destructiveness of the land mines and, with no compensation forthcoming from the government, it remains for the family to look after such victims as best as it can.

In Angola, Mozambique and to a lesser extent Liberia, the basic infrastructure – schools, hospitals and homes – was devastated by war and members of the family scattered. A whole generation of Africans in these countries are therefore growing up without the basic necessities. In fact a major adverse and lasting effect of the civil conflicts in several countries in Africa – Liberia, Uganda, Sudan, Mozambique, Angola – is that 'children have grown up more able to recognise the sound of each different gun' than the alphabets, and are destined to remain illiterate and destitute. Family fortunes have similarly been wiped out. For example, among the Dinkas of Southern Sudan bridewealth used to be around 200 cows; now, as cattle herds have been decimated by drought and war, parents are willing to marry their daughters for only 10 head of cattle (*The Economist*, 12–18 Feb., 1994).

There are, however, more insidious and longer-term effects of war on the family, the consequences of which will be felt for perhaps generations to come: the acclimatization to violence. While death was traditionally feared and appeased by prolonged mourning – indeed an entire village used to mourn the death of one of its members by abstaining from singing or dancing for a week – that practice has now declined as death is so commonplace (*The Economist*, 12–18 Feb., 1994, p. 60). In the recent genocidal conflict in Rwanda for example, children were forced to witness the killing of their parents and siblings; and rape was continued on such a massive scale that nine months later, abandoned babies filled up the orphanages in the predominantly Catholic country where access to abortion is difficult. Such widespread killing and the abandoning of babies runs counter to strongly held family values and may have unknown implications for the victims in the future. High mortality rates in Africa are also in direct contrast to many developed countries where the patterns of mortality are much more predictable, based primarily on the prevailing epidemiological structure.

Just as serious is the issue of child soldiers in countries such as Liberia, Uganda, Somalia and Mozambique, which assumes particular importance within the context of the family. These children are often the product of violence themselves, having witnessed the violent death of one or both parents, siblings and other kin members. As a result, they have grown up feeling rejected and alienated, and, with no familial ties or support, have turned to a culture of violence, drugs and delinquency. Since most are orphaned, they have survived on their own in the bush for years, missing out on education and losing touch in their formative years with societal values and norms. Their future is bleak indeed. They represent a new phenomenon in Africa: a generation virtually delinked from the family. Policies and development efforts now have to contend with them and their problems.

A scantly documented phenomenon is the presence of large numbers of children born to women abducted during times of conflict. At the end of the conflicts, soldiers are demobilized and return to their original wives and children, completely abandoning their wartime families. In Mozambique and Uganda the number of children from such unions is estimated to be in the thousands. In fact in Uganda these children have been nicknamed 'broad-based children', because the demobilization of soldiers which led to widespread public knowledge of their existence coincided with the setting up of a broad-based multi-party government. Few governments emerging from periods of prolonged conflict are inclined to address such social issues, pressed as they are to rebuild their destroyed infrastructures. It is the families or relatives of the freed women who are compelled to take them and their children in and provide whatever rehabilitation they can.

Another consequence of war and internal strife on the family in Africa is the refugee problem. Refugee families are confronted by several problems. In the process of flight, families lose all or most of their belongings, property and land, and consequently often become hopelessly dependent on either local hospitality, if settled spontaneously among kith and kin across the borders, or on food aid if in camps. Family members are often separated, with young men away fighting at the war front or killed, leaving children, women and old men in camps. In the process the family as an organization is severely disrupted.

Refugees are often settled in artificial environments and situations rather than in communities which function normally. Given the gender imbalance in refugee camps, social relations become distorted. Marriages are often no longer contrived as family affairs, divorce tends to be high, and social norms and values are diffused. The loss of the extended family and its traditional base for the care of the disabled, old people and orphans means that other forms of institutional arrangements have to be put in place.

Once the initial trauma is overcome, refugees need tremendous strength to care for themselves. All too often the dangers, uncertainties and risks in refugee camps are overwhelming and refugees lead a life of constant insecurity – physically, socially and spiritually. In several cases, the initial local support and hospitality has turned sour and this has been manifested by resentment in the local recipient population. Men lose self-respect as opportunities for gainful employment are non-existent, hence their dignity is lost in the camps while women are exposed to gender violence and the daily struggle to keep their tattered families together.

Structural adjustment programmes

In several African countries, the transitional costs of structural adjustment programmes through IMF and World Bank conditionalities have had a multiplicity of effects on the African family. At the macro level, the African family has borne the brunt of government reductions in spending in the social sectors. Access to education, health and other social services has been curtailed, thus reducing the overall welfare of the family as a unit – particularly the poorer ones (Adepoju, 1994a). The removal of subsidies on basic food items such as rice in Liberia and maize meal in Zambia has raised their prices far beyond the reach of a significant proportion of families. Also, because of increasing prices of fuel, the family is compelled to turn to cheaper sources of fuel such as firewood and charcoal – with obvious consequences for the environment.

The case of Tanzania is typical. Before structural adjustment programmes were introduced, 90 per cent of women gave birth in clinics. Afterwards only 40 per cent could afford to do so. The rest who could no longer afford to go to clinics delivered at home, sometimes with the help of relatives or traditional birth attendants, but sometimes alone.

The gender division of labour in the family has also been aggravated because two things have happened simultaneously. first, men who were formerly more likely to be in wage employment have lost their jobs through retrenchments. Second, as a consequence women have been forced to seek additional income-generating activities in an attempt to keep family income constant. The result is that women's labour has increased tremendously while that of men has in many instances been reduced. In the process, women's ability to perform their traditional family welfare and nurturing roles has been seriously compromised. One of the phenomena increasingly being observed is mothers delegating their domestic duties to their daughters, often very young ones, so that the mothers can go out and earn some money to buy necessities. Not only are many of the young girls incapable of performing adult tasks, but it is likely that they frequently endanger the lives of their siblings while handling fire during cooking or when using hot water. Also seen is the emergence of families of beggars who are now joining the hordes of street children in urban areas of Tanzania and elsewhere.

Structural adjustment programmes have also had serious consequences for the family at the micro level. Forced to do more with less, the family has developed a variety of survival strategies ranging from selective migration to differential investment in education for its various members. These survival strategies have led to new residential patterns, changing income streams, different types of health seeking behaviour as well as expenditure patterns.

In the context of structural adjustment, therefore, the African family has acted as the safe haven of last resort. It has had to provide social security for its retrenched members; seek whatever employment compensation that it can find and psychologically sustain its large numbers of out-of-work able-bodied men and women. Newly developed social safety nets which are meant to ameliorate some of the negative impacts of the structural programmes are unlikely to challenge this role for the family because they are essentially of a short-term nature and do not cover more than a small fraction of those workers affected. They are little more than a palliative.

Health and the family

Undoubtedly one of the most serious challenges to the well-being of the family in Africa today is the HIV/AIDS pandemic. Because of a variety of cultural and social practices, the African family as a unit is being affected by HIV/AIDS in ways that appear to be quite peculiar to the region. Transmission of HIV/AIDS in the region is almost universally heterosexual; infection through drug abuse, blood transfusion and homosexual contact is so low as to be negligible. This means that everyone who is sexually active is at risk, as well as infants born to seropositive mothers.

There are probably four social and cultural behaviours common to Africa that support the spread of HIV/AIDS in general and promote its spread among family members specifically. First is the early age of first sexual contact. Recent Demographic and Health Surveys (DHS) in several countries in Africa show a very early age of entry into sexual activity. These data are supported in many instances by small-scale sub-national studies in countries such as Kenya, Zambia and Zimbabwe which suggest that entry into sexual activity for a large number of boys and girls at ages of 12 and 13 years respectively is not uncommon. Early age at first sexual contact exposes young people to HIV/AIDS much earlier and consequently for a longer period of their lives, raising the probability of contracting the disease.

Second is a variety of traditional practices that foster the transmission of HIV/AIDS. In many African societies, particularly in East and South Africa, the practice of levirate or 'inheritance of wives by surviving brothers' still thrives. In some areas levirate is responsible for wiping out entire extended families because spouse(s) of the dead man had already been infected with HIV (*The New York Times*, 17 Sept., 1990, p. 14). Despite campaigns to eradicate the practice it has proved to be resistant to change because it is so closely linked to the distribution and right to the wealth and property of the deceased.

Other negative cultural practices are fostered by the family: by parents in the case of young girls, and husbands in the case of wives. Initiation rights for young girls continue and take many forms in Africa. The majority involve the physical violation of the integrity of the female body and primarily the reproductive organs. Married women on the other hand are expected to use herbicides to dry their vaginal secretions in order to heighten male sexual enjoyment. Both practices leave women highly susceptible to lacerations during sexual intercourse. Studies based in teaching hospitals have shown that women who use herbicides are 10 times more likely to contract HIV.

Third is the practice of having multiple sexual partners. This is most common among males because of culturally sanctioned polygynous marriages, concubinage and tacitly acknowledged mistresses and girlfriends. However, studies show that it is also increasing among females as a result of marital dissolutions and the pressure to commoditize sex in exchange for financial gain as the African economies continue to suffer. This is facilitated by the spatial mobility and labour migration of both men and women which is now quite common. So by separating spouses, altering sex ratios and creating markets for prostitution, labour migration has already been documented *inter alia* to facilitate the spread of AIDS (Oppong, 1993; Lalou and Piche, 1994)

Fourth is the African male's unwillingness to use condoms. The combination of non-condom use and multiple partners is particularly favourable to HIV/AIDS transmission. What makes it worse is that, while girlfriends and mistresses are more likely to demand that condoms be used, the same does not apply to wives. What is therefore being witnessed in Africa is very high HIV/AIDS transmission among married women from their husbands. So alarming is this trend that a debate has now erupted over demands that the medical profession suspends client confidentiality and informs the uninfected spouse that her/his partner is seropositive.

The overall impact of HIV/AIDS on the family is also considerable. While perhaps the impact of AIDS mortality is better known, the effects of morbidity associated with AIDS are less visible but no less burdensome. It is the family that undertakes the long-term and time-consuming nursing of its stricken members, while AIDS orphans also become the responsibility of the surviving kith and kin.

The need for linkages

The wide-ranging and complex web of problems and potential strengths discussed in the above sections suggest that, to achieve sustainable development, there is an obvious but critical need to make some conceptual realignment between the management of the population, the management of the environment and the desire for economic growth. This realignment should recognize the centrality of the family as the focal point of any people-centred development. Past attempts to compartmentalize the family into different target groups for each sector have yielded poor results because such paradigms have been, and continue to be, at best inappropriate and at worst irrelevant.

In spite of all the pressures brought to bear on it, the African family has not disintegrated; rather its roles and structure have undergone dramatic changes in response to the economic crisis, environmental deterioration and rapid expansion of the population. Its resilience centred around the norms, values, practices and beliefs that sustain it beyond one crisis after another; these have made it able to withstand the onslaught of westernization, urbanization, formal education and an unprecedented multimedia blitz. Such a steadfast unit is clearly worthy and deserving of more attention than has been accorded to it thus far (Mbugua, 1992).

As a way of redirecting attention to the persistence of the family as the most enduring and fundamental unit of society, the United Nations General Assembly proclaimed 1994 as the International Year of the Family.

Activities related to the Year of the Family were used to create greater awareness of the need to rethink strategies: to strengthen the family, to make it more efficient in its functions and to incorporate it as an integral institution of development planning.

Summary of chapters

Chapter 2 reviews the problem of data availability facing researchers and policy makers concerned with the African family. While persisting institutional and financial constraints present problems that will not easily be solved, rich data sources are available in most African countries. Among the most important are anthropological studies of the family, censuses and demographic surveys. Before examining these in considerable detail, the authors discuss the implications for data collection and analysis of the conceptual distinction between the 'family', as a basic social unit, and the 'household' as an economic unit. The latter offers 'a more flexible concept which allows the collection of standardized data' by means of the practice of 'listing all members of a household in terms of their relationship to the head of the household.' The authors suggest ways in which household data can then be reconfigured to provide insights into family structure and sketch typologies of families and households. The authors go on to stress the need to generate more useful data through studies – both quantitative and qualitative – focused specifically on the family unit.

In Chapter 3, the authors present an overview of the multiple challenges facing the African family and society today. While the family is 'caught in a web of socio-economic disequilibrium [marked by] galloping inflation, chronic unemployment, malnutrition, poverty and illiteracy', it is at the same time 'sustained by a unique set of cultural, institutional and sociological imperatives' that development planners must take into account. The authors examine the rationality of decision making by parents and family heads in a range of contexts, both rural and urban, highlighting the tensions and stresses the family experiences as the development process unfolds. The persistence in Africa of the extended family presents a unique set of constraints to policy makers and researchers. The authors also stress the pre-eminent role of the family in the socialization of young people, despite inroads made in this area by official educational institutions. To the extent that economic and social crises prevent the family from adequately fulfilling this role, young Africans find themselves 'torn between two systems, neither of which is in a position to fulfil [their] aspirations and expectations.' Addictions, delinquency and premarital adolescent childbearing are all too often the consequences.

Regarding the situation of the African woman, the authors highlight her multiple roles as 'wife, mother, housekeeper, worker, kinswoman, and citizen' but also point up how the lives of most African women remain 'closely oriented towards [their] capacities to reproduce and provide for family.' Moreover, 'the complexity of women's roles as child bearers and rearers, as food producers and processors, and as household managers is such that these roles conflict with each other, creating further stress for women.' Structural adjustment programmes sharply exacerbate such stress in women's lives. The authors conclude by urging policy makers to develop 'a better understanding of family systems, modes of domestic organization, and household, economic and demographic decision-making processes' so as to 'reconcile long-term population and development goals and targets with the adoption of strategies that are pertinent and responsive to the conditions prevailing in Africa.'

Ocholla-Ayayo, in Chapter 4, considers a number of disparate phenomena related to the contemporary situation of the African family, in a framework that counterpoises traditional or religious conceptions and practices with those being produced by the rapid and radical changes that have swept the continent in the twentieth century. The former persist inasmuch as – for example – 'within one family or household two totally different worlds may be found coexisting: the children may be attending university while the parents remain illiterate and concerned mainly with cultivating their fields with wooden sticks.' The author examines, in both urban and rural contexts, practices and institutions such as religion, tribal identification, marriage and polygyny, family size, the situation of dependents, funeral ceremonies and kinship networks. On the whole, modernization is seen to be undermining traditional family life and values while failing to replace these with new forms able to meet the needs once served by the old ones.

Within the wide diversity of political, economic and socio-cultural systems that mark Sub-Saharan Africa, Aryee notes in Chapter 5 how the basic features of the marriage institution exhibit considerable common characteristics across the subcontinent. At the same time, the changes sweeping Africa today are in most areas transforming the family. The author reviews the principal features of traditional marriage, which has often been described as an extended process of uncertain duration rather than as a single definitive event or ceremony. One striking feature of change is the coexistence of a wide range of different forms of marriage within the same society, nation or socio-cultural group. Still, the overall trend is toward detachment of the extended family from the nuptial decision-making process, and a consequent shifting of the costs, responsibilities and decisions concerning marriage more and more onto the individuals – the prospective couple. Questioning a common hypothesis that polygyny is structurally incompatible with modernization, the author notes the persistence of the practice in many areas, alongside its metamorphosis into practices such as the 'second office' or 'outside wife'. At the same time, however, consensual and informal unions are becoming more prevalent as traditional strictures against such relationships break down. In general, the author concludes, the ease with which people can get in and out of marriage without any fear of being socially or legally sanctioned is gradually undermining responsible parenthood and promoting the disintegration of the African family. The author recommends that policy makers give priority to the compulsory registration and regulation of unions and to the re-examination, modification or elimination of marriage-related practices that pose a threat to both the physical and mental health of women – such as female circumcision or widowhood and initiation rites. Legal and educational efforts must also be made to encourage responsible fatherhood.

In Chapter 6, while acknowledging that 'there is no typical rural African family', Makinwa-Adebusoye endeavours to sketch the general shape of family organization and working conditions in rural areas. Under the gender-based division of agricultural labour, both men and women take part in productive tasks. But cultural norms bestow a higher status on men than women, who are confined to domestic activities and to a set of 'women's jobs' and the cultivation of 'women's crops'. The chapter then focuses on the demographic and agrarian responses to changes engendered by the development process, the direct and indirect consequences of these responses for the rural family, and their interrelationships and overall implications for population and rural development. The spotlight is mainly on smallholding rural families in the farming sector, where 'feminization' of agriculture and increasing dependence on female labour mean that women are being overworked, especially as male labour becomes scarce owing to migration and other causes related to economic crisis. Moreover, the greater the time and energy a woman devotes to farm and other types of work in order to increase her income, and the further she has to go to fetch water and fuel wood for family sustenance, the less time and energy she has left to devote to caring for children, preparing nutritious meals, or availing herself or her family of existing social facilities such as health care centres and family planning clinics. Women's time constraints thus have grave implications for infant mortality rates and are not conducive to fertility reduction.

Chapter 7, written by Sally Findley, details the many ways that migration has altered family life in Africa and is continuing to do so. Based on a detailed review of data on migration and urbanization trends during the past two decades, the author notes a widespread phenomenon of increased diversification of migration destinations, specifically including more small and medium-sized cities and rural areas. This shift out of major metropolitan areas reflects the serious economic problems confronting the largest cities as a result of the combined forces of worldwide economic downturn, structural adjustment programmes, and disadvantageous terms of trade for Africa's primary products. A trend toward greater international migration is also evident, with both significant movement among African countries and out-migration to Europe and America. Traditional seasonal and circulatory migration patterns are being supplanted by more diverse ones within which migrant itineraries are more complex. With economic success not necessarily guaranteed even with circulation between two places, more migrants find that they must move among several places in order to patch together a living. The data also show a striking increase in migration by women, who traditionally had remained at home while men moved around in search of paid work. Moreover, significant proportions of female migrants are autonomous migrants, moving independently to fulfil their own economic needs rather than simply to join a husband or other family members.

None the less, migration in Africa remains very much a 'family matter', with even non-migrant members of the family intimately involved in and affected by the migration process. Indeed, Africa's extended-family structure is seen to facilitate a subdivision of the family into two or more separate units that continue to function as an economic whole even when spatially disunited. Dual-residence strategies enable families to maintain their extended structure in the face of losses due to migration. Rather than leading to the disintegration of traditional structures migration is seen to facilitate the persistence of such practices as polygyny. For example, a man may use the occasion of migration to take an additional wife in the new location, and the senior wife who remains behind may be better able to cope in his absence since she can call upon co-wives for help in household production tasks. On the other hand, farm productivity has steadily declined in areas of southern Africa where large numbers of men have migrated for long periods to mining zones and women have had to take on a double load. When women migrate as well, they face a number of gender-specific problems such as loss of rights to village lands; lower pay in urban employment owing to lack of education; the need to juggle childrearing and work outside the home; or even separation from their children, who may be fostered to another family or left behind in the care of grandparents. On the whole, however, the author takes a positive view of the effects of migration on the family in Africa, concluding that 'rather than being a brake on progress, families throughout Africa are helping their migrant members establish themselves in new places. By retaining close and supportive relations with the migrant, the family ensures it will share in whatever benefits the migrant attains by his or her mobility.'

In Chapter 8, Mbugua focuses upon the consequences for women's health of social and economic crises and the way these are exacerbated by structural adjustment programmes. Within the context of the family, women are both actors in providing primary health care for family members and especially for children, and acted-upon as they suffer the effects of crisis. As providers, women must largely depend upon their own skills to diagnose and treat ailments; in many instances this is a trial and error affair that can worsen the course of disease. Despite the expert skills of many traditional birth attendants, pregnancy and childbirth present perhaps the greatest health risks to African women. The author details the consequences of high rates of premarital and extramarital sexual activity, teenage pregnancy, and fertility generally. Women's nutrition is harmed by early and frequent childbearing as mothers lack the time and resources to feed themselves properly, coupled with a culturally instilled 'tendency to subordinate their own health'. Mental stress is a further detrimental factor especially for older mothers who, as widows or the victims of marital dissolution, often become the heads of their own households at a time when their resource base is dwindling and their own strength and stamina is fast declining.

Mbugua goes on to examine the health implications of women's role as producers of both health inputs and foodstuffs, finding 'a synergistic relationship between the health of women and the kinds of work they do. ... The physical and mental stress from the amount of time spent working as well as from the types of work done is associated with the rising incidence of high blood pressure, stillbirths, and premature births and deaths – especially during peak periods in harvesting, weeding, or planting.' Additional health problems specific to women in the family context include domestic violence, wife battery, incest and sexual abuse, and harmful cultural practices such as female circumcision.

The author concludes by urging policy makers to transform their ways of thinking about women's health by acknowledging that 'the productive and reproductive activities of women are inextricably linked and therefore cannot be addressed in isolation from one another. ... This can be accomplished by adopting a gender perspective, within which women are not treated as a residual category but where their central but different needs are taken into account in a situation of equity.'

In Chapter 9 the impact on the African family of the demographic changes that have been occurring in a context of economic stagnation, recurrent crises, spiralling debt burdens and the introduction – under international pressure – of structural adjustment programmes (SAP) is discussed. Oppong stresses the gender biases of such programmes, the consequences of which – falling living standards, unemployment, mal-nutrition, and reductions in public services – fall heaviest upon women. Such effects are further exacerbated by continued high fertility levels and the consequent youthfulness of populations. A critique is offered of population programmes, whose failures are attributed in part to policy makers' lack of understanding of the dynamic nature of the socio-economic and demographic systems that they are seeking to affect. Similarly, policies aimed at restructuring economies based largely upon family-run agricultural units and other micro-enterprises are also likely to be doomed to failure if the nature of the underlying family systems is ignored.

The author next examines at some length the various sorts of economic activity in which African women are engaged. She notes:

> Africa is *par excellence* the region of the world where women engage in a life-long struggle to combine reproductive and productive tasks and responsibilities within the family context. Their levels of both fertility and economic activity are higher than for any other region, and they initiate both sorts of activities at an earlier age than do women elsewhere. At the same time, their conjugal roles are characterized by greater autonomy than are the roles of women in other regions. Thus they depend to a great extent upon support from kin in carrying out these heavy and frequently conflicting tasks.

However, in the current context of economic crisis, traditional systems of controlling, monitoring, protecting, and supporting the young, and pregnant and lactating mothers are breaking down, and this collapse is further exacerbated by massive spatial dislocations of people seeking new sources of security and support. The consequences of this for the socialization of youth, for sexual relations (both inside and outside marriage), for fertility control, and for parental responsibility are examined.

Finally, in Chapter 10, using a conceptual framework that both centres upon and challenges the perceived dichotomy between customary or 'traditional' law and Western-based, general law in the African context, Armstrong stresses that family law 'must be investigated not only by looking at court cases or into legal textbooks, but by looking at the customary legal norms of individual families and communities, the practices that have crystallized into "law" by repetition.' Traditional legal functions of the family included making and enforcing law, settling disputes within the family, and representing the family's interests in the community. These in turn depended upon the mutual dependence of family members, power hierarchies within the family, and recognition by the community of the family as legal authority and representative. But under contemporary conditions, each of these conditions is being weakened or rearranged, with important legal implications for the family. Migration is eroding day-to-day mutual support among family members, family hierarchies are being challenged as women take on new roles and family members enter waged employment, and state institutions are displacing the family's central authoritative role.

In the remainder of the chapter, the author examines carefully the changes taking place in a range of institutions central to the family and family law – marriage, polygyny, bridewealth, maintenance of dependants and inheritance. She finds that while on the whole the control once exerted by the family as a group is lessening, its legal role is still more important than that of any other institution in southern Africa – indeed, more important even than the states' laws. Concluding, she urges that 'any study of law ... include a study of the law made and applied by the family. We must rethink our concept of law as something which is state centred and reconceptualize law in its *African* sense as something that is family centred.'

CHAPTER 2

The African family: data, concepts and methodology

Oluwole Adegboyega, James P. M. Ntozi and John B. Ssekamatte-Ssebuliba

The scarcity of quality data in Africa has been decried in many areas of study. Family studies have been no exception. As we approach the twenty-first century, it cannot be denied that the data situation in Africa is much better than at the turn of the century. Even so, progress in data availability has not been at the expected pace. To date, virtually no African country can boast of sufficiently good data in terms of either quantity or quality.

The reasons for the current data situation are many and varied; different countries have had different experiences. Some of the more generalized reasons include: lack of institutional framework; financial constraints; low priority assigned to data collection by planning officials; political, economic and social instability; and low educational levels of the populations. These problems cannot be easily solved in the short term, although African governments and scholars would be advised to start working on them immediately.

The work of a researcher is difficult at present, but it would be wrong to throw up one's hands in despair. In most countries in Africa there are several rich sources of information with varying levels of completeness and quality. Such data can be harnessed, analysed, and disseminated with a view to achieving comparability in data collection and quality at the continental level.

While relatively few studies have specifically addressed the 'African family', valuable analyses may be obtained by exploring the existing data and extracting those pieces which may be relevant. At the same time, such a process can draw attention to the areas where significant gaps exist – areas which should receive particular attention in the new research agenda.

Historical and contemporary perspectives

Anthropological studies Anthropological data on the family in Africa first became available around the turn of the century as anthropologists, mainly from Europe, first began to live among African communities. Data initially took the form of ethnographic literature about African family institutions as seen through European eyes. Books from these studies started coming out in the 1920s, 30s and 40s (e.g., Schapera, 1941; Wagner, 1939; Brown, R., 1950; Mair, 1969). While these studies provided the first systematic investigations of African family systems, they were widely criticized as ethnocentric. The investigators commonly lived among the communities they studied for long periods of time, recorded events, and tried to identify institutions and to impute meaning to them as they saw fit. In general, this is quite a legitimate method of study. However, as a function of the level of development of investigative methodology at the time, many of these researchers lacked what Max Weber (1949) called 'value neutrality'.

These initial studies largely took the form of examining how, in the words of Malinowski (1929), 'savage communities' approximated or deviated from the European 'norm'. The situation was further complicated by colonial governments' practice of using the early anthropologists as advisers on how best to subjugate the various native peoples they studied. Thus though these early studies formed a solid starting point for investigations, their intellectual contributions were greatly compromised by ethnocentric bias.

As a result, a new round of studies was conducted in many African societies from about the 1950s by more enlightened European scholars and by some indigenous scientists as well (e.g., Beattie, 1964; Fax, 1977; Kayongo-Male and Onyango , 1984). This more contemporary approach recognized African institutions as valid ones that had developed within their unique contexts to satisfy the needs and aspirations of their peoples. It was also widely accepted that these institutions were not necessarily evolving towards the European type. This new approach led to a wealth of information, including the identification of a range of family types which had hitherto been brushed aside as deviations.

Demographic approaches   Although the African family was first studied by anthropologists, it has more recently come to be of central interest to demographers – no doubt in recognition of the family's prominence in fertility decisions (Caldwell, 1982; Caldwell et al., 1982). While British-controlled areas collected considerable information in censuses, Francophone countries accumulated a wealth of sample survey data (Brass et al., 1968). Prior to the 1950s, census information was used mainly for official and administrative purposes. By the 1960s, the availability of census and survey information was making possible the first compilations of quantitative data on the family. Censuses usually listed all members of a family unit and their characteristics, making it possible to look at families and family formation in aggregate terms.

With the collection of quantitative data there was need to develop more standardized concepts. Inasmuch as the 'family' may take many forms even within the same country or society, it was found to be a very elusive concept for purposes of data collection. The breakthrough in this regard came with the introduction of the concept of the 'household', which has been defined as 'a group of persons living in a compound and sharing meals together' (Scott and Blacker, 1974). This turned out to be a more flexible concept which allowed the collection of standardized data while at the same time making it possible to investigate the family. Data standardization is facilitated by the practice of listing all members of a household in terms of their relationship to the head of the household. Such information can provide an idea about family types in the society. Censuses also commonly include questions about marital status and age at first marriage. This information can give some idea about family formation and nuptiality patterns.

But census information is limited in terms of the depth to which various phenomena can be investigated. With phenomena that are evolving rapidly, census data may be very unsatisfactory, failing to keep up with the rate of change. In addition, such data often fail to elucidate several important issues concerning families, especially when more detailed or substantial information is needed. Furthermore, because censuses and most official data are often collected on the basis of households, special efforts need to be taken in the collection of data on families due to the important differences between the family and household concepts (see below). Such efforts may involve gathering new and different data or developing methodologies and capacities to reconfigure existing data. For many countries in Africa, collecting new data sets on families may impose intolerable strains on the limited available financial and technical capabilities, so the second alternative is often more feasible.

Surveys have proliferated in most African countries, particularly in the last 20 years. Most national surveys have been essentially demographic and have greatly strengthened the quantitative database in these countries. While this development has been at the cost of a decline in qualitative studies, particularly those of an anthropological nature, certain definite advantages accrue from this proliferation. Surveys have become more specialized, that is they can focus on a few topics and study them in greater depth. Because of their standardized nature, surveys have allowed similar instruments to be administered in different societies and contexts. This permits comparisons not only across countries but also within countries over time. These possibilities were further enhanced with the introduction of world surveys, most notable among which are the World Fertility Surveys (WFS), Contraceptive Prevalence Surveys (CPS), and Demographic and Health Surveys (DHS). These have generated ample quantitative data that can be used to study the African family at the continental level.

In general, survey data is best used to study static situations, that is the way phenomena are exhibited at a given point in time. Introducing elements of trend or dynamics means having to rely on respondents' ability to recall past events – which may not produce very accurate results – resorting to synthetic cohorts where applicable.

Family and household

While it is not always easy to distinguish a family from a household, it is nevertheless essential to draw out the distinction between the two concepts. As noted above most available statistical data are on households and there is often a need to reconfigure data sets to a family basis. For statisticians, the term 'household' denotes a unit of people, consisting of one or more persons – related or not related by blood – usually living under one roof and/or making common provision for food and other living arrangements. Hence a household is basically an economic unit.

The term 'family', on the other hand, is not strictly tied to one location or time, or even, as in some African societies and cultures, to blood relationship. Whatever its internal structure, the family is universally acknowledged to be the basic social unit. Implicit in the concept of the family are certain assumptions about its role and the roles men and women play within it. The most central of these assumptions is the long-term stability of the family (as against the household) as a close physical, economic, and emotional unit within which children are planned, born and reared. It is the duty of the head of the family to see to the welfare of its members – to organize production among family members and to ensure equitable distribution of resources. In most African cultures men are regarded as the heads of families. While all these assumptions may have been valid at some time or other, it is important to monitor their continued validity and detect shifting trends.

Families rarely live together over their whole life cycle: children may move out and spouses may separate through divorce. Children departing to form their own households do not lose their status in their family of origin. In spite of external changes in life, families usually feel as if they belong together. Even when family members die, they may still be considered as belonging to the family.

At the extremes of the African extended family system, a person originating from a family's homestead, village or town may be recognized as a family member – especially if the person and the family are living at a different locality from where they originated. In other situations, a family's domestic worker or farm labourer may, over time, achieve the status of family membership.

Household types While the term household appears to be concise with regard to location and time, it nevertheless has many varieties. In many

weaken family bonds. Cash and other remittances by migrating members of the family often cannot be guaranteed. Even when there are regular cash remittances, the emotional aspect of family obligation is rendered impractical due to the physical separation. Even so, household surveys have indicated that some migrant workers do send money home, in some cases on a regular basis.

Where labour out-migration is substantial, it may be helpful to collect statistical information on the outgoing migrants in order to measure the impact of migration on the family. Generally, out-migrants tend to come from narrow age bands, and the departure of migrants in large numbers may affect the population age structure of society, consequently having a significant impact on family structure. The absence of wage earners in a family may have adverse effects on the family's welfare since there is no guarantee that the volume of remittances from the departing family member will be either adequate or regular. Further, migrants may return with different outlooks on life and social characteristics which may be injurious to the life of the family. In cases where migrants engage in hazardous occupations, such as mining, the migrants may return in broken health or with some severe physical impairments, thus becoming a burden rather than an asset to the family.

Population censuses are major sources of migration data. From such data can be established levels, patterns and streams of migration. It must be conceded, however, that the best way to study these and other related aspects with respect to the family would be through migration surveys. Unfortunately, there have been very few large-scale migration surveys in Africa; accurate relationships between the family and migration processes may thus be hard to establish conclusively. Nevertheless, the national surveys referred to earlier, such as WFS and DHS, do contain some migration data. These surveys asked questions on place of birth, place where surveyee grew up, place of previous residence and length of stay in current residence, therefore, providing migration data that far exceeds that available through censuses and which can be a useful supplement to the census data. Finally, there have been a few small-scale surveys that have focused specifically on migration in some African countries by some individuals and organizations. While issues of comparability and standardization may be problematic in such surveys, they can definitely serve as useful starting points.

The family in rural and agricultural activities

Data for the study of the African family in rural and agricultural activities are not as plentiful as in the cases of migration and nuptiality. Agricultural censuses and surveys have not collected detailed information on the role of the family that can be manipulated for use in family studies. Unlike in the demographic surveys, the main focus of rural and agricultural surveys is usually a higher aggregate unit than the household, such as a ward, village or parish. Surveys that have provided relevant data on the family include a few small-scale surveys which may have been designed specifically for that purpose in a particular area of a country. The problems encountered with such studies is that, due to the differences in design, generalizations become hard even within a single country. Therefore data in this area is quite scanty.

Family survival strategy in the urban informal sector

In the study of the African family and survival strategy in the urban informal sector, little has been done. Recognition of the informal sector as a legitimate mode of living is a relatively recent development. Hitherto the informal sector was seen as testimony to the failure of government development policies, which triggered excessive rural-to-urban migration. In this respect, the informal sector was studied mainly by urban sociologists. The focus here was mainly on individuals who happened to be found in the urban areas at a particular time.

More recently, however, the informal sector has been recognized as a structured and permanent way of living for many people. Even more significantly, it has been revealed that the urban informal sector constitutes a remarkable survival strategy for families in both rural and urban areas. Definite linkages have been identified between rural migrants in the urban areas and their rural homes. Unfortunately, data in this area remains scanty. Most of it comes from isolated and relatively small-scale studies, especially in the slum areas of African cities. Even fewer studies have tried directly to trace the role of the family in this network.

The family, refugees and displaced persons

Although the refugee and displacement situations are having a profound impact on the African family today, not much has been done in the way of research or to increase data availability. Since refugee situations occur during periods of hostilities and are invariably accompanied by human catastrophes, the immediate concern is always the alleviation of suffering. It would indeed be considered callous to try and undertake thorough academic research in such circumstances. Consequently, the only data that is generally available from such situations is from government records kept in refugee reception centres, particularly where refugees cross an international boundary. Another source would be the records kept by relief organizations working in such situations, such as the United Nations High Commissioner for Refugees (UNHCR) and the World Food Programme (WFP). The government records catalogue refugees in their individual capacities as they come into reception centres. By themselves, such records would be of limited use in studies focusing on the family. However, data collected by relief organizations have greater utility, first because they are kept over a longer period than the government records of entrants; second, and more important, in the recent past there has been a proliferation of relief agencies working in the area of refugees and displaced persons in Africa besides the UNHCR. Agencies like the International Committee of the Red Cross (ICRC), World Vision, Medicins sans Frontiers (MSF), and Care International are actively engaged not only in refugee operations, but also in situations of displaced persons within individual countries, where organizations like the UNHCR would not have a mandate.

The records of these organizations could be very useful because they always try, as part of their relief work, to collect information about families whose members may have been torn apart by the refugee or displacement process and to reunite them wherever possible. Records of such a process would therefore be a richer source of family data in both refugee and displacement situations. However, it must be noted that such data are kept for administrative and not for study purposes. Researchers may, therefore, find it inadequate and must strive to produce better designs for generating data in these situations.

Some scholars have studied these situations *post facto*, investigating the problem several months or years later and either trying to reconstruct the original situation, or examining the new situation that has been created and its impact. Such studies may also be an important source of information. In some cases these studies have addressed displacement due to natural disasters such as famine (e.g., De Waal, 1989); in others, displacement due to civil wars and its effects on the population (e.g., Ityavyar and Ogba, 1989; Ssekamatte-Ssebuliba, 1992). There are also a number of studies that have addressed the problem of refugees (Adepoju, 1982; Gorman, 1986; Rogge, 1988; Khasiani, 1989), while other studies have focused on the problematic issue of repatriation (e.g., Rogge and Akol, 1989; Schultheis, 1989).

These studies have focused on both the refugee and displacement problems in Africa and their possible solutions, but they do not directly relate to the family as an institution. It is clear that data on the family would enhance not only an understanding of the problems expounded in these various scenarios, but also facilitate the search for practical and lasting solutions. There is, therefore, a need here for data collection designs that will focus more specifically on the family.

Housing

Another issue with serious implications for the family in most African countries, especially in urban areas, is the housing situation and the consequential family conditions. This situation can be monitored by collecting statistical information on the types of housing unit occupied by families, tenure of occupation, number of rooms available for use, sources of water supply and fuel for cooking and lighting, and type and availability of toilet facilities (data on the latter would be of tremendous importance on health grounds alone).

Censuses and surveys such as the DHS commonly ask about households' sources of fuel or power for cooking or lighting, their main source of water, and toilet facilities. In addition, detailed information is also available from these sources on housing units – type of unit, number of families sharing it, number of rooms, type of tenure, building materials used, and so on. Such information provides a quantitative profile of families' housing and environmental conditions.

Unlike in the case of economic activities, little qualitative data on housing and environmental conditions of families is available. There is a need to know why families live in the conditions they do. Is it by choice or as a consequence of forces beyond their control? The role of culture needs to be addressed as well. Some families, for example, seem to be sitting on plenty of wealth, held in assets such as cattle, and yet this wealth is not translated into better living conditions. To understand such a scenario, we must first be in a position to appreciate such people's perception of wealth. These answers cannot be gleaned from the ample quantitative information that is available to us, and there is thus a need for more qualitative studies to explore relationships between people and land, people and animals, and people and culture.

Family health and family planning

Substantial data is available on family health and family planning. From the decennial censuses one may derive measures like infant and child mortality rates, which are generally accepted as indicators of the health conditions of an area. Although these are aggregate indicators, since the overall data is collected by household, disaggregating the household and hence family linkages may not be too difficult a task.

Furthermore, in almost all African countries, there have been health-related surveys over the past 20 years. Again the most prominent of these have been the Demographic and Health Surveys. These produced a standard health module that has provided considerable data on infant and child health in a household context. Such data include information on the areas of immunization, morbidity and growth. In addition, general topics on household hygiene and living conditions could generate data on the larger family health picture. Besides the DHS, which could be used to produce a continental health profile, numerous national health or health-related surveys have been conducted in which the health conditions of all household members have been recorded. These surveys may also be disaggregated to derive families and family types and to permit an assessment of health conditions for all members of the family.

In the area of family planning, there has been an even greater proliferation of data. Although by the mid-1960s hardly any African country had a Knowledge of Attitude to and Practice of Family Planning (KAP) study, by the mid-1970s many countries had had at least one KAP study. These studies of family planning in Africa were followed by the Contraceptive Prevalence Studies (CPS) of the late 1970s and early 1980s. Around the same time, the WFS studies were also conducted in Africa. Like the CPS studies, the WFS asked very detailed questions about family planning such as knowledge about the various methods, attitudes towards them, extent of use, and plans about future use. Similarly, a number of national surveys have been conducted using the WFS family planning module. These data sets are perfectly comparable, making possible a comprehensive continental profile.

The DHS which followed a few years after the last WFS added to the wealth of information on family planning in the region. Beside the WFS's standard KAP module, the DHS also addressed issues of non-use. Reasons why women may not be utilizing family planning services were explored, including some myths and misconceptions about family planning. In addition to this wealth of data, in almost all African countries family planning services are offered as standard practice, either in family planning clinics or as part of maternal and child health services. These outlets provide a wealth of data, particularly on family planning acceptors and drop-outs. The answer to why, in almost all African countries, the acceptance rates and prevalence levels of family planning are still extremely low after several years of family planning activity may actually already be held by these units. Unfortunately, many countries have not bothered to compile the wealth of information at the family planning outlets into a form more accessible to researchers. Providers are also yet to agree on a standardized set of information to be collected from all clients in a region to facilitate utilization that goes beyond the purely administrative requirements of the providers. Improvement in this area of data compilation might lead to them asking acceptors for information about their families.

The family and the law

In the area of the family and the law, there are virtually no particular data sets that one could readily consult. Although a number of books have been written about family law in Africa, there are as yet very few sociological studies that have addressed the issue of the African family in the legal context. Consequently, the best available source in this area would be court records involving family cases. The obvious shortcoming here would be that the majority of African family disputes are handled by traditional courts, which do not record their proceedings. There is therefore a great need for innovation in designing this type of studies. (See Chapter 10 for a detailed discussion of law and the family in the Southern African context.)

Conclusion

The foregoing analysis shows that while the dearth of good and reliable data in Africa is still a barrier to family studies, the situation is not totally hopeless. A lot can be achieved in the study of the African family even using existing data sets in many African countries. Nevertheless, it must be emphasized that to accord the family the significance it deserves in social and other studies, there is need for more studies designed specifically around family units. Presently, most data sets and databanks in Africa utilize the concept of the 'household'. This concept is more suitable for quantitative analysis and easier to handle than the more elusive one of the 'family', in all its various structural and cultural varieties. Again, although some households coincide with the family, it would be a mistake to assume that the two can be used interchangeably. But combining the two concepts should not only be easily accomplished, but also more fruitful, leading to more analytical and policy-relevant conceptual frameworks.

Although quantitative and qualitative study designs are presented above in a comparative context, they should not be viewed as isolated or competing designs. There are some topics that can best be studied with quantitative information, and others by use of a qualitative design. Yet others may be done equally well using either. However, it is undeniable that one design can supplement whatever data are generated by the other. Nevertheless, in Africa today, there are very few instances where these designs have complemented each other in generating information about the same phenomena. This complementary approach may well be the best way forward for future research development in the region.

CHAPTER 3

The African family: an overview of changing forms

Aderanti Adepoju and Wariara Mbugua

In Africa the family is still primarily an economic organ, as a unit of both production and consumption; it is indeed a multi-functional unit. As a social institution, it procreates, socializes and educates the children. In rural areas, the household is virtually a self-sufficient economic unit: it provides almost all factors of production – labour, land and capital. In such a subsistence economy, the main and indeed crucial factor of production is labour, which is traditionally recruited mainly from within the family unit (Adepoju, 1977; Locoh, 1988a).

In order to perform its various roles effectively, family size is usually tailored to these needs of the family. In the rural economy, the largest share of income originates from farming: land is therefore a central source of income for villagers. In such a situation, it becomes necessary for households to have more than one worker, especially as some workers earn income from more than one source simultaneously. The system also depends on using all sources of labour: women and children are fully deployed in various duties on the farm, thereby contributing to aggregate family income. The productive process still involves using very simple technologies to produce goods and services, and indeed all the essential daily needs. Necessarily, the household economy is thoroughly integrated into the family structure (Adepoju, 1977, 1992).

With these points in mind, it is pertinent to examine the family structure in order to establish the rationality of parents in the decision-making process. As the structure of the traditional economy – and the family – has been substantially transformed over the years, an examination of these changes can greatly enhance our understanding of the present and suggest implications for the future. This chapter, therefore, discusses the African family within the context of the development process, highlighting the tensions and stresses being experienced with a view to suggesting how population and development policies can be improved by making them responsive to the dynamics of the African family.

Family formation

Marriage is the traditionally recognized point of entry into family formation in most parts of Africa. Marriage in Africa is a complex affair – an arrangement between families rather than individuals. Identification of a bride (or groom), consolidation of the search through payment of bridewealth, formalization of the rites of marriage, consummation of marriage – all these components of the process are arranged by families which also have an enduring responsibility to ensure stability of the union through a variety of controls and a mutual-support network (Adepoju, 1992; Locoh, 1988a).

Marriage is a virtually universal event, an essentially group activity that society is very insistent upon. A permanent state of celibacy is foreign to most cultures, being regarded as abnormal for men and unthinkable for normal, healthy women. Traditional marriage is the most common type. While the economic prerequisites for marriage – gifts, bridewealth and expensive ceremonies – act as constraints on the propensity to take more than one wife, the incidence of polygyny is nevertheless widespread. A major incentive for polygynous marriage is the provision of social, domestic and economic assistance by the women, but for the African male polygyny also demonstrates social status and is therefore a source of immense prestige (Oppong, 1991b; Mbugua, 1992).

Most African men are involved in long-term relationships with more than one woman at any given moment, a situation that for the majority of African women has led to the inevitability of being in a polygynous consensual or formal union. The logical and rational causes of polygyny in Africa are many and include such imperatives as the institution of the levirate, which prescribes the automatic inheritance of widows by members of the husband's lineage; men's need to demonstrate power and wealth; and women's inability to acquire or create resources without the assistance of male relatives, most commonly spouses. Wide age gaps between wives and husbands added to higher male mortality rates ensure that there is always a large pool of women available to be drawn into polygynous unions (Mbugua, 1992). Average age at first marriage, particularly for females, is low, as is average age at first pregnancy. In rural areas, nearly all females marry before their twenty-fifth birthday and about 70 per cent are married before the age of 20. The situation is not very different in the towns (UN, 1990).

A surprisingly wide variety of different marriage forms and types of conjugal relationships exist in virtually all parts of Africa south of the Sahara. Such variation arises as a response to changing economic circumstances as well as to emerging functions of the African family. A common type of union which is being observed in West, East and Southern African countries is polygyny without cohabitation. This type of union is evident among both the educated and the uneducated in both urban and rural areas. For educated women polygyny without cohabitation arises out of the need to link up with spouses who will not insist on coexistence with other co-wives, thus permitting the educated wife autonomously to maintain her own residence and pursue her own, often crucially important, economic activities. In contrast, for poorer women such unions offer protection from unwanted male suitors as well as from interference by kin as they pursue their often quasi-legal economic activities in the peri-urban areas of Africa's cities (Ngondo, 1992). In both cases the man periodically visits the mother–child(ren) units and offers them whatever material support may be necessary, but more importantly provides a mutually satisfying emotional support and security blanket in an environment where the predominance of patriarchy undermines the ability of non-attached women fully to realize their potential (Mbugua, 1992).

In recent times scholarly attention has focused on the structure of family formation in Africa, raising the question of whether the African family is becoming more nucleated or not. Evidence from qualitative studies, particularly in West Africa, demonstrate that the lineage still exerts a great deal of influence over young couples and effectively discourages nucleation in terms of exclusive emotional attachment (to spouse and children), resource allocation and living arrangements (Locoh, 1988a, 1988b).

The extended family in Africa is being sustained by several factors. The better-off members of the lineage are obliged to share the benefits of their education or businesses (in which other lineage members, more often than not, have invested) by looking after poorer relatives, either through substantial financial outlays or through accommodating and sheltering them. The family has also become an economic refuge for unemployed members – especially for the increasing number of jobless young people – in the absence of alternative state arrangements. For divorced and widowed women, the family also acts as an emotional and economic refuge, when as such women are disinherited by husbands' kin in societies where the concept of 'community property' – which would enable wives to share the wealth of the marriage – is non-existent (Mbugua, 1992).

Childbearing

Decisions on when to have a child, on how many children to have and at what birth intervals, and on when to cease childbearing are all, directly or indirectly, taken by the family. In some cases, the family acts as the arbiter of communal norms and values. In several African societies, the community expects and the family ensures – through subtle, sometimes overt pressure – that marriage is quickly followed by pregnancy. Everyone waits very impatiently to observe the obvious manifestation just a few months after wedlock. The young woman is expected to demonstrate her fecundity immediately, otherwise the equation changes and, after a period of infertility, her family must provide a substitute. This often happens among some ethnic groups in Cameroon and Swaziland so as to fulfil the covenant implicitly entered into between the two families – childbearing. A woman is also expected to cease bearing children, irrespective of her age, as soon as she becomes a grandmother (a status she can attain at the age of 35 or even less) (Adepoju, 1992; Lule, 1991).

For a significant proportion of African women, childbearing continues to be a life-threatening endeavour, and raising children is punctuated with grief as many families continue to watch helplessly as their children die. While a lot of progress has been made in reducing the levels of maternal and infant and child mortality, the reality of the situation is that the death of parents, spouses and children is an experience with which most African families are well acquainted. Mortality rates among all age groups in Africa continue to be the highest in the world (Sadik, 1991; Page, 1988). Generally, less than 80 per cent of Africans born live to reach their first birthday, and perhaps no more than 70 per cent can expect to reach their fifth. On average Africans expect to live no more than 55 years, perhaps a little more for women and a bit less for men. Sadly also, 10 per cent of pregnant women lose their lives and those of their unborn children at delivery. Such is the devastating experience which average African families have lived with – and some have seen worse days. Historically, mortality – among infants and adults alike – was a much more fearsome experience in the face of poor hygiene, ignorance, poverty, environmental hazards, poor medical facilities, and so on. Little wonder that, with such a collective memory, the average African family produces a large number of children just to ensure the survival of a few. In demographic jargon, families hoard children as an insurance strategy to perpetuate the lineage. These families have learned painfully that in the absence of state provision, surviving children are the only social security they have to support them in old age, though this may be changing now (Adepoju, 1992).

For most families, recounting or being enjoined to recall past experiences of the loss of their dear ones, especially children, can be so emotionally devastating that responses are, understandably, inaccurate. One rural survey in Bendel state, Nigeria, encountered a harrowing case of a family that had three surviving children out of a total of 40 (from three wives). Demographers wield questionnaires and tenaciously request that such respondents recall each event – including dates and, unrealistically, causes of death – in neat chronological order (Adepoju, 1992). Thanks to anthropologists, such survey approaches are becoming less fashionable.

Childrearing

It has been suggested in the literature that children in many societies are in part an economic good and that the number of children desired by parents is in part determined by the costs and benefits of having and raising a family. We shall examine this matter in terms of the contribution of children to household expenses, earnings and possible savings at various ages and by sex for various family sizes.

In rural Africa, with few services such as hospitals, piped water, schools and recreational facilities, the family bears almost the entire cost of rearing a child. To the extent that each family bears all – or a large part of – the costs resulting from decisions about childbearing, and eventually reaps all the benefits arising therefrom, it is to be expected that families will make decisions so as to maximize net benefits. Among most African societies, that decision is for a large family, averaging about six children (Adepoju, 1977).

In the traditional African cultural setting, a child is regarded as both a symbol of joy and an economic asset from birth through adolescence and up to the time when he or she is capable of supporting an aged parent. Children are productive assets and parents usually derive immense satisfaction from having them. While the child is an extra mouth to be fed and clothed when young, even at that age he or she is regarded hopefully as a potential member of the family labour pool – restricted, of course, by clearly defined sex roles. From around the age of six, the child is gradually integrated into the family's productive activities: running errands, doing menial household chores and looking after the younger ones (Oppong, 1991b).

Thus children perform various services which in the more industrialized and lower fertility societies usually eat up a large share of the family budget. Even at such a tender age, children's productivity is not zero; if one were able to cost their activities in the way the market does in a more advanced economy, the value of their production may well be shown to be considerably more than their consumption costs (Adepoju, 1977).

As the children mature, they follow their parents to the farm (if they are farmers), help in cooking, fetch water from the stream and do many other tasks which enable the parents to concentrate on more arduous ones. They also sow seeds, harvest and transport small quantities of farm produce – as well as having the general responsibility for carrying firewood and water home in the evening. This is to be expected since, in a sub-sistence economy, labour is the most crucial factor of production. For school-going children these activities are performed before and after school. During peak planting or harvesting seasons, parents often withdraw children from school to help. Children therefore enter the family labour force at an early age, and, by so doing, are able to defray some of the costs of their maintenance while preserving family income that otherwise would have to be used for hiring extra farm labour (Adepoju, 1977).

Under this system, children work for their parents until adulthood. When they are about to assume some measure of socio-economic independence, usually at age 20 or beyond, they are given a share of the family farm. This usually precedes the time that boys marry and become fathers themselves. The predominance of agriculture tends to overshadow other important secondary jobs, such as craft activities like drumming, weaving, blacksmithing, carving, and many other applications of skill. Most of these trades are determined largely by the sex and lineage of the individual concerned. Skills are passed from one generation to another, and apprentices and journeymen to these craft activities are drawn mainly from family members. This ensures the continuity and exclusiveness of the craft. The number of children needed to manage or inherit the trades and ensure their continuity depends upon the number and diversity of crafts, as well as on the degree of specialization by sex. The exclusiveness of most family concerns ensures that the proceeds from such undertakings are retained within the family. Even modern businesses in the informal sector are typically family enterprises that continue to benefit substantially from the labour input of children (Adepoju, 1979).

The family thus depends largely on the productive efforts of its members to sustain itself. It is because of this that marriage and child-bearing assume such prominence in Africa. Although education has the potential to erode these arrangements, the poor returns to education now being experienced in Africa and the low proportion of highly educated Africans means that traditional family systems are still functional for the majority of African families (Sawadogo, 1992).

Youth

In all circumstances the youth are the most vulnerable and find themselves living with unfulfilled hope, aspirations and expectations – increasingly sandwiched between tradition and modernity, between childhood and adulthood, and between the family and the state (each of which is less and less capable of fulfilling its obligations to youth). Indeed, Africa's youth face an uncertain future, a future for which they are ill-prepared and bear no responsibility in the first instance and over which they have little control (Adepoju, 1992; UNESCO, 1981).

The African family is still the most crucial agent of socialization. It moulds the formative stage of the infant whose initial survival probabilities are also conditioned by norms, practices and values of the society, re-inforced at the micro level by the socio-economic condition of the family (Locoh, 1988b). As *1994 International Year of the Family* (IYF) asserts, the family continues to provide the mutual framework for the emotional, financial and material support essential to the growth and development of its members, particularly infants and children, and for the care of other dependents. It can, and often does, educate, train, motivate and support its individual members thereby investing in their future growth and acting as vital resources for development. (UN, 1991a)

The educational system has taken over many of the socialization roles of the family, but all too imperfectly. Stated differently, the family seems to have gradually abdicated its socialization role to the educational institutions. At the beginning, all seemed to be well as missionary schools – Christian and Muslim alike – sought to inculcate specific values and discipline with the support of parents and society (UNESCO, 1981; Bona, 1990). But the school system is now seriously handicapped by inadequate facilities, breakdown of discipline, overcrowded enrolment (a teacher is often expected to supervise up to 100 children), declining morale among teachers and the elimination of moral education from secular school curricula (Ly, 1981). The majority of Africa's youth are, sadly, illiterate. Less than half the school-age population is enrolled; several thousands drop out each year, and for the few who remain in school the chances of advancing to the next stage are slim. At the tertiary level, less than 10 per cent of the cohort who start the first level (primary) are able to complete the university courses.

Unemployment in urban areas of Africa is concentrated among the youth. Initially localized among primary school leavers in the early 1960s, the pool of unemployed now includes both secondary-school leavers and university graduates. A large proportion of these unemployed university graduates are under the age of 25 and constitute a potentially unstable and politically volatile segment of the population, ready to explode at the slightest provocation after seeing their intellectual efforts go unrewarded.

Unemployed youth constitutes a dormant labour force – a waste of human resources on whose education parents and society expended scarce financial resources. The unemployed continue to depend on parents and are thus inadvertently unable to fulfil their roles of supporting parents and assisting siblings, and thereby 'recycling' their education. They are faced with several obstacles, being unable to prepare for independent households, marriage and family life. They are socially and economically dependent, disillusioned and bear deep grudges against society – a society that seems uncaring of their future and their plight. They are easy recruits for involvement in political activities, social upheaval, theft, violence, and even for revolution (Adepoju, 1991a; Essone, 1990).

Young Africans are frustrated, and understandably so, being torn between two systems neither of which is in a position to fulfil their aspirations and expectations. The children turn in vain to a subsystem, the vague outer world where they quickly learn all the seamier aspects of life

– drunkenness, addiction to drugs, crime and other forms of delinquency. The street-children syndrome is a manifestation of such malaise. There are millions of such children in Africa's cities today, including abandoned infants, and victims of drought, desertification and war (Agnelli, 1986).

The girl-child and the young adolescent girl are particularly vulnerable members of the African family. Subject to an onslaught of discriminatory practices – cultural, institutional and legal – the adolescent girl is growing up in a life of hopelessness that condemns her and her offspring to cycles of poverty. Denied equal access to educational opportunities and often forced to marry at a very early age, usually to a man considerably older than she is, the African adolescent girl starts bearing children early, exposing herself and her infants to a series of health problems. Lack of information about child spacing leads to too frequent births; by the age of 25 she may well have five or even six children. Her unmarried counterpart fares no better as the spate of adolescent pregnancies shows (Mbugua, 1992).

Adolescent pregnancies have become pervasive in societies which once exercised strong cultural restraints on premarital childbearing. Such pregnancies are increasingly tolerated, even in rural villages. Average age at marriage has increased in several African countries, but, rather ironically, the incidence of child mothers has similarly increased, as has the incidence of abandoned babies and unnecessary deaths among pregnant adolescents in the process of illegal abortions. In spite of this stark evidence of the unmet needs of the youth, most population policies and programmes in Africa are still adamantly opposed to the provision of contraceptive information and supplies to young people. One-third of the 18 countries surveyed in a recent United Nations study still did not provide contraceptives to unmarried teenagers and only one country in five indicated that family life education is included in their school curricula (UN, 1989; Sadik, 1991).

Because of their youth, adolescent girls, married or unmarried, contribute the greatest proportion of gynaecological emergencies. At delivery they are subject to a host of medical complications including toxaemia, anaemia, premature delivery, prolonged labour, cervical trauma, even death. Another medical consequence of early pregnancy, vesicovaginal fistula (VVF), leads to the ostracism of the young girl by both the husband's family and her own family because of the unpleasantness of the condition (WHO, 1990). A recent study carried out in Nigeria showed that about 60 per cent of the 241 VVF cases studied involved girls under the age of 15.

Very few reform institutions are available to rescue the family in such circumstances of apparent helplessness. If anything, those institutions which have the potential to ameliorate the desperate situation of the African adolescent girl are aggravating the problem. The majority of schools in Africa are intolerant of school-girl pregnancies and prohibit pregnant girls from continuing with their formal education, at a time when they most need it (Bledsoe, 1989). Some 8,000 teenagers were forced to drop out of school in Kenya in 1988 because of adolescent pregnancy. Similarly, 18,766 primary and secondary school students were expelled from school due to pregnancy in Tanzania in 1984. The irony of all this is that those responsible for these pregnancies – boy-students, older men and even male teachers – go scot-free, no doubt to repeat their actions.

Thus the joy and jubilation that welcome the arrival of newborn babies elude teenage mothers unlocked from the protective custody of families. This unwholesome development is increasingly visible in both rural and urban areas but is most evident in the towns, where social controls on youth have weakened considerably and where the vacuum left by the family has not been filled – and seems unlikely to be so.

The African family has been caught up in a web of struggle – for the newborn child's very survival, to salvage the youth from hopelessness, to provide for material needs and a future of hope for its members. This has become more and more evident since the late 1980s and is still more bitingly during the 1990s. The structural adjustment programmes have had an ineradicable impact on the African family in the sectors of education, health and employment (Adepoju, 1993).

Gender and the African family

In every society, women play important roles. Differences in culture, traditions, religion, historical development, economic life and political systems are reflected in the participation of women in various activities in their societies. In most African cultures, women's roles are basically those of procreation and care of the home. But if this were all they were responsible for it would be an irrational decision for men to marry more than the number of wives capable of maintaining the home and providing an optimum number of children.

The prevalence of polygynous unions owes something to the levirate system; to the likelihood of taking a second wife after the failure of the first wife either to bear a child at all or to bear a male one; and to the cultural importance attached to the institution itself (Ngondo, 1992). From an economic perspective, moreover, wives are viable economic assets to their husbands, as are their children. This becomes apparent as one critically examines not only women's procreative roles but their productive ones as well.

In the traditional system, women are usually subordinate to their husbands, both socially and economically. But this does not imply that they are wholly dependent upon them financially. Women provide necessary help on the farm, particularly in the spheres of planting, harvesting, processing and marketing. Indeed, marketing is a speciality of many women in West Africa while planting, harvesting and processing in subsistence agriculture is most common among East African women. In most of Africa the employment structure is such that men predominate in plantation agriculture, industry, commerce and transportation. Thus men tend to migrate alone and leave their wives behind. The cultural factors which until recently favoured the education of males over females had the effect of confining women to the lower rungs of formal employment, the more so since employment in the organized labour market is highly correlated to education. Hence, women are confined largely to commerce and distributive trade (Adepoju, 1983).

The African woman performs multiple roles – wife, mother, house-keeper, worker, kinswoman and citizen (Oppong, 1988). In the traditional subsistence situation, early marriage is the norm, and the life of the female is closely oriented towards her capacities to reproduce and provide for family. The early age of female marriage and childbearing, pregnancy wastage, limited access to productive and remunerative work, and, in rural areas, the drudgery of life and work have all severely constrained women in the effective performance of these multiple roles. Nevertheless, in some parts of Nigeria, especially in the east, and in all countries of East Africa, women have been and continue to be responsible for much of the demanding agricultural work, especially weeding and harvesting. They are also responsible for the energy-sapping and time-consuming tasks of food processing, food preparation, and marketing of farm produce, conveyed to the periodic markets over considerable distances. Apart from trading, other non-farm occupations in the informal sector – weaving, dyeing, crafts, and so forth – generate substantial private revenue which supplements family income. The complexity of women's role is such that individual aspects of it conflict with each other, creating further stress for women; in the best of circumstances, they may complement one another (Oppong, 1988).

The proportion of female-headed families and single-parent families is increasing in both rural and urban areas. These result from divorce, male migration or death of the male head of household. Whatever the reason, considerable pressure is placed on the females who have to combine and balance work and familial responsibilities. Economic stress has reduced the attraction of marriage and joint residence among adults. Marriage tends to lose its formality and to become increasingly fragile and unstable (Makinwa-Adebusoye, 1988).

In some parts of the region, such as in Kenya, female-headed house-holds constitute more than 30 per cent of all households nationally, the figure being as high as 45 per cent in certain high out-migration, high mortality districts. The increasing prevalence of female-headed households has implications for population and development policies that are yet to be articulated. Widowed female heads of household tend to be older, responsible for a large number of grandchildren and considerably poorer. The sociological consequences of large proportions of grandparents who are forced to act as the primary parents to their grandchildren have yet to be researched and documented. Furthermore, there are some indications that these heavy maternal responsibilities and the work patterns that they entail are having negative consequences for infants. In Kenya, for example, it has been postulated that high infant mortality rates in some urban areas are partly a result of the employment of childminders or babysitters who are too young and inexperienced in looking after infants. These youthful childminders are brought to the urban areas by women desperate for help around the household to enable them to pursue income-generating activities outside the home. Unfortunately the childminders that they bring from the rural areas may fail to understand how all the facilities and gadgets work, thus giving rise to many fatal infant accidents through improper use of electricity, gas cookers, hot water and the like.

In female-headed households, moreover, the problem of juvenile delinquency is fast becoming evident, particularly among boys who in the absence of their fathers rebel against the mother's authority. All these issues point towards a need to understand and thoroughly document through research the dynamics obtaining in female-headed households so that appropriate policies and interventions can be mounted. Some of these interventions, for example, need to examine how the fatherhood role can be strengthened, since it is clear that large numbers of African children are growing up without ever having experienced the richness of family life and familial bonds that emanate from the active participation of both parents in bringing up the children.

Gender bias in the structural adjustment programmes (SAPs) has had a particularly devastating effect on women and, consequently, on the African family. These programmes have reallocated resources to the detriment of women because they have failed to take note of women's reproductive, productive and socializing roles. By cutting down on social programmes, the SAPs have shifted the greater burden of sustaining the family on to the women. Women's incomes are now disproportionately devoted to the welfare of the family: almost the whole of their income, earned at a cost of a longer and harder working day, is now spent on food, clothes, and health and shelter for the children (Palmer, 1991).

Questions must arise sooner or later regarding the extent to which the African woman will continue to be the pillar of the African family, with all the stress that this entails, without herself breaking down (Sawadogo, 1992). Already, newspaper reports are replete with stories of women abandoning their children; of women killing their spouses, husbands and boyfriends with little apparent provocation; and of women killing their children and committing suicide after. Many African cities are also now witnessing increasing numbers of women beggars, many of whom drag their children along with them and introduce them to a life of begging at a very tender age. Unless policy seriously addresses gender issues in the African family, what now appears to be an inconsequential ripple of family breakdowns will gradually become a tidal wave.

The economic crisis

Conforming to IMF conditions, African governments have had to reduce the size of the public sector – the dominant employment sector – through early retirement, retrenchment and redundancies. The private sector has followed suit. This has resulted in family heads being out of work at a time when inflation is at its highest and is fast increasing. These jobless household heads add to the existing pool of unemployed youths. The impact is often more than dehumanizing (Adepoju, 1993).

Concurrently, governments have removed subsidies on health, education and major staple food items. Cost-recovery strategies call for parents to pay the full cost of health and education services. The cost of these services to families has escalated at a time when a large proportion of family heads are jobless. Parents unable to pay the prevailing school fees reluctantly withdraw their children. Unable to meet the cost of health care, families turn increasingly to traditional or religious forms of healing. Others watch helplessly as the health situation of their children deteriorates (Adepoju, 1992). The gains of the last decades in health status and consequent declines in mortality rates among infants are being eroded, indeed reversed, and malnutrition is more severe now than at any time in the past decade. The impact is heaviest on poorer families, Africa's majority. A UNDP report (1992) noted emphatically that the average African in the 1990s is less educated, less well fed and lacking in remunerative employment to a greater extent than at around the time of independence.

It is apparent that the dramatic changes in Africa's economic fortunes have undermined the ability of families to meet the basic needs of their members. One emerging consequence is the weakening of family control over the youth who, driven by desperation, often engage in illicit activities (drugs, crime, delinquency, alcohol abuse) both as an act of defiance and in a survival strategy to fight what they see as an uncaring society (Adepoju, 1991a).

Education for children has moved beyond the reach of most women and families, with the consequence that growth in primary education has slowed by as much as 50 per cent in countries affected by structural adjustment programmes. Living standards and nutrition have been decreasing across the board, and increasing rates of malnutrition and infant and child mortality bear witness to this. Structural adjustment demonstrates the price to be paid for failing to recognize the strong and intricate interrelationships between the productive and reproductive functions of the African family. Until economic policy takes these issues into account, more of the same negative consequences are to be expected (Palmer, 1991).

The AIDS pandemic

HIV infection is of special concern in Africa, with the number of reported cases of Acquired Immune Deficiency Syndrome (AIDS) increasing daily. Much more important is the large pool of asymptomatic seropositive cases that several surveys and researches have reported, each of which carries a threat of life-long infectivity to the public. The size of this pool is increasing in a geometric progression, and one area of special concern is the impact of the infection on the family. In some countries of Sub-Saharan Africa between 10 and 29 per cent of pregnant women in some localities have been found to be infected. These percentages are much higher for special groups such as prostitutes. Current estimates suggest that up to 50 per cent of the children born to these mothers will be seropositive and that half are likely to develop AIDS and die from it (UNDP, 1991).

The AIDS pandemic has several serious consequences for the African family. The disease is likely to become the major cause of perinatal and infant mortality in many parts of Africa. At the same time, AIDS will also be responsible for the creation of untold numbers of orphans, as both parents in a family die of the disease. Besides the severe strains that AIDS is already placing on the already overstretched public and clinical health services, the social aspects of its ravages will have a potentially devastating effect on the family. The burgeoning number of orphans will come at a time when surviving relatives are themselves financially unable properly to care for them. These orphans are therefore likely to grow up educationally, emotionally and financially deprived, thus becoming a likely pool of future delinquency. Already many African families have demonstrated their inability to cope with family members suffering from AIDS – abandoning them and disassociating themselves from other kin members whom they suspect, often without proof, of having been exposed to the virus. Large numbers of male heads of household have already died from AIDS in such countries as Uganda and Zambia. Such households immediately become female-headed, with all the attendant problems that female-headship entails (Oppong, 1992a).

Besides the high mortality rate that AIDS brings to the African family, HIV is also contributing to very high morbidity status in the family. Persons infected with the HIV virus are likely to present the following symptoms for prolonged periods of time: severe weight loss, fever, night sweats, diarrhoea, tuberculosis and other pulmonary infections, pneumonia, Kaposi's sarcoma and other malignancies, neurological disorders, and a host of other opportunistic infections. Even at the best of times the current health systems cannot cope with the variety and intensity of morbidity arising from HIV; the burden of dealing with HIV morbidity, therefore, has been largely shifted to the family, further draining family resources (Mbugua, 1992).

Family survival strategies

Within the context of the pressures being exerted upon them, African families are responding by adopting a variety of coping mechanisms. These have implications for population and development policies because they are used for crisis management and cannot, therefore, be sustained long term. Among such strategies are migration, marriage, child fostering, and formation of women's groups. Depending on the circumstances, some of these strategies are more successful than others.

A family adopting a survival strategy may endeavour, for example, to sponsor one or more of its members to engage in the labour migration system. The expectation is that the migrant will maintain close touch with family members left behind through visitations and especially remittances. The family may also expect to reap rewards from its investment in the education of one of its members – usually the firstborn male – who has been groomed for migration to the urban formal sector (Oucho, 1990). The migrant member typically feels compelled to remit regularly a substantial proportion of his earned income to support family members left behind. For many families such remittances are a lifeline, the dominant source of income to pay house rent, medical expenses, school fees and a variety of communal commitments (levies, contributions, rituals, etc.), or to build a house or set up small enterprises in preparation for the migrant's return home. Several surveys focusing on the remittance mechanism point out that the migrants often remit up to 60 per cent of their earnings, regularly, to the homeplace through formal and informal channels. In some resource-poor countries of Africa, the importance of remittances – especially foreign currency remittances such as those received in some countries around the Horn of Africa from the Arab world and elsewhere – has been given full recognition by governments, which accordingly encourage such labour migration (Adepoju, 1990; Oucho, 1991).

Traditionally, men have migrated and left behind wives and children, who may join them subsequently. Cases of family or joint migration are rare as women normally either accompany or join their husband later. Autonomous female migration was negatively sanctioned by a variety of customs and made more difficult by job segregation and discrimination in the urban labour market where the gender bias is all too pervasive (Makinwa-Adebusoye, 1988; Adepoju, 1983). But all this has now changed, with female migration burgeoning in recent years. Most striking, however, is the relatively new phenomenon of females migrating internationally, leaving their husbands behind to care for the children – a turnaround in sex roles. This feature is increasingly visible among professionals in Nigeria and Ghana (Adepoju, 1990).

Sponsored, selective migrations are designed to ameliorate the dramatic impact of structural adjustment programmes (SAPs) on the family. As SAPs bite harder and deeper, the pressure on migrants to support other less-privileged family members could become very compelling indeed. Indeed, a new phenomenon of dual households has emerged among African migrant families trying to maximize economic returns from both the home area as well as from the destination. The emergence of such dual households obviously has implications for development planning.

As large numbers of women are left alone in rural areas – and increasingly in urban ones – to cope with the total welfare of their families, their lack of information, skills and technology to lighten their burden leads them to pool resources and experiences with one another. Traditionally informal networks of women's groups existed but their functions were limited to the celebration of births, marriages, deaths and other rites of passage. In recent times, however, these groups have been transformed into income-generating groups. They raise money through activities such as labour-for-cash; chicken or pig-rearing; crafts, both making and marketing; brick-making; and song-and-dance for cash (especially at political functions). Besides raising income, women's participation in these group activities is an attempt to combine their community roles as workers with their domestic roles as wives and mothers, so as to minimize the role conflict that they often feel as a result of polarized dissension about their expected roles among different members of the family and community. In countries such as Kenya the formation of women's groups as a survival strategy has achieved considerable success in the area of home improvement, with women taking responsibility for upgrading their homesteads – from thatched roofs to corrugated iron and brick roofs, from mud walls and earthen floors to wooden and sometimes stone walls and cement floors, from river and well water to piped water. These tasks were traditionally the domain of men but, after their migration in droves, women have successfully stepped in, albeit at some cost to their health (Oucho, 1990, 1991).

Family survival strategies do not always work well. One of the emergent problems is the inability of the young migrant or the new school-leaver to secure a source of income which will enable him or her to contribute to the support of the family, most often the aged parents, in the rural areas. The shrinking of both the formal and informal sectors, both of which have seriously been aggravated by structural adjustment programmes, has rendered jobless massive numbers of young able-bodied males and doomed the expectant parents to a life of destitution. As a result, old men left in the villages are finding it expedient to marry young girls specifically to ensure that there is someone who will take care of them in their old age. Sadly, but inevitably, however, such girls are soon widowed and with their children are thrown into a life of destitution because they are quickly rejected by their husband's family, especially by the sons and daughters of the first wife. In other circumstances, such young wives of older men fail to obtain sexual satisfaction from their husbands and consequently form other liaisons. In countries such as Kenya and Uganda newspaper accounts have documented cases in which young wives have been killed by their much older husbands upon the discovery that they have taken lovers. This is clearly one survival strategy which is causing serious problems at both family and community levels.

Child fostering, which has been a very common practice in African families, is also experiencing difficulties as the potential foster parents themselves face severe economic distress. African families have traditionally both fostered out and received children for varying lengths of time. The relatively better off were recipients of poor relatives and even of non-kin. Many African families even today have no strong objection to sending a child to live with a relative should it be thought necessary, and almost all African families are prepared to delegate child care on a daily basis. The infertile and subfertile look for children to foster as a substitute for their own. With the economic crisis, however, there is an increasing reluctance to accept foster children from other kin members. Even among those who are willing, their own economic circumstances sometimes take such a sudden and dramatic turn for the worse that they are forced to abandon their foster children (Ingstad, 1994). In a study of some borstal institutions in Ghana it was observed that 70 per cent of the inmates had both parents living out of the city or the country and many had been left with foster parents.

Conclusions and policy recommendations

As this chapter has suggested, the African family and society are currently caught in a web of socio-economic disequilibrium: galloping inflation, chronic unemployment, malnutrition, poverty, and illiteracy at the micro level; and overburdened debt payments, internal strife, mismanaged economies, drought, desertification, and so on at the macro level. All these render living conditions in the 1990s inferior to those prevalent in, say, the late 1960s. At the global level, African countries can hardly feed, educate, and clothe their teeming populations or provide adequate shelter and health facilities – the basic needs required for a decent standard of living.

At the same time the African family is driven and sustained by a unique set of cultural, institutional and sociological imperatives quite distinct from those observed elsewhere in the world. The combination of these factors means that population and development policies must henceforth adopt paradigms that address the situation as it actually exists rather than as development planners think it should exist. The evident failure of development strategies, reflected in the decline of the majority of Africa's economic and social indicators of development, has evidently been a result of the use of inappropriate models based on Western stereotypes. It is now clear that such internationally determined frameworks are almost wholly predicated upon definitions and classifications concerning production, reproduction, resource allocation, gender relationships and so forth derived from the experience of industrialized countries but largely inapplicable to Africa.

With regard to the African family, for example, there are certain unique features with which policy makers and decision makers must henceforth be concerned:

1. Decision making within the family is a diffused process achieved through consensus rather than through edicts by an omnipotent head of household. Decisions about which members of the family should migrate, where to and when, are made jointly, as are decisions pertaining to the education of children, marriage, adoption of family planning, the wife's economic and productive activities, and so forth. Therefore development planners who conveniently isolate certain members of the family as the targets of their strategies are unlikely to succeed.

2. Gender inequities in the African family are major and pervasive, and continue from infancy to old age. Studies have shown that conjugal relationships are characterized by separate resource generation and allocation. Husbands and wives ordinarily do not pool their resources in managing their households, and neither do they share leisure activities. This contradicts the new home economic theories commonly used in social demography and uncritically applied to Africa, which are based on the fundamental premise that sees 'the genders as different but equal'. Couples in such theories are assumed to view children as a household good whose production is only constrained by the household budget and the desire for other goods. The decision to have children is thus viewed as having been arrived at through consensus between the husband and wife.

   In reality, in African families the least powerful participants in all household or family decision making are the women, followed of course by the children and adolescents. In many African societies, the company the wife keeps, what dress she wears, where she goes, even when and what she eats, and when and where she seeks medical treatment are sanctioned by senior members of the husband's family, rather than by the husband. Yet these are minor issues compared to the questions of how many children to have and when, whether or not to use family planning, and how to utilize the greater proportion of the household resources – all matters that are completely under the control of the husband and his family.

It is therefore important that the conceptual frameworks used in trying to understand the dynamics of the productive and reproductive endeavours of the African family, and how these are in turn reflected in the structure of the population, are relevant and appropriate to the situation. Currently, official discourse regarding population issues in Africa is largely de-gendered and continues to be dominated by demographic projections and goals. It is becoming increasingly clear, however, that African population policies and programmes cannot succeed without taking into account the strong linkages between women's productive and reproductive activities and how both are driven by the prevailing cultural norms, especially those of patriarchy, as well as by the global economic crisis.

3. African families have still a disproportionately large number of young people. In spite of this, the youngsters in the family are often called upon to assume adult-like productive responsibilities from a very early age, in order to contribute to the general welfare of the family. Inevitably, perhaps, the young of Africa also partake of adult pursuits in matters of lifestyle. Thus a very large proportion of them enter into regular sexual activity at very early ages.

In spite of this, population policies and programmes pertaining to youth have tended to treat early sexual activity as an exception rather than the rule. Consequently, family-life education programmes are introduced all too late in high schools, and the content is diluted to such an extent that it is less than useful. Most family-life education programmes start in secondary schools, on average about three to four years after at least half of the recipients have begun engaging in sexual intercourse. Such programmes also focus heavily on the biology of reproduction and thus fail to equip young people with the skills and knowledge necessary to cope with their own turbulent emotions, self-esteem, sexually transmitted diseases, and problems associated with early pregnancies, contraception and the risks of abortion. It can be summed up as a case of too little, too late.

4. Lastly, most policies have failed to appreciate the centrality of the African family as a productive unit or to tailor the training of young people accordingly. In spite of the formal and informal sectors of African economies, most productive activities in the region are still based at the family level. These include both farm and off-farm activities. Yet the educational systems of the continent continue to provide training that, at best, ill-prepares the youth for these activities and, at worst, alienates them altogether. A redressing of the situation is now well overdue as the droves of young unemployed attest.

Thus development and population policies in Africa, supported by the necessary legal frameworks, need to have a better understanding of family systems, modes of domestic organization, and household, economic and demographic decision-making processes. They should also take particular cognizance of inter-generational and sexual power relations and resource allocations, in order to ensure that the strategies and programmes devised will be supportive of familial tasks and activities that are vital to national economic and demographic goals concerning production, mortality, fertility, and spatial distribution of populations. Such an approach is based on the urgent need to reconcile long-term population and development goals and targets with the adoption of strategies that are pertinent and responsive to the conditions prevailing in Africa. Only in this way can the integrity of the African family be maintained and a sustainable and acceptable quality of life for all be promoted.

CHAPTER 4

The African family between tradition and modernity

A. B. C. Ocholla-Ayayo

The traditional family in Africa

The family is the basic social unit in which norms and values, beliefs and knowledge, and practical living skills are imparted to the young members of the society. The family is the basic economic unit which provides survival chances for infants and children. And the family is the biological unit in which reproductive performance and maintenance of biological continuity takes place. In Africa, it is at the family level that the society feels most acutely the pain of underdevelopment and social change: the family suffers from poor housing conditions, poor health status, food shortages, lack of potable water, nutritional deficiency, and unemployment (Ocholla-Ayayo, 1985, 1991).

Among African peoples, the family has a much wider circle of members than the word connotes in Euro-American usage. Although changes have of course occurred, the concept of family has not changed significantly in Africa during the last 50 to 80 years. In traditional settings, the family includes parents, children, grandparents, uncles, aunts, brothers and sisters – all of whom may have their own children and other immediate relatives (Mbiti, 1969; Ocholla-Ayayo, 1970; Obunga, 1988). Typical of many African societies are what anthropologists term 'extended families', meaning that two or more brothers (in patrilocal societies) or sisters (in matrilocal societies) establish families in one compound or close by one another. Together, these households form one large family. In such cases the number of family members may range from 10 persons to as many as 100 when several wives belonging to each husband are involved.

For African peoples, the family also typically includes departed relatives, whom anthropologists have termed the 'living dead' (Mbiti, 1969; Evans-Pritchard, 1956; Wagner, 1949; Egil, 1974; Ocholla-Ayayo, 1970, 1976). As the name implies, these are kept 'alive' in the memories of the surviving families and are thought to remain interested in the family's affairs. The 'living-dead' solidify and mystically bind together the whole family. Surviving members must not forget the departed, lest misfortune strike them or their relatives. (That survivors nowadays do very often forget is a sign of change.)

African families likewise include unborn members who are still in the loins of the living (Mboya, 1938; Ocholla-Ayayo, 1970, 1976; Mbiti, 1969). These are the locus of the family's hopes and expectations, whereby the family makes sure that its own existence is not extinguished. African parents are anxious to see that their children find husbands and wives, since failure to do so means in effect the death of the unborn and a diminishing of the family as a whole. Hence the generally negative attitude towards 'barren women'; a woman or a man who is incapable of establishing a family is viewed with a mixture of scorn and sympathy (Ocholla-Ayayo, 1988a, 1990, 1991).

Household and family The household in Africa is what in European and American societies would be called 'family'. The household is the smallest unit of the family, consisting of the parents and children, and sometimes the grandparents. Mbiti (1969) has called this unit 'the family at night', for it is at night that parents have only their immediate young children in the same house (the more grown-up ones may have been transferred to other relatives' families). Private household affairs are discussed, and the parents educate the children in matters pertaining to domestic relationships.

If a man has two or more wives, he has as many households, since each wife typically has her own house, erected within the same compound where the other wives and their households live. Such a structural arrangement is not practical in urban settings, where households may be situated in different parts of town. In other instances, some family households may be in urban while others are in rural areas.

The area or compound occupied by one or more households is the homestead or village, in the African context of these terms. The homestead may include houses, gardens or fields, a cattle kraal or shed, granaries, a courtyard, threshing grounds, a men's outdoor fireplace, the children's playground, and family shrines. In many societies the village has a fence round it, marking it as a single village or a set of households. As a rule traditional African houses are round in shape and are built around the village compound so that the houses form a circle or semicircle, generally facing the centre of the compound and the main entrance into the village. Thus each household's members can see what is taking place in the centre of the compound. The circle of the village also symbolizes security: every house can be watched, and granaries surrounding the cattle shed at the centre can be kept safe from intruders (Ocholla-Ayayo 1980).

Ceremonies The food and libations offered by the family at the death of one of its members are tokens of fellowship, communion, remembrance, respect and hospitality, extended to those who are the immediate pillars of the family and to those who have come to say farewell to the deceased. Family households are generally led and represented by the head of the family, whether male or female, in making family offerings, libations or prayers where these still occur. Each community has traditionally had elders or other recognized leaders who take charge of communal rites, although these have diminished in many communities due to social change. Today, many ceremonies and functions such as weddings, settlement of disputes, initiations, festivals, rites of passage, cleansing ceremonies, and upkeep of shrines and sacred objects have been taken over by authorities appointed by either the central government or the church (Bernadi 1959; Evans-Pritchard, 1948).

Changing African families

The traditional African concept of time is mainly unidimensional, implying that human life is relatively stable and almost static; a steady rhythm of life was the norm, and radical change was either unknown, resented, or so slow that it was hardly noticed (Mbiti, 1969). But beginning in the second half of the nineteenth century and swiftly gaining momentum towards the middle of the twentieth century, rapid and radical changes have been taking place everywhere in Africa. These changes are total and involve not only the family but the entire existence of African peoples, making an impact upon religious, economic, political, and social life.

Religion and values   African people are deeply religious and experience these changes in religious terms. Hence the resistance, for example, to fertility control and the use of contraceptives (Ocholla-Ayayo 1985). Once a society has been deprived of its values, it is like a person without clothes who feels shameful and either runs to hide or follows a person with new clothing; it is easy to manipulate and exploit vulnerability. Africa is caught up in a world revolution so dynamic that it is almost beyond human control; no people or country can remain unaffected. In Europe and North America, this revolution goes back five to ten generations, but in Africa it is a relatively recent phenomenon – only the first and second generations of experience of such change (Mbiti, 1969). This has happened without warning and without physical or psychological preparation. African families must now listen to the new rhythms of the drums of science and technology, modern communications, and cities and towns. Families are being divided, forced to live apart in order to labour, and to accept new lifestyles never before practised (Achebe, 1958). The African family must get up and dance, for better or for worse, in the arena of this world drama.

Christianity from Western Europe and North America came to Africa, not simply carrying the gospel of the New Testament but as a complex phenomenon made up of Western culture, politics, science, technology, medicine, schools, and new methods of conquering nature which African families must adopt effectively if they want to survive (Hunter, 1962; Southall and Gutkind, 1956; Herskovits, 1964). Young members of African families, both women and men, must assimilate not only new religions but also science, politics, technology and the modern market economy.

It is these same young people who are becoming detached from their tribal roots. Those attending schools and working in the urban centres and towns, bring back modern innovations and 'all that glitters' to the rural populations. They become the vehicles for carrying the new changes and introducing them to their families and villages. Gradually, new forms of medical care, both preventive and curative, have began to reduce infant and child mortality and bring under control diseases such as smallpox, malaria and cholera that had always been the main killers of African families. In most parts of Africa, better health care is resulting in increased population, and a growing population brings with it problems which the rate of African economic development has been unable to solve (see Henin, 1981; Ominde et al., 1983).

Detribalization? These changes, which affect all spheres of life, have been termed 'detribalization' on the grounds that the traditional lifestyle is being so deeply undermined that tribal identities are fading away as other identities make claims on the individual and the community (Mbiti, 1969). But if one looks at Africa in the 1990s, one sees a more complex picture in which tribal identities survive. In traditional terms, the family is the nucleus of both individual and corporate existence, the space within which a person experiences personal consciousness both individually and in terms of other members of society. Now, the family is the unit of African life most severely affected by change. Within one family or household two totally different worlds may be found coexisting: the children may be attending university while the parents remain illiterate and concerned mainly with cultivating their fields with wooden sticks. In such a family, there are two sets of expectations, economic standards, cultural concerns, and world views (Van den Berghl, 1965; Rees, 1959; Mbiti, 1969). These changes show themselves outwardly in many ways, such as education for both sexes, styles of clothing, housing, food, means of transport and moral behaviour.

Consequences of modernization In the final analysis, it is the family and the individuals within it who really feel the change – experience it, accept or reject it, and hasten or slow it down. Modern change has brought many families and individuals in Africa into situations entirely unknown in traditional lifestyles. Some are forced directly or indirectly to practise prostitution or work in mines, factories or European-style farms or houses, leaving their land, families and relatives. Sudden detachment from the land and family – to which Africans are mystically bound – and being thrust into situations where corporate existence has no meaning have meant that individuals are severed, cut off, and pulled out of the context of corporate morality, customs and traditional solidarity (Mbiti, 1969; Ocholla-Ayayo, 1991; Van den Berghl, 1965; Rees, 1959; UNESCO, 1956). People lose their values and norms and have no firm footing any more. Mbiti (1969) refers to these as people who are 'uprooted but not necessarily transplanted'. They float from the rural world to the urban and back again, but they are dead to the corporate humanity of their forefathers. Lacking the moral values of the traditional set-up, their social behaviour brings them only misery and untimely death, as witnessed in the current AIDS pandemic (Ocholla-Ayayo, 1990).

Individuals are involved in these changes and yet alienated from them; becoming alienated both from traditional ways of life and the new lifestyles brought about by modern change (Rees, 1959; Southall, 1961; Mbiti, 1969; Ocholla-Ayayo, 1991). They are poised between two positions: the traditional solidarity which supplied land, customs, ethics, rites of passage, a burial place upon death, customary law, religious participation, and historical depth (ethnic identity); and a modern way of life of economic activity, education, transport, communications and political debate which are very important for individuals but are externally controlled and manipulated (Ocholla-Ayayo and Igbozurike, 1973).

The traditional life of the family is fast being swept aside, and the further it recedes into the past the more golden it appears. African families today can neither return to the past nor find much hope in the future. Families are divided into two, blaming each other for having supported change or for not having resisted it firmly enough. (Thus the father may blame the mother for having encouraged the daughter by accepting her premarital child, to which the mother responds by saying, 'She is not the only one with a premarital child – how about the many around us right here, and why didn't you try to stop them?')

Urbanization and family crisis Modernization in the urban centres has brought problems of housing, employment, earning and spending money, alcoholism, prostitution and corruption. Unwanted children, orphans, criminals, delinquents and prisoners, all of whom need special social care, present problems beyond the family's abilities to cope. In the traditional set-up, some of these problems would have been dealt with through kinship networks, but today such networks are disintegrating, and in any case the ties of kinship have not the same power in the city as they had in the country. Individualistic urban life demands its own code of behaviour. Emphasis has shifted from 'our' to 'mine', from the 'we' of traditional corporate life to the 'I' of modern individualism. Today, people say, 'I take my child to school', 'I go to church', 'I go to the market to sell my crops', and so on. When a child falls ill, perhaps only one or two other people know about it and come to visit; when one is hungry he or she finds that begging food from a neighbour is either shameful, unrewarding or both; when bad news arrives from relatives in the countryside, a person cries alone even if hundreds of other people rub shoulders with him or her in the workplace; and even when being attacked in the street by robbers, the individual cries and struggles alone. The masses around the individual and his or her family are both blind and deaf to the family's situation, indifferent to them as people; yet the solution to individual socio-economic problems is in corporate life of a kind not necessarily equivalent to traditional life, but which considers the welfare of the many and that of individuals as well.

The family experiences great stress and strain in this changing situation. Everywhere in Africa, families are being told to raise funds for school buildings, to pay school fees, to contribute towards health care, to pay one-tenth of their income to the church. They are taxed on every item they buy in the shop, and if they are in the towns and cities, they have to pay house rent, pay for water and electricity, and pay for sewage and trash collection. If they are workers, their salaries are below the level of subsistence. Living conditions are universally appalling. In the urban zones families are housed in slums and crowded rooms, and in the rural areas they still live in round huts of the type used by their ancestors. African families lack clean water and have no regular means of transport. In most regions the few health centres that exist are continually without medicines and people must walk long distances for any of these services. Famine and drought are common, conflicts and wars that displace people are frequent and widespread.

The size of the family is shrinking: from the traditional extended family concept to one in which the parents and their children constitute the family in the modern sense of the word. The authority and respect that parents used to enjoy under traditional morality and customs are being challenged by the younger generations or transferred to the central authority. In many homes there is rebellion of children against their parents because norms and values that used to bind the generations together have been eroded by changing values and the realities of life as it is lived today. The fact that children and young people are living away from home for most of the year in order to attend schools, colleges, universities or to look for work, tends to undermine family solidarity and authority. When a young man wants to get married, if he can raise a few heads of cattle from his own salary, he need not go to his parents for permission to wed. In most cases, parents just hear that a couple is living together as husband and a wife. The education of children has been passed from parents and the community to teachers and has become more a case of book learning as an end in itself rather than an education which prepares the young for mature life and future careers.

Whereas under the traditional set-up both boys and girls received preparatory education concerning marriage, sex and family life – especially during and after their initiation rites – modern schools provide little such education. Some parents who never went to high school find it difficult to provide their children with even an informal education, while the schools spend more time teaching young people about dissecting frogs and colonial history than about how to establish happy homes and family life (Mbiti 1969).

Marriage and family instability have increased considerably under modern strains, giving rise to higher rates of divorce and separation than in traditional life. Polygyny is gradually dying out in many parts of Africa, while concubinage is rapidly increasing in the towns and cities; in Kenya it has spread throughout the rural areas as well. Married men often must leave their wives at home in the countryside and go to work in the towns, where they remain for several months or even years without going back to their families. At the same time, families may insist on bridewealth for their daughters before marriage, so quite often, the boy takes the girl and runs away with her to the city. Prostitution can be found in every African city and town in the 1990s, this being an economic necessity or convenience for women since it helps them to earn some money, find somewhere to live, and meet some of the demands of city life (Ocholla-Ayayo, 1989, 1990).

One of the most serious problems African families are currently facing is due to the men being forced to work in towns, plantations or mines while their wives and children remain in the countryside. This is partly because of housing shortages in the town or workplace, and partly because the men cannot afford to keep their families with them as someone is needed to remain to take care of land and livestock. Geographical separation of families creates great strains on the emotional, psychological, sexual and marital lives of husbands and wives. On the one hand, children grow up without a father at home and have an image of their father as someone existing in a distant town from where he occasionally sends money for clothes and school fees, and comes home once a year or every two years. The father hardly shares in the daily responsibilities and concerns of childraising; the wife becomes both mother and father to the children. It is important to note, however, that many wives in these situations have tried very hard to create a home and meet the problems with courage and rectitude.

It has been observed that greater marital strain arises in marriages where there is a wide educational gap between husband and wife – especially where, after marriage, the husband receives university or overseas education while his wife has had only primary or junior secondary school education. A number of these marriages seem to succumb under the strain and are wrecked as a result of a gap in values and world view between the partners.

In many parts of East Africa, traditional cultural values and modern socio-economic circumstances have interacted over time to produce, so to speak, a new African 'social contract' where grandparents (and particularly grandmothers) increasingly take on the role of economic providers for their grandchildren. Premarital teenage pregnancies, in particular, are having a serious effect on inter-generational relations as grandparents now assume new support functions amid economic hardship.

Rural vs. urban families Although rural life in Africa retains many of the social features prevalent in the pre-colonial era of about a century ago, many modern lifestyles have also arisen. The majority of African families continue to be oriented to an agrarian lifestyle and depend on the family labour force for subsistence foods and cash crops. Within a family, as in the past, women and children are the most important source of farm labour. For this reason large families are still desired by both men and women, and polygyny is seen as means of increasing family size and thus providing additional free labour. In a recent study of western Kenya, most families interviewed responded to the question 'What do you like most about your children?' by saying, 'They help a lot in domestic and farm activities.' (Kilbride, 1990). Most families in rural areas still expect their children to help with various activities. Rural family life continues to be very much a collective enterprise, constituting an interpersonal, inter-dependent system within which kinship, and age and gender roles are clearly utilitarian and reciprocal (Kilbride 1986, 1992; Ocholla-Ayayo, 1990; Obunga, 1987).

Family life in urban areas has changed much more. Urban children contribute much less economically. Older children may help clean the house or be sent out to buy vegetables and a loaf of bread, but that is about all. Urban African families tend to experience children as a burden, while rural children are still highly valued, serve important economic roles in the family, and are the responsibility of extended family members in situations where parents are unable to provide care.

Demographic change and economic growth

Three aspects need to be examined when considering the effects of the demographic situation in a country on its economic development: (a) population size (family size); (b) growth rate (family total fertility rate); and (c) age distribution (birth spacing, age distribution within the family). These factors are closely interrelated and often difficult to separate. Their interactions and consequences are discussed below.

A favourable demographic situation at the household level can mean different things to different families. To some it means that families can consume more; to others it means that the national economy saves and invests more of its annual gross national product (which is rare in Africa). To still others, it may mean more capital per worker, so that output per worker is increased, which is the essence of economic development. It is not necessary to decide which of these views is the more correct, for all these manifestations of economic development are associated with higher output per capita even at the level of household units.

One of the most stubborn tendencies in popular thought about the family is to refer to families as being 'small' or 'large' in size. Elementary logic suggests that there must then be a state in which the family has just the 'right' number of children – the optimum family size. But in the present state of affairs nothing is easier than to show how impossible it is to argue that birth spacing or large family size alone is a major factor in determining family economic prosperity. No matter how it is measured, density can be high and low or family size can be large or small in countries that are poor or rich, without the slightest systematic tendency.

Indeed, it is plausible that in very sparsely settled regions of Africa a larger population or a larger family size would be better able to make use of natural resources. There would be economies of scale, the division of labour would be facilitated by greater density of settlement, transportation costs would be lower, and so on. Beyond a certain point, of course, there might be diminishing returns and the advantages of a larger population or larger family size would vanish. For the time being, if the optimum family size seems larger than the actual one, it is easy to believe that population growth does not constitute a problem. The central flaw in such an argument is that it is vague in relation to the role of technological change and capital formation, which will displace the point of 'optimum' family size (or population) even while the actual family size (or population) is moving towards it.

If there is any relationship at all between the rate of family size change and the rate of family capital formation and technical change, then the fastest way of raising family income per head is not necessarily to increase family size. In some conditions it may well be, and there may be reasons to encourage it, but the entire argument breaks down if the growth in family size competes with family capital formation. Thus female migration and wealth dissipation have serious consequences for both fertility and economic growth for those who practise patrilineal exogamous family formation. By and large, however, size seems to be of subordinate importance. At a macro level, neither the present nor the future size of population constitutes a major economic problem; the real problem, according to Henin (1981), is the excessive rate of population growth which impedes the progress of modernization.

At the micro, or household level, the real problem is not only the high total fertility rates (TFRs) detrimental to economic savings and investment, but also birth spacing (which impacts upon age distribution within the family). The dependency ratio is based on the fact that every member of a society is a consumer but only some members are producers. Africa is a continent with a smaller proportion of its population producing goods and services while a larger proportion of its population consumes and enjoys the services being produced by the few.

Dependency and economic development   The burden of dependency (the ratio of persons who are in a dependent status because of their age – too young or too old to work – to persons at ages making them eligible for productive work) is relatively high in areas characterized by persistent high birth rates, and low in areas with low birth rates. The burden of dependency is, therefore, lower in contemporary Europe than in Africa. African families deviate in this respect in two important ways from their counterparts in Europe. First, fertility levels are certainly very much higher and indicate a long road ahead if African families are to match the fertility levels prevailing among European families. The second important deviation lies in the fertility differences between regions and countries in Africa. What factors lead to such differentials?

Little is known of the reasons for these differences in fertility either between or within countries. Various factors such as differences in levels of education, age at marriage and in proportions marrying have been suggested (United Nations, 1965; Henin, 1981). Such distinctions, however, could only play a rather minor role in bringing about the observed differences, since available information shows that in most African countries most women are married by the age of 20.

Another factor that has usually been suggested is the prevalence of polygyny in African families or marriages (United Nations, 1965; Henin, 1981). Lower fertility on this count may arise from the lower average frequency of coitus among women in polygamous marriages. Henin mentions favouritism, which means that some wives may be preferred to others; this may also result in a number of wives being deprived of sexual relations. Ocholla-Ayayo and Ottieno (1987, 1988) have shown, however, that fertility differential in polygynous families depend more heavily on coital frequency rules than on preference. Other factors which may be important are frequency of divorce and early widowhood, the latter resulting from excessively high mortality in Africa generally. Further reductions may result from prolonged separation when husbands migrate in search of employment (United Nations, 1965). Prolonged lactation and taboos surrounding it likewise have an effect in many parts of Africa, though this is fading as a result of mothers taking jobs outside the home.

Funerals and dependency Deaths and the resulting funeral ceremonies impose conditions on African families that are contrary to the principles of production, consumption and savings. Funeral practices in Africa typically involve large numbers of people – both consanginal kin and affinal relatives, plus friends and onlookers who come to witness the send-off of the deceased member of the community. In many societies, such persons not only come to bid farewell to the departed but also expect the bereaved family to feed them during the period of the funeral, which may last several days or even weeks. Consequently it is common after a funeral for the family to have no food, no money for the children's school fees, and no means of transport. All previous savings may be used up within a week of the death of a family member; the granaries are emptied and cows, goats and sheep are slaughtered for the mourners. Communities with high death rates also, of course, have high funeral rates, meaning large numbers of consumers who come to consume what they did not produce and make no contribution. Thus funerals further raise the dependency ratio.

Insofar as population is increasing, the number of consumers at funerals also increases and the dependency ratio rises. At the village or family level this can have far-reaching consequences; the impact of funerals on family economic development is very real when examined from the standpoint of the size and structure of the family. According to some African customs a family with many married daughters always has more 'oche', or in-laws, during a funeral. Each brother-in-law must have an animal sacrificed in his honour at a funeral for his father-in-law, mother-in-law or any grand-parents of his wife – indeed any close relative of his wife. On the other hand, a family with many sons, married or not, would have many agnatic kin at the funeral ceremony.

Family ties in the urban setting

Thoroughgoing urbanization entails considerable socio-cultural and socio-economic autonomy from the rural way of life commonly practised by the majority of African societies. But the increasing number of people moving to live and work in small and secondary towns throughout Africa implies a merging of the urban ways of life with the traditional systems, inasmuch as these minor urban centres will be required to interface with agriculture to provide all the forms of support which may be required (Ocholla-Ayayo, 1989). The contact networks required for the achievement of socio-economic goals in the new African urban–rural setting have been studied through the lens of kinship networks. Social security is a mechanism that aims at transferring financial and other economic benefits from the working generation to those who cannot work because of age limits, disability, or other dependency status; however, it should be linked closely to the principle of kinship ties, which provides a traditional form of social security. Despite the existence of formal, government-supported social security schemes, in many African states the aged and the young have preferred to depend on parents and certain other categories among the members of kinship groups (Ocholla-Ayayo, 1984). In societies where the family is a tightly integrated unit, the aged would not be of concern beyond the immediate family, especially in urban settings. Under-aged children without parents may look for guidance from a member of the kinship group who has moved to the urban areas, since there are no under-age children's homes (orphanages, etc.) in the rural areas.

The effects of urbanization on the role of the extended kinship are thus fundamental to the principle of socialization and solidarity among the members of kinship units. While Wirth (1938) once contended that urbanites are characterized by secondary rather than primary intimate relationships and that the urban family, wherever it may be, is free from the large kinship group leaving members free to pursue their own interests, Ocholla-Ayayo (1986, 1989) and Obunga (1987) have concluded that Wirth was referring either to Euro-American families or to long-term, permanent city dwellers who have become completely cut off from any rural relationships over the passage of time. In most African countries, such a situation is only just beginning to emerge. The predominant situation, rather, is that urbanization has led to split families and to very loose kinship structures that play down the importance of relatives. Even the communal responsibility to care for one another has been eroded as emphasis has shifted to the individual family.

In many African countries, including Kenya, Uganda and Tanzania, urbanization is already close to reducing kinship down to the conjugal family (parents and children). Elsewhere, many studies have been carried out which attempt to refute the idea that economic and other needs formerly met within the network are now being served solely by non-kin agencies. But Smelser (1967) has argued that even the most developed countries still show some viable extended kinship structures. Studies of Kenya by Ocholla-Ayayo (1986) and Obunga (1987) stress that the process of decline of extended kinship should not be oversimplified. While some features of it may be eroding, others – such as social security for the ageing and under-age – may survive for long periods, not only in Kenya but also elsewhere in Africa. These studies have also shown that the kin network often plays a positive role in residential migration, with an economic and residential foothold being carved out in an urban area by one individual who is followed later by another kin member.

There is also the question of kinship obligation whereby an urbanite feels obliged to relate to and assist the other kin. Such assistance is a crucial factor in binding kin relationships and in contributing to social welfare. In fact, to the adjustment-oriented urbanite, selective obligations to kin is one method that the family uses to adapt to industrialization. The urban African is dependent upon rural products. Kinship obligation is not based on the social responsibility norm, but rather upon the fact that the existing relationship is an ethical one which includes a moral obligation to provide support. Relatives are, to a great extent, a 'given' in the individual's social milieu; he or she does not choose them. They may be scattered or clustered, numerous or few, remote or proximate, depending upon the fertility, migration and interpersonal history of previous generations (Adams, 1968).

Kinship links in the secondary towns of Africa are perhaps more intensive and more a matter of daily routine than the kind of links found in major cities. Also, inasmuch as these are relatively young towns, one would expect kinship loyalties to persist among the majority of their residents. But in major cities such as Nairobi or Lagos, kin networks have begun to take a different pattern. Kinship networks in Khartoum, for instance, are seldom entirely dispersed but are held together only by telephone calls, letters and periodic weekend visits. Most Nairobi or Harare residents are still only first and second generation residents of the city (Obudho, 1981); most, having been raised in rural parts of the country, still have more attachments to the rural areas than exclusive links developed within the urban area itself. Thus it is natural for a kin web to be already firmly established within the city. Most of the kin are found in the urbanites' rural homes of origin and it is to these homes that they travel or unite to seek assistance of one form or another (Ocholla-Ayayo, 1986, 1989; Obunga, 1987).

In major urban centres like Nairobi, Harare, Dakar, Lagos or Addis Ababa, residents have distinct categories of interaction, which may be professional, official or business-related. Even the more social and religious ones, such as attending football matches or going to church, do not bring relationships much closer than the kind we find in kinship networks. While some churches have recently begun to provide some elements of moral support by coming to the aid or comfort of their members who are bereaved, the church does not take on the responsibility to support individuals' education, health expenses, marriage, food and other daily expenses which are associated with kinship obligations. (Ocholla-Ayayo, 1989) Thus, while socio-cultural obligations have much to offer, the responsibilities of kinship cannot be easily taken over by any individual or organization.

Mukras and Oucho (1986) have shown how urban–rural remittances can reaffirm kinship ties. Ocholla-Ayayo (1986, 1989) and Obunga (1987), examining the extent of kinship dependency and the exchange of remittances, have pointed out how rural residents also transfer their agricultural products, food in particular, to urban dwellers. Rural kin also secure property for urban dwellers. All these do not balance the urban remittances to rural kin, however, and as a result the urban dweller with many rural kin cannot save and invest for future development.

Kin dependency and flows of wealth Caldwell (1980) has argued that the prime mover behind fertility transition is education: 'In traditional family-based production, family morality dictates that children work hard, demand little and respect the old. Wealth flows upwards and high fertility is profitable.' But such a family morality cannot, according to Caldwell, survive the change brought about by national education systems. Public education is seen to:

1. increase both the direct and indirect costs of bearing children;
2. decrease the child's potential as a worker both inside and outside the home;
3. make the child – as a future producer rather than a present producer – dependent upon the household for support;
4. promote agendas, such as increasing production in a capitalist economy, that differ from the parents' values; and
5. propagate individualistic values.

Caldwell adds that where occupational–educational chains exist, older children who have been educated often hold jobs which enable (or oblige) them to send the younger children to school. The strategy for parents is then to educate the first three children, for example, and thereby reduce considerably the educational expenses for the remaining children. Caldwell did not see this as perpetuation of kinship morality, whereby older sons would be obliged to support not only their younger brothers but also other members of the extended family. Caldwell (1989, 1982) noted that the persistence of such kin networks lessen the impact of education on large households.

Wealth will continue to flow upwards in Africa so long as kinship lineages and ties persist. Indeed, recent studies suggest that the direction of wealth flow in urban–rural remittances continues to be upwards, that is, from children to parents for the bulk of the children's working lives and only briefly from parents to children during the latter's schooling period (Bradley, 1992; Mukras and Oucho, 1986).

Studies conducted in Kenya by the present author between 1986 and 1989 had the following conceptual hypotheses:

1. Kinship obligation and kin dependency are normative and are likely to persist because they have a moral basis.
2. Kinship obligation and kin dependency are based on both social responsibility and the fact that kinship relations exist.
3. Urbanization has not given rise to values that have completely isolated

the nuclear family from its kin, even though the kinship unit has been reduced – indeed minimalized.

4. The importance of relatives has been undermined by urbanization, to the extent that communal mutual responsibility to and for each other has eroded.

5. Kinship dependency affects the family socially and economically since family relations have been reduced to mere money relations and are appreciable only if economically or financially rewarding.

The empirical findings of the Kenyan studies were as follows:

1. A large majority of urban dwellers in the city of Nairobi and in Migori town were found to be staying with kin or affines, whatever the nature of the dwelling.

2. Urban dwellers were found to be supporting the education of their kin or affines, regardless of their income.

3. There was no urban dweller who did not support in full or in part the education of a kin or affine.

4. Most urban dwellers have been asked for some assistance, either financial or material, from kin or affines.

5. Help in job placement is a common request from kin or affine, one which every urban dweller expects to receive.

6. A kin and affinal relative may be welcomed regardless of whether he or she brought a gift.

7. A kin or affinal relative may arrive regardless of invitation or notification of intention to come.

8. A clan member is obliged to welcome a kin or affine regardless of his or her socio-economic status.

9. Kin or affines who come to stay for an extended period with relatives living in the urban area are coming to look for jobs or are working but have no housing or school.

10. Kinship ties are important as social and economic security.

11. Members of the kinship group will be the most willing to collect money to transport the body of a deceased clan member, regardless of whatever financial difficulties he or she may have.

Additional findings of the Kenyan studies (Ocholla-Ayayo 1986, 1987) should be mentioned here. Some 62.2 per cent of families were staying with kin or affines and supporting fully or partly the education of their relatives. Of the 2500 persons interviewed, 63 per cent had been obliged to provide financial and material assistance toward the burial and funerals of relatives who had died at home or in urban centres. Some 90.7 per cent had accepted responsibility, in one way or another, for assisting kin or affines. Thus compliance with such requests was quite high, an indication that respect for kinship and affinal ties was flourishing. The findings also suggest that the dependency ratio remains quite high, and that without this kind of security the unemployed and under-aged, the aged, and the handicapped would simply perish. Such a high degree of compliance to kin demands further encourages kin dependence. Most of the respondents said they were under social or moral obligations to stay with relatives. While it is evident that the respondents had not invited kin to stay with them in the urban areas, moral obligations were motivated by custom (Ocholla-Ayayo, 1976; Baylis, 1958). When respondents who had come to seek help from those working in the city were asked if they had any other dependants at their rural home or anywhere in Kenya who relied on them for their livelihood or anything else, 57.6 per cent of them said they had.

Those urban dwellers who had kin staying with them but felt unobliged said it was too expensive or there were others in the town with whom these relatives could stay quite comfortably, but that they just preferred staying with them. The working kin felt that their income was far too small to pay rent for a reasonably decent house, feed their own family, and still have something to share with relatives coming to the city or remaining at home in the countryside. It should be noted that the dependent kin who were said to be working were either casual labourers or temporarily employed.

As to whether kinship relations were regarded as intimate or important in one's total life situation, 61 per cent indicated that they were and only 39 per cent – mostly of the younger generation (between 20 and 29 years) – maintained that they were not important. Those who maintained that it was unimportant to keep kinship relationships intimate argued that keeping such relationships was expensive and cumbersome, ruined families and discouraged independence and privacy on the one hand, and led to poverty on the other. Those who said they were important gave various reasons, such as mutual benefit in time of need, companionship, consultations, harmony, unit of continuity, social security, solidarity, 'family-hood', upholding tradition, 'who else could we go to', and the sheer fact that relatives could not easily be ignored. Many concluded by saying such things as 'blood is thicker than water'; 'charity begins at home'; 'if he does not help us when he can, he will not expect others to help him, say, when he is thrown out of his job'; or 'who will bury him?'.

Although urbanites recognized the economic strains of the extended family, they still held that kinship relationships were necessary, especially in times of happiness and sorrow. Those in urban areas perhaps realize this more than anyone because in time of need, it is the kin and affines who come to one's aid. Urbanites are also aware that there is a real need for socio-economic development, but this can only be effected through saving and investment. With extensive kinship ties and support networks, however, this is not possible. They also felt that the persistence of the extended kinship system was one sure way of upholding the African tradition of mutual love and dependence.

African social life is built upon the principle of kinship networks of distribution and consumption, but consider the level of production. The concept of *harambee* at the household, lineage and clan levels suggests that kinship ideology and kinship systems of production, distribution and consumption are more positive than any system that could be introduced in Africa. The fact is, no government will come to support an individual or a household unit – the family – in time of need, but the kinship network can do this and has done it. In this author's view, then, the problem is how to perfect the system in the light of modernization. Even so, a positive view of the kinship support network should not obscure its disadvantages. The view is widespread that kin are a nuisance to the urban household, especially as their presence is seen to affect the family negatively in terms of financial and material well-being. Moreover, decisions on matters relating to routine welfare (shelter, education, food, education, clothing, health) usually provoke very trying moments for the family.

Sacrificing for investments of all kinds always entails a degree of suffering. That is perhaps one aspect of development. One must make some saving to use as security in old age. The security that kinsmen provide at old age is what one invested in their well-being. Homes for the aged cannot provide the kind of social security one can receive from the members of one's kinship group. Thus most people who supported a kinsperson in one way or the other said they felt obliged to do so. But this obligation should not be seen as merely social. It is a socio-cultural and socio-economic obligation.

Conclusions

Support networks provided by extended family ties comprise stable relationships, not sporadic ones. The functions of the extended family through kinship networks in the development of the new rural–urban patterns is an area which has yet to be adequately researched. Whether the system is disintegrating due to urbanization in Africa is still debatable and, therefore, remains an interesting area of study. The fact that the income of one person has to be redistributed to many others who fall within the kinship network ought to be of concern to government. An African worker's income helps to educate, clothe, provide shelter for, and feed others in addition to his or her own immediate family. Adherence to the demands of extended kinship therefore seems to be one way of developing one's larger family and the community in general. To this extent, a more relaxed taxation system could be one way of encouraging individuals to support others in a newly introduced cost-sharing policy in many African countries. On the other hand, it is certainly the case that some individuals in urban centres find themselves unnecessarily over-burdened by kin who could have been enabled to become more productive in their rural homes. Thus development plans could take care of such anomalies by promoting the development of rural areas and the creation of jobs. Migrants move to urban areas because of the lack of facilities in the rural areas; an urban centre is viewed as a place of relief and hope, where one can receive educational opportunities, medical services and, above all, employment. If the new African rural–urban centres are to be viewed in this way, then they must provide the opportunities and facilities badly needed by the rural population.

CHAPTER 5

The African family and changing nuptiality patterns

A. F. Aryee

Sub-Saharan Africa is known for its diversity of political, economic and socio-cultural systems, and for societies which until fairly recent times lived in relative isolation from each other. It is remarkable that, within this wide diversity, some social institutions tend to exhibit certain common characteristics. One such institution is marriage, the basic features of which have been extensively documented in the ethnographic literature.

There are still many areas of Africa today where the avalanche of changes sweeping the continent has hardly made a dent in the rigidity or sanctity with which these traditional institutions are maintained. In some remote or rural areas of 1990s Africa, it is still possible to encounter marriage practices, beliefs and rituals that have changed very little from ancestral practices. In the greater part of Africa, however, traditional African marriage has, like many other institutions, succumbed to the forces of urbanization, migration, modern education, Christianity and so on.

The major catalyst of these changes was the colonial penetration of the continent, especially from the middle half of the nineteenth century when the 'scramble for Africa' started in earnest. Colonialism took on different shapes, but invariably included a Christian religious component in the form of new doctrines and practices, a new economic system oriented towards the metropolitan centre, and new political and educational structures. Another major world religion, Islam, had reached Africa centuries earlier, and in Western and Eastern Africa particularly had acquired deep roots through both trade and proselytization. The result has been the emergence of a multiplicity of practices and systems which are markedly different from the traditional systems and yet are so widely practised that they have acquired, to varying degrees, a legitimacy or acceptance of their own.

To understand these complex forces and the ways in which they have affected the institution of marriage, it is useful first to outline the main features of traditional marriage in Africa before going on to discuss ongoing changes.

Main features of traditional marriage

The first, and probably the most important feature is that marriage cannot be separated conceptually from the institution of the family. Marriage is only a means to an end, and its most important *raison d'être* is the production of children to enhance the size, status and power of the larger family, lineage or clan. Marriage is thus, in essence, a union between two families rather than between two individuals.

The importance of this *raison d'être* for marriage is expressed in most societies by the payment of some dowry or bridewealth by one family or lineage, usually that of the prospective bridegroom, to the other family, usually the bride's. In a matrilineal system – such as among the Ashanti of Ghana, for whom the 'benefits' of such a union accrued more to the woman's lineage than to the husband's – the dowry paid was relatively insignificant in value, and the ceremony itself perfunctory. On the other hand, the 40 head of cattle traditionally paid for a Nuer bride, and the elaborate ceremonies which accompanied the transaction, served to emphasize the seriousness with which the society assessed the relative gains and losses in the bridal exchange between the two families. While in the matrilineal case, the woman's fertility served ultimately to enhance the interests of her lineage, in the patrilineal case the situation was reversed.

The importance attached to marriage as a means of acquiring rights over the woman's reproductive capacity is underlined by the fact that in many African societies the final marriage payments are not made until the woman has given proof of her fertility. In other societies, the return of all or part of the bridewealth is obligatory if the woman is unable to produce children to seal the marriage bond. The institution of the sororate provided additional insurance: guaranteeing that if the wife died too early or failed in her duties, a sister would replace her in the marital relationship to perform the basic function of reproduction. What all this means in essence is that in traditional African marriage, the rights *in genetricem* took precedence over the rights *in uxorem*, and the rights and interests of the family superseded those of the two individuals linked in the marital relationship.

Acquisition of rights over the woman's reproductive capacity partially explains why African marriage is often described as an extended process of uncertain duration rather than as a single definitive event or ceremony (Radcliffe-Brown and Forde, 1950; Aryee and Gaisie, 1982). Where child betrothal is practised, as among the Konkomba of Northern Ghana, several years may elapse before the couple actually start to live together as man and wife, but symbolic ties and mutual exchanges are maintained during the intervening period as an expression of the union between the two families.

Polygyny was also the norm rather than the exception; while the practice was limited by the demographic factor of numerical gender balance, various institutional mechanisms such as a substantially lower age at marriage for women or early remarriage of the divorced and widowed served to increase the pool of women available for marriage. The largely subsistence economic system favoured early economic independence and therefore early marriage, especially as the labour of the wife and her children constituted an important asset.

The rules or customs pertaining to the living arrangements of the couple also varied widely. Neolocal residence was the more common, but other residential forms such as virilocal, uxorilocal, patrilocal and matrilocal were widely recognized and practised. There were other situations in which the couple never shared the same living quarters throughout their entire married lives. In this case, visiting by the wife was the norm; children of the couple alternated between the father's and mother's households, with age and sex being the primary determinants of a child's usual place of residence.

Contemporary form of marriage or types of union

The variety of ways in which marriage is contracted in African society in the 1990s provides one of the clearest testimonies to the transformation which marriage has undergone in modern society. In most societies, the vast majority of marriages are still contracted by the performance of the customary rites, but these rites have been considerably modified, both in form and substance. Not only are the ceremonies more elaborate, but even more significant is the fact that the amount of monies paid and the range of goods demanded or offered as part of the bridewealth have increased sharply – to the point where they have become a serious deterrent to marriage. Where once only a few cowries and a bottle of local gin were exchanged, now huge amounts of money, imported beverages, sewing machines, and other expensive gifts have become the norm. The simple nuptial ceremony at which friends and family gathered to sing and dance has now been replaced in urban Africa with a public ceremony complete with formal invitation cards, hired musicians and lavish public entertainment.

Among the Fulani, for example, it has been reported that marriage has become a substantial economic burden involving a variety of gifts in cash and kind. The lengthy and costly process may start with an advance payment of about £60 plus additional gifts of clothes. It is followed by the engagement ceremony, which involves gifts of two calves or goats. At the marriage itself – which may easily cost £200 – more gifts in cash are presented to the bride's family along with three heifers for the bride (Hill and Thiam, 1987). It is easy to see why the larger family retains such a pre-eminent role in the decision-making process. In the urban areas of Africa, many families and couples are known to borrow heavily in order to finance weddings, often with very dire consequences for the financial health of those involved. One study among the Ibo illustrates vividly how bridewealth payments have evolved over the years, from a simple system in which bridewealth was settled primarily through the prospective bride-groom's offer of labour to the current situation in which bridewealth varies from 2000 naira for girls with primary and high school education to 10,000 naira for university graduates (Isiugo-Abanihe, 1987).

Another striking feature of change is the coexistence of a wide range of different forms of marriage within the same society, nation, or socio-cultural group. An examination of African survey data on form of marriage may show the customary form of marriage coexisting with a civil or religious ceremony, a consensual or free union (variously described as mutual consent, common-law, *conviviente*, visiting unions), a 'blessing' (in church), or combinations of two or more of these. The civil ceremony may take place before a marriage registrar, and the religious ceremony may take place in a church or before the cadi or the *djemaa* in countries such as Algeria, Chad or Madagascar.

The Liberian DHS data showed that as many as 38.3 per cent of women of reproductive age in the sample surveyed were living with partners in such informal or transient unions. The comparative proportions were relatively low, but still significant, for countries such as Nigeria (7.4 per cent), Botswana (10.8 per cent), and Uganda (13.5 per cent).

The same relationship may also be marked by different kinds of ceremonies at different stages of the union, depending on factors such as the couples' social and financial status or religious affiliation. It is now not uncommon for marriages to begin with the performance of very simple customary rites. Pressures from family members (especially the bride's) or improvement in the couple's financial status may lead later to a more elaborate Western-style ceremony, either in a church or at a registry office. Similarly, a 'blessing' in church may take place after several years of marriage to symbolize the church's official acceptance of the union.

A recent study in Ivory Coast illustrates the complex nature of these marital unions in contemporary society. Unions in which the marriage ceremony, the consummation of the union and co-residence of the spouses began simultaneously constituted just under half (46.3 per cent) of the ever-married women in the sample surveyed. But nine other types of sequential marital arrangements were also identified; these proceeded in stages extending over varying periods of time (Meekers, 1992). It was clear from the study that religion, ethnicity and education were important determinants of a respondent's type of union.

Emerging forms of marriage – looking to the future One significant feature of contemporary African marriage (as noted above) is the large proportion of couples who are living together in informal or consensual unions. Of course, this phenomenon is not peculiar to Africa. Rindfuss and Van den Heuvel (1990) report that one of the fundamental changes in male–female relationships in American society today is the growing popularity of cohabitation among virtually all segments of American society. In America, Africa and other places where the practice in its various forms is increasingly in vogue, there is no doubt that a certain proportion of such relationships are merely transitional stages towards formalization of the marriage. But there is a great deal of evidence to suggest that for many couples, especially in Africa, no further nuptial rites are contemplated or possible.

The reasons for this are diverse, but they revolve basically around the high cost of marriage. Many young men find this prohibitive, especially in the absence of familial or kin support and amid general feelings of insecurity imposed by life in an increasingly harsh market economy. Poverty is a crucial factor here: however committed a man may be to a relationship, his continued inability to acquire the necessary means to formalize it may erode his confidence or interest, thereby precipitating a break-up.

Such informal unions generally lack the security and institutional support for the wives and children that the customary or legally sanctioned marriage provides. The refusal of families or kinsmen to recognize the legality of such unions may have very serious consequences for all concerned, especially with regard to inheritance, family property rights and so on. In many areas of Africa where traditional values still exert a dominant influence on daily life, it is not uncommon to see husbands being denied even the simple right to bury their deceased spouses, or having all their children 'taken away' from them because of their failure to perform the customary rites of marriage.

Among the Ijaw in Nigeria, for example, it was reported that whether or not a man acquired social paternity over his biological children depended on how much of the bridewealth he had paid. If he had paid only palmwine, the children belong to the wife's family; if he had paid half the bridewealth in a recognized currency, he acquired paternity over the sons while daughters went to the wife's family. Only if he had paid the bride-wealth in full did he acquire social paternity over all his biological children (Phillips, 1953).

Even where the union has been properly solemnized, family disapproval is always a lurking threat to the stability of the union. In the case of a disruption such as the death of a partner, the family may wreak full vengeance on the other partner by depriving him or her of all accumulated properties, and subjecting him or her to various kinds of indignities. Such conflicts are increasingly a feature of modern African marriage, especially as the number of inter-ethnic marriages grows. As far back as 1950, Busia reported that the proportion of inter-ethnic marriages was as high as 30 per cent in the port city of Sekondi-Takoradi in Ghana (Busia, 1950).

Given the fact that the rights of wives and children have not been fully entrenched in the laws of African countries, the increase in such unstable unions contributes significantly to the growing phenomena of single-parent or female-headed households and uncared-for street children. The practice also largely accounts for the high rate of marital disruption and remarriage in Africa, since the woman's search for security may prompt her to drift into multiple relationships. Recent data from DHS show that 36 per cent of ever-married women in Sub-Saharan Africa had experienced a marital disruption due to divorce, separation or widowhood. The rates varied from 7 per cent in Mali to 61 per cent in Ghana (Demographic and Health Survey data, 1992).

One obvious reason for the increasing popularity of consensual unions is the relative ease with which people can get in and out of them – the restraining influence of kin or family is absent or minimal in urban settings. Modern education has also endowed the young with a power that puts them beyond the reach of the social power that age has traditionally conferred on their parents. The advice or objections of illiterate or semi-educated parents or kinsmen regarding these unconventional living arrangements are likely to be belittled or ignored. This newly acquired independence is also reflected in the choice of partner, with the family's role increasingly limited to one of merely expressing approval or consent. In one study of university students in Ghana, about one-third of those interviewed insisted that they would not require parents' advice, guidance, blessing or ratification before entering into marriage (Kumekpor, 1972).

In many areas of western, eastern and southern Africa the high bride-price has also been identified as a major contributory factor in the popu-larity of consensual unions. Further modifications of these requirements may provide the necessary incentive to the young to marry formally. In this connection, Mali's low rate of marital disruption may be instructive. In Mali, Burkina Faso, Niger and Senegal, the French colonial powers made systematic attempts to modernize the marriage laws. The Malian code of marriage and guardianship enacted in 1962 requires that marriages be celebrated and registered before an official of the state. Attempts have also been made in all these countries to regulate rather than abolish the bride-price. Among the Gourma in the east of Burkina Faso, for example, the bride-price is limited to not more than 5000 CFA (US$22), nine cloth wraps, and a prescribed amount of labour that the husband must con-tribute to his new family-in-law (Boye et al., 1991).

The law is not always the best mechanism for dealing with the problem of high bride-price, however. In 1980, the government of Imo state in Nigeria introduced the Dowry Limitation Law pegging the bridewealth at 60 naira, but the law failed because even prospective husbands appeared unwilling to antagonize their future in-laws by paying this low amount (Isiugo-Abanihe, 1987). In some areas, especially in western Africa, where the Pentecostal or African-Christian sects have extended their influence, a significant increase in young marriages has been observed in recent years as a result of church insistence on exercising strict control over all aspects of the marriage ceremony – including responsibility for the wedding reception, which is usually held on the church's premises to ensure the use of alcohol or other forms of wasteful expenditure are avoided. This underscores the important role that religious institutions can play in initiating or supporting social reforms.

Compulsory registration of marriages, regulation of bride-prices, and legal guarantees or protection for spouses and children are all measures that need to be seriously examined if the institution of marriage is to be strengthened.

Polygyny

Historical context of polygyny   A distinctive feature of African marriage today is the widespread practice of polygyny. It is probably futile to speculate on to the origins of the practice, but it is pertinent to point out that it has been practised throughout the ages in various parts of the world (Goode, 1963). Polygyny is clearly consistent with patriarchy, which, with rare exceptions, has been a distinguishing feature of African social organization. Wives, and by implication more children, constituted crucial resources for enhancing a man's image and furthering the larger interests of his lineage; it seems reasonable therefore that those with the means and opportunity to do so would acquire more wives. In the typical African community, it was the chief, the elder, the wealthy or the distinguished warriors who acquired more wives than others. Whatever the origins of the practice, certain social norms, practices and factors provided strong institutional support for the practice of polygyny.

One of the most important of these were the intermittent wars, conflicts and skirmishes between different ethnic groups; these typically led to periodic decimation of the male warrior population. The capture of women and slaves as spoils of war has, historically, also been widely practised. The consequence of this for most groups was an excess of nubile females in the population, which undoubtedly facilitated the practice of polygyny.

In the absence of wars to create the excess pool of females, the wide gender differential in age at marriage served the same purpose, again creating a reservoir of nubile females. While it may be difficult to disentangle cause from effect, it seems reasonable to assume that age-old practices such as prolonged post-partum abstinence, rules of endogamy and exogamy, the levirate and sororate, and ritual prohibitions against menstruating women all served to support the institution of polygyny. The extension of Islamic influence throughout Africa in the pre-modern

Table 5.1 Proportion of women in polygynous unions, according to education, selected African countries, percentage

Country	Years of education	
	None	Seven or more
Benin	38.7	24.0
Cameroon	44.8	18.8
Ivory Coast	42.3	28.5
Ghana	37.6	30.0
Kenya	34.0	22.0
Lesotho	10.6	6.4
Mauritania	21.0	11.0
Senegal	49.3	33.6

Source: UN, 1988: p. 331.

period further reinforced the institution by providing religious support for its practice.

Polygyny in contemporary Africa It has generally been hypothesized that polygyny is structurally incompatible with modernization. This assertion is based on the assumption that a combination of factors inherent in modernization tends to undermine the institution, rendering it manifestly dysfunctional and unviable in modern society (Goode, 1963). These factors include changes in the structure and functions of the family, physical and social mobility, emphasis on egalitarian marriage, education, extension of Christian influence, legislative pressures and the gender balance.

None the less, recent data from the World Fertility Survey (WFS) indicate that polygyny remains widespread throughout Africa. Its incidence may be gauged by measuring the percentage of men or women in polygynous unions, or the mean number of wives per married man. Data from the WFS show that the proportion of women between 15 and 49 years in a polygynous union ranges from 7.5 per cent in Lesotho to 46.6 per cent in Senegal.

Recent analysis has shown that polygyny is still widely practised in West Africa; that is, in what is described by Lesthaege as the Atlantic polygyny zone. This area stretches far inland from the Atlantic coast and (with a few exceptions) as far south as Angola, incorporating all climatic and cultural zones, and over 40 per cent of married women are to be found in polygynous unions within its informal boundaries. The typically high rates for West Africa are exemplified in the rates for Benin (36.5 per cent), Cameroon (37.2 per cent), Ivory Coast (38.5 per cent) and Ghana (30.8 per cent). In contrast, polygyny rates are generally lower for eastern, southern and central Africa (Lesthaege et al., 1989), where the rates are generally in the range of 20 to 30 per cent. The proportion of women in polygynous unions is only 27.1 per cent for Kenya and 14.8 per cent for Mauritania (UN, 1987). As for predominantly Moslem North Africa, it is quite surprising to find that the incidence of polygyny is generally very low in that zone.

Data from the WFS show an inverse relationship between years of schooling and incidence of polygyny in all the countries studied. Table 5.1 presents the figures for selected countries; these data offer overwhelming support for the depressor effect of education – and, by implication, of modernization – on the incidence of polygyny.

Age at marriage

The early age at marriage in traditional society was facilitated and sanctioned by a number of factors. First, the economy was largely based on subsistence agriculture. Even among nomadic herdsmen such as the Masai and Fulani, cattle were seen more as family wealth to be preserved and increased than as marketable goods. Such social formations permitted and indeed obliged family members to participate in productive activities at a very early age. Physical maturity, signified by one's performance of the puberty rites, was the crucial factor in determining when to get married, rather than economic independence. Moreover, very little if any of the resources required for the marriage ceremony came from the couple themselves, since the arrangement was essentially one between two families. Age mates, friends and relatives were also available to assist in putting up the simple hut or cottage which the couple needed to start life, thereby obviating the need – widely prevalent today – for a prospective bridegroom to acquire a substantial amount of resources of his own before marriage.

In societies in which prolific childbearing was desired and honoured, early marriage made a great deal of sense. It not only lengthened the reproductive span but enabled the couple to provide both the family and community with proof of their fertility and, by implication, full attainment of adulthood. Many traditional societies also had very strong prohibitions against premarital sex and pregnancy. Among the Krobos of Ghana, the abhorrence with which society viewed such behaviour was so strong that girls who flouted these norms were expelled or banned from the society. Early marriage provided some guarantee against such behaviour.

There were some notable exceptions or variations within the general pattern of early marriage. The Rendille of Kenya traditionally favoured late age at marriage, for reasons related largely to the very harsh conditions of their camel-based economy (Hawthorn, 1970). In almost all societies, boys married at considerably older ages than girls. There were two main reasons for this. First, a girl's attainment of physical maturity was easier to determine than a boy's since, in societal terms, it was usually identified with menarche. In most societies the puberty rites which marked the transition into womanhood coincided with the onset of menstruation. The significance of these rites was that they formally proclaimed to the community as a whole the availability of the celebrant for marriage, and also ensured that the girl was physically, psychologically and emotionally ready for marriage.

Boys' transition to adulthood, on the other hand, was physiologically more difficult to determine and even where initiation rites for males were practised – as among the Kikuyu – the age ranges may have been significantly higher than those for females. Besides, African traditional society was basically male-centred and strongly held the belief that the man carried the responsibility for his family. This further implied that physical maturity alone was not sufficient to justify entry into marriage; one also had to demonstrate other qualities of both mind and body. In other words, the requirements for marriage were more stringent for men than for girls, and this partly accounts for the age differential between grooms and brides at marriage.

Variations in age at marriage also occurred between girls because of differences in physical maturation and in customs relating to practices of puberty rites, engagement and marriage. Where marriage payments are fairly substantial, for example, it is easy to understand why the sixth brother may find it very difficult to marry when all the family's resources have already been used in acquiring wives for his older brothers. Similarly, however desirable a girl may be her chances of early marriage may be considerably affected by the fact that she has four older sisters still waiting to be married off. Among the Mosi of Burkina Faso, for example, younger brothers often have to migrate abroad to acquire the necessary resources for marriage, since older brothers have already used the family's resources for their own earlier marriages (Capron and Kohler, 1978). Practices such as child and *in utero* betrothal promoted early marriage for girls, since bridegrooms were anxious to assert their nuptial rights at the earliest possible opportunity. On the other hand, it generally resulted in a later age at marriage for males, and a wider age differential between groom and bride.

Changes in age at marriage It is reasonable to expect significant increases in age at marriage with increasing modernization and education. The more pertinent aspects of the modernization process are the increasing nucleation of the family and, by implication, a concomitant decline in the influence of the extended family in the nuptial decision-making process.

One general consequence of the transition from a purely subsistence economic system to that of a market economy has been that the average individual is increasingly compelled to depend on his known resources in various aspects of his social life, and particularly in decisions relating to

Table 5.2 Singulate mean age at marriage (SMAM), by sex and region, Africa

Area	SMAM (males)	SMAM (females)	Age difference
Eastern Africa	25.1	20.0	5.1
Middle Africa	24.7	18.3	6.4
Northern Africa	26.4	21.1	5.4
Southern Africa	28.0	23.2	4.7
Western Africa	26.6	18.2	8.4
Africa	25.9	19.5	6.3

Source: UN, 1988: pp. 66–7.

marriage. More often than not, the young man growing up in the towns of Africa today must himself find the resources to secure suitable accommodation, acquire basic household facilities, pay for the cost of marriage and maintain a family. This is a situation which obviously favours postponement of marriage, especially in situations where entry into the labour market may already have been considerably delayed by prolonged schooling.

The detachment of the larger family from the nuptial decision-making process also means that a great deal of pressure may be imposed on the couple, thereby delaying even further the marriage decision. In the traditional setting, the family shouldered a greater portion of the responsibility for selecting the bride, assessing her qualities and making all the crucial decisions about marriage. These are responsibilities which are now largely the couple's, and the natural desire to avoid making mistakes while at the same time securing the approval of the larger families tends to delay the marriage process.

Using current data, Lesthaege et al. (1989) distinguish five broad geographical patterns in age at entry into first union in Africa. These are, first, a broad zone in the western and central savannah and sahel regions characterized by early marriage for women. In this zone the singulate mean age at marriage (SMAM) for females is generally below 18 years, although variation is seen along the Atlantic Coast (from Liberia to Namibia except for Gabon and Angola), where the SMAM for girls is generally above 18 and quite often above 19.5. There is a second belt of later age at marriage (generally above 18) extending from central Kenya, Burundi and north-east Tanzania to South Africa, where ages above 19.5 years are the norm. Within this broad zone, however, there are pockets of early marriage (under 18) in areas such as central Uganda, southern Malawi and northern Mozambique.

A third zone of later age at marriage covers Saharan nomadic groups, such as the Tuaregs and Hassania of Mauritania, while a fourth zone

Table 5.3 Effect of schooling on singulate mean age at marriage for selected African countries

Country	Year of survey	Singulate mean age at marriage	
		No schooling	7 or more years of schooling
Benin	1982	16.9	24.1
Ivory Coast	1980	17.1	21.8
Ghana	1979/80	17.4	20.5
Lesotho	1983	18.3	22.3
Nigeria	1983	16.9	22.0
Rwanda	1983	18.8	20.8
Tunisia	1983	18.4	21.4
Zaire	1982	15.3	16.3

Source: UN, 1990: p. 91.

covering Sudan, Ethiopia and Somalia seems to have moved from an earlier era of low age at marriage to a present regime of substantially later age at marriage.

Finally, Lesthaege et al. discern a fifth zone covering Central African Republic, eastern Angola and north-western Zambia, which originally may also have been characterized by low age at marriage, but which is currently in a process of transition to higher ages at marriage.

For males the overall pattern is one of higher age at marriage; husband–wife differences in age at marriage range from 3 to 11 years, with the largest differences recorded in West Africa. Though there are wide variations both within countries and throughout the continent, Table 5.2 provides an overall picture of the available information.

In general outlines, the pattern shown in Table 5.2 appears to be consistent with Lesthaege's typology. The southern African pattern of late marriage age for both males and females contrasts sharply with the low age at marriage for western and central (middle) Africa, for females in particular. Northern Africa and eastern Africa exhibit an intermediate pattern of moderate age at marriage for both males and females. Table 5.2 also confirms the pattern of a large age differential between spouses in western Africa. In countries such as Guinea, Mali and Senegal, the average difference in age between spouses is over 10 years; this is partly the result of the practice of polygyny, in which younger wives are preferred in successive marriages. For all countries, however, the much later age at marriage for males is undoubtedly also a reflection of male–female disparities in school enrolment and duration of schooling.

Faced with a choice, most parents would prefer to send their sons rather than their daughters to school, for a variety of practical reasons. Gradual elimination of such a disparity in educational opportunity may ultimately lead to significant increases in the age at marriage for females and to a narrowing of the differential between spouses. The importance of education as a determinant of the age at marriage can be seen from Table 5.3. Girls with seven or more years of schooling marry on average five to seven years later than their counterparts with no schooling.

Universality of marriage

The traditional value system which promoted early marriage also enjoined universal marriage. While there were exceptions to this general rule – such as in the cases of eunuchs and slaves, and of priests or priestesses for whom spiritual purity forbade relations with the opposite sex – the phenomenon of non-marriage for adults was very rare throughout the sub-region. Severe sanctions, both religious and social, were invariably applied to those whom society thought unduly delayed in getting married, and the families of such persons might as a last resort forcibly acquire a partner for the recalcitrant member in order to avert disgrace.

With modernization now shifting the costs, responsibilities and decisions concerning marriage more and more onto the individual, it is reasonable to expect a gradual increase in the proportions of those who voluntarily choose not to conform to traditional mores. Non-conformity may be expressed in a variety of living and sexual arrangements, but in extreme cases non-marriage may result. Even so, all the available evidence points to the fact that marriage remains virtually universal for both sexes in Africa. Data for the period 1970–85 demonstrates that universality remains the norm, with proportions married by the age of 50 of almost 100 per cent for most countries in Africa (exceptions are South Africa, Reunion, Mauritius, Madagascar and Botswana) (UN, 1990).

Non-marital sexual relations

The weakening of the marriage bond and the concomitant decline in family or kin influence over male–female relationships are also reflected in sexual activity before and outside marriage. Contrary to Caldwell's assertion that African societies did not sanction chastity and that changes in that direction began only with the arrival of foreign religions (Caldwell et al., 1989: 194), there is a great deal of evidence to support the view that women's involvement in premarital sex and sex outside marriage has, historically, been severely penalized. The importance attached to this norm was exemplified in the widespread practice of some kind of public demonstration of a bride's virginity on her wedding night. Nor was it uncommon for nubile girls to be punished, ostracized and, in extreme cases, banished from the tribe for an infraction of this rule of sexual purity, especially in cases where the puberty or initiation rites had not been performed (as among the Krobo of Ghana).

Among the Igbo of Nigeria, Basden reported that a new bride was compelled to divulge before an idol and in the presence of her husband's family the name of any and every man with whom she had had any sexual relations (Basden, 1921). The fear of such exposure constituted a strong deterrent against the temptation of sexual licence and served to emphasize the society's insistence on the virtues of chastity and fidelity. Among both the Fulani and the Gas, a white cloth was spread on the bed on the wedding night in order to obtain proof of the wife's virginity (Azu, 1974). Yoruba society similarly attached a great deal of importance to female virginity (Orubuloye, 1981). The widespread insistence among many African societies on withholding part of the marriage payment if the woman's virginity is not demonstrated clearly supports the view that the principle of bridal chastity has been the norm rather than the exception.

It is, therefore, more reasonable to suppose that the changes one finds in sexual behaviour today are more the result of the general process of modernization or urbanization. The permissiveness, anonymity and economic consideration which facilitate or promote free sexual behaviour in the modern environment did not exist to any significant degree in traditional society. Practices such as child betrothal and early marriage served to obviate the need for any extensive sexual experimentation. The increase in age at marriage today, however, means a widening of the gap between physical maturation and the onset of marriage, thereby precipitating increased adolescent sexual activity.

Nuptiality and fertility

A full discussion of the implications of nuptiality and fertility behaviour is beyond the scope of this chapter. It is pertinent, however, to highlight some aspects of the relationship which are particularly relevant in the African context, especially in view of the current attempts to slow down the continent's rate of population growth. One of these is adolescent sexuality and its impact on population growth. On the basis of available DHS data, it appears that 15 to 20 per cent of all births in sub-Saharan Africa are to teenagers. While teenage fertility appears to have declined in some countries such as Botswana, Burundi and Senegal in recent years, it has remained constant or increased slightly in other countries such as Ghana, Liberia and Mali (PRB, 1992). Such early entry into childbearing lengthens the reproductive span and therefore increases the possibility of high fertility. Early childbearing also involves serious health risks to both the mothers and their babies.

There has also been a great deal of debate about whether polygyny results in higher levels of fertility, both at individual and societal levels. The evidence obtained from various studies across Africa is rather inconclusive and sometimes contradictory, but a recent analysis based on WFS data shows that differences in fertility between women in polygynous and monogamous unions were small or insignificant for Cameroon, Lesotho and Senegal, and virtually non-existent for Ghana; the differences were significant only for Kenya and Ivory Coast (Pebley et al., 1989).

Policy issues

Adolescent sexual behaviour   World Fertility Survey data on age at first sexual intercourse indicated median ages of 16 years for Ivory Coast and 15 years for the Yorubas of Nigeria. It is interesting to observe that in the traditional environment girls would have been married or about to get married at these ages, and thus there would have been no need to indulge in any premarital sexual experimentation.

All across the African continent, there is increasing evidence that teenage pregnancy and out-of-wedlock births are becoming a major social problem (Gyepi-Garbrah, 1985). Early and uncontrolled sexual activity has serious health and social implications, for both the teenage mothers and their offspring, many of whom die or grow up to join the growing population of street children. Increases in premarital sexual activity and the related increases in adolescent pregnancy, abortion and baby dumping or abandonment thus constitute a serious challenge to policy makers, parents and society at large. Data from the DHS showed that in sub-Saharan Africa as many as 36 per cent of girls aged 15–19 who had given birth at the time of the surveys were not married. The proportions were high for Kenya (40 per cent) and Liberia (42 per cent), though small or moderate for other countries such as Nigeria (4 per cent), Senegal (11 per cent), Togo (22 per cent), Uganda (17 per cent), Ghana (20 per cent) and Burundi (19 per cent). In Zimbabwe, Boohene et al. (1991) report public concern about the growing incidence of 'baby dumping' by young girls, either for economic reasons or in order to pursue their educational careers. Though the evidence is scanty, abortion among adolescent girls, particularly unmarried ones, is said to be high in Africa and rising (Gyepi-Garbrah, 1985).

There is also the threat to society's very survival posed by the burgeoning spread of AIDS, which in Africa is known to be transmitted largely through heterosexual contacts. Adolescent and indeed non-marital sexuality generally often involves multiple and much older male partners, especially in west and east Africa (Caldwell et al., 1989). Participants involved in multiple partner sexual activity are particularly susceptible not only to AIDS infection but also to other sexually transmitted diseases in a severely constrained health-resource environment. Such sexual activity, often by young schoolgirls, is prompted largely by economic considerations: a growing girl needs clothes, shoes, finery, school fees and so on, which many impoverished parents are not in a position to provide. This has given rise to the 'sweet 16 sugar daddy' phenomenon, in which schoolgirls or young working women become regular girlfriends or mistresses of financially secure older men.

Polygyny Beliefs, norms and attitudes pertaining to the practice of polygyny are deeply implanted in the psyche of the average African, and decades of Christian indoctrination and Western education have done very little to lessen its appeal. There are two major reasons for examining its relevance or continuance in modern society. First, the social and economic conditions which justified its persistence in traditional society are no longer pertinent; second and more importantly, polygyny is in essence a total negation of the now universally accepted principle of equality between the sexes. No woman, whatever her social, educational or economic status, deserves the humiliation of having to compete with another woman for another human being's favours.

None the less, the question of how to eliminate the practice is the more intractable considering that even women may oppose its abolition. In many areas of Africa where polygyny is widely practised it derives its legitimacy not only from custom but also from Islamic doctrine; in an age when Islamic fundamentalists worldwide are campaigning for a return to pure Islamic principles, it is not certain whether polygyny can easily be legislated out of existence in Islamicized societies.

There are additional reasons for its persistence. Existing social and economic structures have contrived to make women highly dependent on men for social, economic and even psychological fulfilment. In a status-conscious society, polygyny may be the only avenue open to some women for enhancing their self-esteem and social or economic status by getting married to a rich, successful or 'powerful' man or by having children. Many women, even highly educated ones, would prefer being second or third wives to a doctor, lawyer or other such 'successful' man to being in a monogamous union with an ill-educated or unsuccessful man. Thus polygyny has been one way of ensuring security and adequate care not only for the woman but, even more importantly, for her children. Even for women who are financially independent, such as the well-known market 'mammies' who dominate the commercial sector in western Africa, such a polygynous relationship may confer respectability, social status and children without requiring the woman to sacrifice her independence and freedom to pursue commercial activities. One study of women in Ibadan indicated that as many as 60 per cent of the women surveyed did not mind sharing their husbands; only 23 per cent were openly opposed to the idea (Ukaegbu, 1981).

Some countries have tried to legislate against the practice; in Tunisia, for example, it is officially prohibited (Duza and Baldwin, 1979). Specific measures to regulate polygyny have been enacted in Francophone countries such as Ivory Coast, Senegal, Togo and Zaire (UN, 1990: 88), but it seems to have metamorphosed into the now widespread practice of the 'second office' or 'outside' wife or wives. In Ghana, attempts by the orthodox Christian churches to prohibit the practice have been largely unsuccessful, and have led rather to a situation in which polygynists, in order to be eligible for either communion or Christian burial, officially abandon wives and children of several years' standing (Aryee, 1967).

Conclusions

There is overwhelming evidence, discussed in this chapter, to support the view that the weakening of the marriage institutions has had some very serious consequences for the stability of the family in African society. The facility with which people can get in and out of marriage without fear of being socially or legally sanctioned is gradually undermining responsible parenthood and promoting the disintegration of the African family. The father is slowly disappearing as an integral part of the unit responsible for the care and nurturing of children, while the mother's responsibility has correspondingly increased. The tragedy is that the most vulnerable group in this process of disintegration and disorganization is children.

The beliefs, norms and values relating to marriage are deeply rooted in customary practices and are therefore not easy to modify or eliminate, despite the obvious evidence that many of them are no longer functional. Still, however complex or difficult the problem, the overriding need to preserve the family's fundamental role as the substructure of society demands that policy makers in Africa seriously address the issue. It is a problem which obviously calls for a multifaceted approach. Education, both in its formal and informal aspects, should constitute the core of any such programme. One measure towards this end is the incorporation of sex and family life education in both school and adult education, using a variety of media. But this should be complemented by the judicious and selective use of social and legislative sanctions, both positive and negative.

Of the more specific measures that need to be instituted, priority should be given to the compulsory registration and regulation of unions. Such regulation should cover issues such as the cost of marriages, the bride-price, minimum age at marriage and legal responsibilities of spouses, especially fathers. It must also extend to a re-examination, modification or elimination of marriage-related practices that pose a threat to both the physical and mental health of women – such as female circumcision or widowhood and initiation rites. This requires a comprehensive inventory and codification of the laws relating to marriage in order to ensure that among the conflicting demands of Christianity, Islam and traditional religions, some basic principles to strengthen the marriage bond and protect the rights of children are formulated and incorporated into the existing legal system. In Botswana, for example, discriminatory laws which deny citizenship to children of women married to foreigners (but not vice versa) actually force many women in such unions to opt for an informal rather than a formal relationship.

Such measures or laws are likely to face a great deal of opposition, especially from men. Again, if sufficient care is not taken in the use of the legal mechanism, it may well turn out to be counter-productive, creating a situation in which the undesirable practices seemingly disappear only to emerge in new forms that are essentially indistinguishable in content or character from the banned practices. Cultural, religious or ethnic diversity will also undoubtedly complicate this task, and local sensibilities or concerns must be acknowledged. The endless debates going on throughout Africa as to whether adolescents should have access to contraceptives, or whether sex education should be taught in schools at all, or whether pregnant schoolgirls should be allowed to continue schooling after childbirth all attest to the sensitivity and complexity of the dilemmas facing both parents and policy makers.

In the southern African countries (Zimbabwe, Botswana, Zambia, Lesotho, etc.), where attempts have been made to encourage responsible fatherhood through the use of legal mechanisms such as Child Maintenance Acts, experience has shown that women sometimes refuse to take advantage of these laws because of pride, unfamiliarity with the modern court system and its bureaucratic requirements, fear of antagonizing the man or his family and thereby destroying any chances of marriage, or fear of physical reprisal or abuse from enraged fathers (Armstrong, 1992).

Ghana has had a Maintenance of Children Decree with provisions enforceable through a Family Tribunal Court system since 1977. But, as one researcher reports, the tribunal is generally seen as a weak and ineffectual system because of its limited jurisdiction, lack of coercive and enforcement powers, the time-consuming and expensive procedure for prosecuting claims, and the stigma of pauperism attached to the process (Mensah-Bonsu, 1993). Additionally, as the Francophone example of 'second office' or 'outside wife' shows, legislation will not necessarily ensure the registration of wives or guarantee children's rights so long as the considerable power which men wield in society permits them to manipulate the system to their advantage. The empowering of women in all areas of socio-economic life should therefore constitute an essential element in the overall strategy of strengthening the institution of marriage. Several factors have hitherto combined to perpetuate African women's low status in society and poor self-esteem; among these are disparities in access to modern education, employment, professional training, credit or loan facilities, and ownership of property. Elimination of these disabilities will ultimately serve to enhance not only women's self-esteem, but also their position in marital relationships.

CHAPTER 6

The African family in rural and agricultural activities

P. K. Makinwa-Adebusoye

There is no typical rural African family. The vast cultural, economic and social diversity within and between countries does not permit such generalization. Even so, it is possible to sketch the general shape of family organization and working conditions in rural areas.

Agricultural employment predominates in Africa's rural areas, where about 70 per cent of the population lives. Other rural workers (about 30 per cent of the rural population) are engaged in the non-farm sector – in small-scale industrial activities such as food processing; in commercial and service activities such as transportation and various forms of trade; in artisanal activities such as masonry, brick making, tailoring and carpentry; and in infrastructural development activities such as irrigation works and reforestation. Some few rural residents are formally employed as professionals and administrative personnel (ILO/JASPA, 1990).

For the purposes of this chapter, 'family' will be defined in terms of the sharing of a common residence (a single building or a compound comprising several dwelling units). A family can be nuclear, consisting of a man, his wife or wives and their children; or extended, embracing members from two or more generations. A family can also extend beyond any boundary-maintaining unit to include all participants in cooperative activities in consumption, production, and childrearing.

There are notable differences in traditional African family structures, reflecting the multiplicity of the continent's ethnic groups and cultures. Some ethnic groups practise patrilineal inheritance of property, succession (to office), and descent (to social groups). Others are matrilineal, and yet others engage in both patrilineal and matrilineal practices concurrently (Goody, 1990). Internal factors such as these combine with external ones such as state policies on education and wages, and the differential ways that changes in market and non-market activities affect rural families, to shape living conditions.

Reflecting the low level of economic development in much of Africa, rural enterprises are typically family-owned and operated. Family groups coordinate production of goods and investment in human and non-human capital as smallholding farmers or as self-employed entrepreneurs in the non-farm sector. Both male and female household members participate in labour activities, but cultural norms place men on a higher status footing compared to women, who are considered inferior. The gender-based division of household tasks ensures that women are confined to domestic activities and to a set of 'women's jobs' in both the farm and non-farm sectors. Certain crops are also regarded by certain ethnic groups as 'women's crops' and are cultivated solely by women (Henn, 1983; Makinwa-Adebusoye, 1988; Makinwa-Adebusoye and Olawoye, 1992).

Family organization and the system of agricultural production are so closely related that any change in the latter can have an immediate impact on the former. This chapter examines this close relationship, focusing on the demographic and agrarian responses to changes engendered by the development process, the direct and indirect consequences of these responses for the rural family, and their interrelationships and overall implications for population and rural development. The spotlight will be mainly on smallholding rural families in the farming sector.

Conceptual framework

A useful way to begin the discussion of work and living conditions of rural African households is to consider the theoretical model proposed by the 'new household economics', which views family relations as though they were market relations based on efficiency. Based on the experience of Western Europe, the model assumes a cohesive, resource-pooling household with a unified demand system (a common preference function), based on altruism of the household head (Becker, 1981). But such an assumption is untenable in most African countries and especially so in West Africa, where the non-pooling household is the rule rather than the exception (Fapohunda and Todaro, 1988). Moreover, the tradition of socially sanctioned inequality between the sexes and the distribution of family resources in favour of the most powerful members (the men and the elderly) result in divergent preferences or conflicts which are not considered in the model. Systematic examination of daily activities and family decisions regarding allocation of time and resources among market production, food production, childrearing and leisure must consider not only market efficiency and areas of cooperation in the household, but also how these differ between women and men.

Indeed, most rural African women are in polygynous unions, in which each wife and her children form one among several matrilocal 'hearth-holds' or cooking units, depending upon the number of wives (Ekejiuba, 1984). In most cases, wives not only provide food but are also responsible for children's school fees and other related expenses. As a result, the fertility goals of women do not always coincide with those of their husbands.

Another important feature of traditional family structure is that all members of extended families share obligations. This permits biological parents to share childrearing costs with members of the wider kinship group through the institution of child fosterage (Isiugo-Abanihe, 1985).

These characteristics of rural family organization affect and are affected by the supply of labour, the mode of production and agricultural productivity in the traditional farming system.

Traditional farming systems

Gender-based division of labour, a land tenure system that vests ownership of arable land in communities or lineage groups rather than individuals, slash-and-burn methods of a shifting cultivation based on rudimentary implements – these well-known features of African rural life will be examined in the following paragraphs.

Organization of farm labour All household members are obliged to work on the common or household fields. Private plots belonging to individuals in the household are separately maintained by their owners. In addition, whole villages or members of extended families form groups that work on members' farms.

Under the gender-based division of farm labour, male members of a community are generally responsible for performing the more arduous tasks, such as felling trees and clearing the land for farming. Women and children work at the sowing, weeding, harvesting, and processing of food. The different climatic zones in which farming occurs – rain forest, savannah, sahel – help to determine the exact nature of women's activities. Rearing of small animals within or outside the compound is considered women's work. Where men cultivate farms the scale of production is usually larger, mainly because men can more easily call on wives' labour; women who cannot demand the labour of husbands or relatives manage smaller farms. The distribution of farm products is also affected by gender differences in the responsibility for family provision. Table 6.1 summarizes the traditional gender division of agricultural labour for selected ethnic groups.

Women have long supplied the bulk of labour required in food production. An early survey of 140 Sub-Saharan ethnic groups revealed that in 85 per cent of the cases women were responsible for all the work and in 45 per cent women did all the work except land clearing (Henn, 1983, citing Baumann, 1928). More recent studies have corroborated these findings. For example, the World Bank (1988) reported in the late 1980s that women produce the bulk of the food in Sub-Saharan Africa. In Kenya, women manage at least two-fifths of smallholdings (the core of Kenya's agriculture) and provide three-quarters of the labour required on

Table 6.1 Gender-specific division of labour among selected ethnic groups in Africa

Ethnic group	Type of land	Female tasks	Male tasks
Kikuyu (Kenya)	Household fields	planting, weeding, harvesting, storing	clearing fields, some assistance in weeding, animal husbandry
	Men's plots	assistance	cultivation, animal husbandry
Ewe (Ghana)	Household fields	planting, weeding, harvesting (except yam)	clearing fields, digging mounds, planting yam, weeding and harvesting yam
Yoruba (Nigeria)		root crop production: planting, weeding, harvesting, transportation, processing	clearing land
Ibo (Nigeria)		clearing land, planting, weeding, harvesting, transportation, processing, storage	clearing land, growing yam

Sources: Kershaw, 1975; Makinwa-Adebusoye and Olawoye, 1992.

these farms (Herz, 1989). In Nigeria, women's contributions span all aspects of farming (Makinwa-Adebusoye, 1988). In Nigeria's Imo and Anambra states, women increasingly perform *all* farming tasks, including those pertaining to land preparation (clearing, stumping, burning and removal of burnt stakes) that were traditionally considered men's jobs (Uwaka and Uwaegbute, 1982; Ezumah, 1990). In fact, in Imo state more women are farmers than men. According to the chief agriculturalist for the Imo State Agricultural Development Project, women there 'contribute more to food production and family labour than men. It is estimated that 95% of the rural women are small scale farmers who produce most of the food and bear the burden of day-to-day family subsistence.' The situation in Kenya is vividly captured in this portrait of a rural Kenyan woman:

A rural woman in Kenya is likely to be a young farmer. She is likely to be literate, the wife of a man who is often absent, and mother of several young children. Compared to her grandmother, she probably has a substantially higher standard of living, better health and education, and more independence. She spends 12–14 hours a day working at home or in the fields. Like her grandmother she is largely responsible for growing, storing, and preparing the family's food, and she probably helps grow and market cash crops (food and others). She is responsible for finding the family's fuelwood and water, and for most household chores. And in Kenya as elsewhere, it is primarily women who care for young children and see to their health and learning. (Herz, 1989)

Feminization of agriculture and heavy dependence on female labour mean that women are being overworked, resulting in grave consequences for food production and the type of crops grown – especially as male labour (for whatever reason) becomes scarce or non-existent. This problem is exacerbated to the extent that women lack access to land and capital.

To ensure that large tracts of land are cultivated, men and women who belong to the same lineage or village community combine to form groups that move from one member's farm to another. Such working groups constitute another traditional source of rural labour. Members of working groups may be members of the same lineage, such as the *gandu* among the Hausa (Smith, 1965), or they may belong to the same age cohort, such as the *otu* among the Edo. In the latter case, the *iroghae* involve youth from their early teens to about 30 years of age, the *ighele* are adult males aged 30 to 45, and the *edion* are elders above 45 years' old (Bradbury, 1973). All participating households and individual members have free access to the services of the group.

Rural land tenure system   Traditional land tenure systems vested owner-ship of land in communities and not in individuals, who enjoyed only usufructual rights. The community – variously defined as a village group, a clan, or members of a lineage – owned the land, which was held in trust for members by the clan or lineage leader or village head. Details of land allocation to individuals varied widely. For example, Gluckman (1943) reported a hierarchical mode of land allocation among South African ethnic groups where the highest ranking chief allocated land to his sub-chiefs, who in turn allocated portions to village heads under their juris-diction. The latter then allocated land to family heads (Mabogunje, 1990). Among ethnic groups in West and East Africa, land was owned by lineage groups whose patriarchs allocated plots to family heads as necessary. But women were regarded as legal minors and had only indirect access to land through male kin (husbands or adult sons).

Like all other aspects of rural life, this system of land allocation is gradually changing. In recent years, the development of large-scale, com-mercial, food-crop farms has resulted in the increasing commodification of land with a consequent rise in individual land ownership.

Rudimentary technology   Another notable feature of rural agriculture in Africa is the persisting use of simple farming tools like the hoe and matchet which depend solely on human power. Despite efforts at rural mechanization, Africa remains the world's least mechanized region, with only about 1 per cent of farm tasks performed by mechanical means, about 10 per cent by animals, and the remainder by human power (Ajayi et al., 1990). Besides the low income of rural families, which limits the extent to which they can afford to mechanize farming, there is the added problem of ignorance of the use and maintenance of modern farming tools:

> Employing the technology presents some problems; but the organization of its production and the maintenance of the plant involve the greatest difficulties, even in the case of relatively simple products such as the ox-drawn plough; and such difficulties in turn lead to a heavy and fragile dependency upon outside supplies and upon outside funding, sources that are subject to constant interruption, both for external and for internal reasons. (Goody, 1990: 122)

Although the hoe and matchet are less disruptive of fragile lands and are thus considered environmentally friendly tools, their use entails a great deal of back-breaking labour with low yields per person. Other vital tasks such as the fetching of water and collection of fuel wood for household use also depend on human labour, mainly that of women. It is therefore necessary to continue present efforts towards mechanization and improvement of the level of technology for the small-scale farmer, not only to reduce the drudgery of his or her tasks, but also to increase food production.

The greater the time and energy a woman devotes to farm and other types of work in order to increase her income, and the further she has to go to fetch water and fuel wood for family sustenance, the less time and energy she has left to devote to caring for children, preparing nutritious meals, or availing herself or her family of existing social facilities such as health care centres and family planning clinics. Women's time constraints thus have grave implications for infant mortality rates and are not conducive to fertility reduction.

Demographic responses

The strategy of out-migration   As development proceeds, the traditional farming systems described above are undergoing rapid transformations. Structural changes which accompanied colonial rule, notably the improvement of transportation, monetization of the economy, and the imposition of levies and taxes created the need for wage labour. The creation of farms producing cash crops, which gave rise to oases of agricultural prosperity, also increased the demand for labour. Other colonially inspired types of farming which existed side by side with peasant agriculture are the settler farms, which required land alienation from indigenous populations, and outgrower schemes involving cultivation of plantation crops in contiguous set-ups (Mabogunje, 1990). These changes dictated the direction of migrations, with the settler farms (including plantations) and outgrower schemes depending on migrant labour. Thus began voluntary, seasonal movements (during the dry, slack season) of agricultural labour from the dry sahel interior to plantations of cocoa and coffee in better-watered areas of Ghana, Côte d'Ivoire (Ivory Coast) and southern Nigeria. Similar migrations took place to the tea, sisal and cotton plantations in Kenya and Tanganyika (now Tanzania).

Other migration-inducing policies in the colonial era included the designation of new or old settlements as administrative headquarters and the opening up of mines which attracted migrant labour. The mines of South Africa were particularly noted for attracting migrant labour from present-day Zambia, Zimbabwe and the BLS countries (Botswana, Lesotho and Swaziland). The new administrative centres enjoyed electricity supply and other social amenities which attracted migrants. The urban-centred development strategy of the 1960s likewise furthered rural–urban migration.

At the outset of the first United Nations Development Decade (the 1960s), conventional development theory held that rapid development could be achieved by shifting perceived 'surplus' agricultural labour into urban-based industry where labour could be more productive. The great hope was that industrial development would in time provide the much-needed economic stimulus for the African continent. In implementing this project, most countries concentrated development resources on certain urban centres designated as 'growth poles', from which development was expected to trickle down to rural areas. By the early 1970s, however, it was becoming evident that this strategy was failing to yield expected results. Despite growing output, development failed to 'trickle down' as expected and rural areas suffered continued unemployment, under-employment and low productivity.

The mode of peasant farming also contributed to out-migration from some rural areas to others or to urban centres. Where the traditional system of slash-and-burn bush–fallow cultivation is practised, virgin forest is cleared to grow yams, cassava and other food crops; the fragile tropical topsoil becomes infertile after one or two harvests. In optimum situations – where arable land is plentiful – the infertile land is left fallow for a period of five to eight years and the cultivator moves to other sites. But rapid population growth, spurred by persisting high fertility levels and reductions in infant mortality, has brought mounting pressure on arable land. The resulting land shortage, soil exhaustion and poor harvests literally 'push' people out of poor rural areas.

In the years immediately following independence from colonial rule, most African governments spent significant proportions of their annual budgets on improving educational and health facilities. As with industrial-ization policy, most of the new facilities were located in urban centres and further encouraged the trend of movement into towns. The number of children enrolled in primary schools increased tremendously. The white-collar orientation of primary school curricula, coupled with the urban location of most secondary institutions, further encouraged out-migration from rural areas. Desirous of white-collar jobs and higher education for their children, rural parents actively supported their children's migration.

Depending on the type of urban job, migration can be cyclical or seasonal. The former has been more typical of southern Africa, where migrant workers from neighbouring countries are usually contracted to work for specified periods, after which they return to their homes for short stays before returning again to the mines. Seasonal migrations characterize movements from the sahelian countries to the rich, cash-crop producing areas along the coast of western Africa.

Until recently, migrants were mainly male (Adepoju, 1983; Makinwa-Adebusoye, 1990). The relatively low level of female migration was not unconnected with the gender-based division of farm labour, which saddled women with the growing, weeding and harvesting of food crops – tasks which require constant attention. Men's farming responsibilities are largely seasonal (felling trees and preparing the land), and hence they are freer to migrate during slack farming periods (Stichter, 1985). In some countries, particularly in southern Africa, specific ordinances and other obstacles, such as refusal of the required pass or a demand for marriage certificates, also blocked female migration. A further constraint was women's lack of education, a major prerequisite for employment in the urban formal sector.

Consequences of out-migration   The loss of farm labour created by the removal, either temporarily or permanently, of large numbers of adult males from rural areas resulted in changes in the composition and organization of rural labour supply. Responses to labour loss due to out-migration vary by community. Among the Mambwe of Zimbabwe, for example, the absent migrant's wife could replace her husband in the cooperative work group and so ensure sufficient labour on her absent husband's farm (Watson, 1958, cited by Mabogunje, 1990). The Tonga of Malawi regulated male out-migrations in such a way that at no time were their hamlets entirely devoid of men.

Most rural communities were not so successful, however; these suffered declining productivity and increasing poverty. Rural areas of Zambia and of other countries which were the traditional labour reserves of South Africa typify the resulting disorganization and poverty in areas of out-migration. The Travers Lacey Committee, appointed in 1936 to inquire into migrant labour in Zambia, reported the following:

[T]here was not one of us who realised the seriousness of the situation. As our investigation proceeded we became more and more aware that the uncontrolled and growing emigration brought misery and poverty to hundreds and thousands of families and that the waste of life, happiness, health and wealth was colossal. … Huts, grain stores and fences fell into disrepair; gardens and farms were not properly cultivated; attempts to effect improvements in the village were stopped by lack of manpower. (Gluckman, 1943)

Village elders in Edo state, Nigeria, complained during a 1977 survey about the loss of labour for productive activities in their villages (Makinwa, 1981). As a result of the temporary or permanent absence of male heads, increasing numbers of women are becoming *de jure* or *de facto* heads of households (Makinwa-Adebusoye, 1988). Female-headed households accounted for 45.2 per cent of total households in Lesotho in 1980 (Safilios-Rothschild, 1986). The National Sample Survey of Agriculture in Malawi estimated in 1980–81 that 20 per cent of rural women were married to absentee husbands who had moved away in search of employment, either within the country or abroad.

Several accounts suggest that female-headed households are among the poorest in the world (Mueller, 1977; Kossoudji and Mueller, 1983; Youssef and Hetner, 1984). The reasons for such poverty lie in the fact that female heads of household are usually unable to muster the necessary unpaid or hired farm labour, machinery, and other farm inputs to maximize production and profits on farms abandoned by migrating men. In many cases, women seek to alleviate the increased workload by shifting from the cultivation of more nutritional though labour-intensive subsistence crops to less nutritional ones requiring less labour. Among the Saboke in Liberia, for example, women replaced cultivation of rice with the less arduous cultivation of cassava. In eastern Zaire, women likewise shifted from plantain cultivation to cassava cultivation.

Together with natural and man-made causes such as drought and civil war, loss of farm labour helps to account for the current food crisis in the region. In an attempt to increase food production, governments have adopted several strategies, including 'back to the land' movements and the introduction of modern, large-scale irrigation farming requiring expensive inputs. These are, in turn, responsible for changing modes of production and noticeable shifts from communal to individual land ownership.

High fertility levels Fertility levels in many African countries are much higher than world levels, but they are higher still in rural areas. Persistently high fertility coupled with declining mortality rates make African countries the fastest growing areas in the world. Early and universal marriage and continual childbearing throughout their fertile years are characteristic of women in Nigeria's pro-natalist society. The rationale for large family size lies in the organization of farm production. A land tenure system that grants only usufructuary rights tends to make family size a limiting factor in land availability. Women also need children's help with housekeeping, childrearing and other tasks. In societies lacking public social security systems, surviving children are seen as providers of old age security for parents and as potential foster parents to younger siblings. Thus labour-intensive subsistence farming regimes, added to women's multiple roles, encourage the large family ideal.

It has been argued that high fertility is economically rational in pre-transitional, subsistence economies which rely heavily on child labour. In such societies, children who work from around the age of five do not have first claim on family income and, as a rule, live modestly (Caldwell, 1977; Caldwell and Caldwell, 1987). In other words, children are valued as a source of cheap labour. Boserup has explained the need for child labour in African economies in the following terms: 'Where women and children perform nearly all the agricultural work, the father of a large family is likely to become a rich man, while the father of a small family will remain poor. Therefore, this system provides motivation for a much larger family size' (Boserup, 1985: 386).

Although African growth rates remain high by world standards, several countries, notably Botswana, Kenya, Mauritius and Zimbabwe, are beginning to record appreciable declines. In other countries, persisting economic recession appears as a major factor in a perceived re-evaluation of the benefits, real or imagined, of large families. Economic recession – with its attendant structural adjustment programmes (SAP) and spiralling inflation – has greatly increased the economic burden of children for parents, while reducing the expected gains from their labour. (Makinwa-Adebusoye, 1991). But the situation is too complex to produce corresponding reductions in fertility in a simple fashion. Falling school enrolment resulting from the implementation of SAPs does not portend imminent reductions in fertility, for example. Similarly, SAP-induced cutbacks of government subsidies in the health sector may keep infant mortality at current unacceptably high rates, with grave repercussions for future fertility reduction. Replacement fertility is a real danger, and parents' need to ensure they have surviving children as a form of old-age security has not diminished.

Responses to agrarian crisis

Agricultural stagnation and resulting food shortages, added to population growth have created a crisis situation in Africa. In response to the food crisis and the poor economic condition of most countries, many urban salary earners have taken to 'salaried farming' (Goody, 1990). In Nigeria, this new breed of educated farmers includes retired military officers and senior civil servants who have had the resources and connections to acquire large parcels of land. More generally, it appears that there is an emergence of a class of functionaries and members of the educated elite who use family plots, or land newly acquired from the traditional headman, to cultivate cash crops on a relatively large scale.

Modern farming Many African governments have also used assistance or loans from donor agencies and the World Bank both to establish large-scale irrigated farms and to introduce large numbers of agricultural extension workers to aid small farmers. In Nigeria, the Agricultural Development Programme (ADP) is responsible for executing such projects. ADP efforts seek to increase agricultural productivity, and food production in particular, thereby raising living standards in the rural areas. A 'female farming system approach' that would equip women with necessary skills for more efficient production has also been incorporated. The programme has had mixed results as old prejudices persist. Recent evaluations of 10 villages revealed that women farmers continue to suffer unequal access to credit and farming inputs (although their access to training has improved). While 30 per cent of male farmers received bank loans, not a single woman did. As a precondition for loans, female applicants were required to produce written permission from their husbands. Those able to do so subsequently failed to secure loans because they lacked collateral. Women fared only slightly better in access to farm inputs: 26 per cent reported that inputs were sometimes available, while 56 per cent stated that inputs were rarely available. In comparison, 90 per cent of male farmers reported that inputs were readily available. Similarly, extension officers made regular weekly visits to only 10 per cent of women, compared to 70 per cent of men farmers; and whereas all men claimed to have received some training from extension agents, only 36 per cent of the women said they had received any training. Women's unequal access to both extension workers and farming inputs was explained by the fact that all extension agents were male and might have been biased against women who did not fit their concept of 'farmer'. Other factors were thought to include the high costs of inputs and the fact that husbands were expected to share credit, farming inputs and knowledge with their wives. But this 'trickle down' approach – again – did not work (Elabor-Idemudia, 1991).

The latter study points to the importance of engaging female extension workers to counteract the perceived bias of male extension agents towards female farmers. There is also a need to regard each farming couple as two individual farmers in their own right, since couples do not always maintain a joint account from which all family expenses can be met. The tradition of wives keeping separate incomes and performing different obligations with distinct expected returns often results in couples pursuing different objectives with different demands, whether for agricultural inputs or for a particular number of children.

Summary and conclusion

The traditional features of farming organization in the rural household – gender-based division of labour; a land tenure system which vests ownership of arable land in communities or lineage groups rather than individuals; slash-and-burn shifting cultivation based on rudimentary implements – are undergoing profound changes in response to modernization. This chapter has highlighted the implications of unequal distribution of household responsibilities and women's time constraints not only for farm production but also for infant mortality and fertility levels.

Although the mode of agricultural production is changing, the rate of mechanization remains low. Changes in the land-tenure system and commodification of land have mainly benefited the rich and powerful, to the virtual exclusion of small-scale farmers – including women – who remain responsible for most food production.

The gradual transformation of rural families brings into sharp focus the nexus between population, agriculture and the environment. Although initiated by the need for cash earnings, the rapid growth of human and animal populations is mainly responsible for shortages of farmland and for rural out-migration. Land shortages lead to the shortening of fallow periods and to the over-cropping and over-grazing which, together with urban-centred development policies, have resulted in massive loss of male labour and of male heads of households. (The ability of migrants' remittances to offset rural losses in Africa has not been established.) In turn, this situation has not only produced great poverty in the rural areas but has also brought about a dramatic change in the traditional composition and hierarchical structure within rural families as more women assume greater authority as household heads. Additionally, these changes have had profound effects on the organization of rural labour and are encouraging the trend towards individual land ownership.

With the social changes accompanying rural transformation, Africa's family structure has changed considerably, as is evident in the growth in female independence as women become *de facto* and *de jure* heads of households. Rapid population growth under conditions of economic depression and in the context of structural adjustment programmes are exacting a toll on family resources and the natural environment. Efforts to improve conditions of living in rural areas include several components which should receive attention concurrently. In particular, the population problem should be considered alongside the need to ease women's time constraints, while efforts are made simultaneously to conserve forests and soils.

CHAPTER 7

Migration and family interactions in Africa

Sally E. Findley

Africans throughout the continent have a long history of migration in search of a better economic future. Drought and low agricultural productivity have prompted millions over the years to go from dry, interior areas to wet, coastal zones. Others, lured by jobs in mines or on plantations, have spent months or even years working away from home to supplement their farm earnings. Seeking new, possibly richer lands to farm, many families have completely relocated to less hostile areas. Millions have headed for the cities with great hopes of finding their dream of a stable salaried job. And while most African migrants have stayed within Africa, not insignificant numbers have found their way north to Europe.

These migrations are transforming the demographic landscape of the continent. Cities have grown and rural populations have redistributed themselves. This ongoing spatial redistribution is accompanied by a transformation in rural and urban lives which reaches into many dimensions of African family life: work, marriage, childrearing.

This chapter reviews the ways that African migrants have altered family life. It begins by reviewing major migration trends in Africa, especially Sub-Saharan Africa. It then discusses significant ways that these migrations have intersected with family life. The chapter concludes with a discussion of the implications of continued migrations for African families.

African migration and urbanization trends, 1970–90

Although migration is not the only force spurring the growth of cities, continued high rates of rural–urban migration in Africa have driven the rapid urbanization seen throughout the region in past decades. Africa has the highest rates of urban growth in the world. In 1985–90, African cities had an average annual growth rate of 5 per cent, with a high of 6.8 per cent per year in east Africa and only dropping below 5 per cent per year in southern Africa. In the rest of the developing world, urban growth rates peaked in 1985–90 at 4.5 per cent per year. By 2005–2010, the latter rate is expected to decline to 2.9 per cent per year. In contrast, African urban growth rates are expected to remain above 4 per cent per year through the year 2010 (UN, 1989, 1991a).

Despite the fact that some 350 million people will live in Africa's cities by the year 2000, Africa will remain the least urbanized region of the world, with only 40.7 per cent of the total population living in cities. Of the African sub-regions, the least urbanized will continue to be eastern Africa, where only one-third of the population will live in cities. In contrast, in southern Africa, almost two-thirds (61 per cent) of the population will live in cities (UN, 1989, 1991a).

Compared to the rest of the developing world, fewer of Africa's urban populations will live in the largest cities, in metropolitan areas with one million or more persons. In the developing world, 77 per cent of the total urban population will be in cities of one million or more; in Africa only 25 per cent of city residents will live in such large metropolitan regions (Findley, 1993). None the less, Africa's largest cities will almost double in size between 1990 and 2000. In the 1990–2000 decade the population living in Sub-Saharan African cities of one million or more population will increase by 59 per cent from 33,150,000 to 52,774,000. By the year 2000, 20 per cent of the total Sub-Saharan urban population will live in these metropolitan regions (UN, 1991a). In Sub-Saharan Africa, 18.5 per cent of the 1990–2000 urban growth will be concentrated in the largest metropolitan areas comprising one million or more persons. In the rest of the developing world almost twice as much of the total urban growth (30.5 per cent) will be concentrated in metropolitan areas of one million people or more.

Continued domination of the African urban landscape by smaller cities implies that Africa's urban migrants will tend to end up in these smaller cities. The migration studies reported below indicate that this trend has already started, as more and more migrants seek alternatives to the over-sized metropolitan areas with undersized job opportunities.

Current migration levels in Sub-Saharan Africa   By any measure, millions of Africans are migrating from one place to another within their countries. Without regard for migration type, Table 7.1 indicates that one in five Africans is no longer living in his or her birthplace. Applying this proportion to the estimated 1990 African population of 648 million gives an estimated 130 million lifetime migrants in Africa at that date.

Migration to urban areas or particular cities ranges from 12 per cent to 66 per cent of the population surveyed at the destination (see Table 7.1). In many cities and regions, the proportions are well above 33 per cent: Ouagadougou, Burkina Faso; Banjul and Kombo, The Gambia; Accra-Sekondi, Ghana; Abidjan and the entire south-western region of Ivory Coast; Monrovia, Liberia; Brazzaville, Congo; Addis Ababa, Ethiopia. In some cities, one out of every two residents is a migrant.

Consistent with the United Nations projections for continued domin-ance of African urban populations by the smaller and medium-sized cities of Africa, migrants are spread out in the urban hierarchy. In Senegal, for example, the 1980 labour survey yielded estimates of 360,000 rural–rural migrants and 175,000 urban–rural migrants, in addition to the 616,000 urban in-migrants. Similarly, statistics for Ghana show that at least half of the migrants are residing in urbanized regions excluding Accra-Sekondi, Ghana's metropolitan area.

Due to the relatively recent institution of national census and survey programmes in Africa, very little is known about long-term migration trends. However, there is evidence that rural–urban migration declined during the 1970s and 1980s. As shown in Table 7.1, the proportion of in-migrants in Ghana's Sekondi dropped from 63 per cent to 49 per cent between 1970 and 1984. In Sierra Leone, net urban in-migration dropped from 234,622 to 165,968 between 1963–74 and 1974–85.

The reduction of migration to selected cities reflects a broader phenom-enon of increased diversification of migration destinations, specifically including more small and medium-sized cities and rural areas. This shift away from major metropolitan areas reflects the serious economic problems confronting the largest cities as a result of the combined forces of worldwide economic downturn, structural adjustment programmes, and disadvantageous terms of trade for Africa's primary products. Cities like Abidjan that once had thriving modern sectors now struggle to keep their economies going (Demble and Hugon, 1982; Dubresson, 1990). Structural adjustment programmes imply that it may be difficult to raise funds for secondary job creation in the urban informal sector (Berry, 1985; Lootvoet, 1989). In Ivory Coast, such urban sector changes have been reflected in greater migration to the smaller cities (Dureau, 1989; Lootvoet, 1989). Surveys in Ivory Coast show that 19.5 per cent of villagers had previously resided in a large city and another 26.7 per cent in a smaller city (Dubresson, 1990). Migrants have traditionally gone from Burkina Faso to Abidjan, but in recent years thousands of Burkinabes go to other rural areas to work on cotton plantations or to settle and farm in areas more favourable than their home zone (Ouedraogo, 1989). Similar reports of migrant preferences for small cities and rural areas are found in Ivory Coast (Dureau, 1989), Togo (Marguerat, 1989), Ghana (Ohadike and Teklu, 1990), and Nigeria (Berry, 1985).

Despite the observed shifts away from the largest metropolitan areas, most of Africa's migrants will continue to be oriented towards the cities. Even though the economies of African cities were already in crisis by the 1980s – when most of these surveys were collected – statistics continue to show heavy in-migration rates and hence a continued need to cope with these migrants.

Table 7.1 Estimates of Sub-Saharan African internal migration, 1970–90

Country	Migration type	Dates	Migration level
West Africa			
Burkina Faso	To Ouagadougou	1975	55% in-mig.
	Lifetime migs	1975	30% of total pop. is in-mig.
	Rural–rural	1975	55% in-mig.
The Gambia	To Banjul/Kombo	1983	39% of Banjul, 52% of Kombo
Ghana	To Accra	1982	36% in-mig.
	Western, Sekondi	1970	63% in-mig.
	Western, Sekondi	1984	49% in-mig.
	All regions	1982	18% in-mig.
Ivory Coast	International	1975	22% immig. of total pop.
	Rural–rural, SW	1975	35% in-mig. of region pop.
	Urban areas	1978–79	66% in-mig., Abidjan, other cities
	To smaller cities	1970–79	43% in-mig. last 10 years to cities
Liberia	Rural–urban	1962–74	23% of urban pop.
	Net to Monrovia	1974	30% of Monrovia 1990 pop.
Mali	Lifetime migs	1987	16% of resid. pop. not at birthplace
	Out-mig., Kayes	1982–89	37% of adults had migrated
	To Bamako	1987	44% of residents
Nigeria	Rural out-mig.	1977	66% of households have out-migs
Senegal	Lifetime migs	1978	13% of total population
	U-U mig. to Dakar	1980	27% of Dakar pop.
	R-U mig. to Dakar	1980	12% of Dakar pop.
	Total R-U migs	1980	13% of urban pop.
	Youth in Dakar	1986	73% of Dakar's youth
Sierra Leone	Net urb. in-mig.	1963–74	40% of urban pop. 1970
	Net urb. in-mig.	1974–85	21% of urban pop. 1980
	Mig. to Freetown	1963–74	12% of Freetown 1990 pop.
	Mig. to Freetown	1974–85	17% of Freetown 1990 pop.
Togo	Mig. to Lomé	1981	41% of Lomé population
	Int. migrants	1981	22% residents outside birthplace
	From south Togo	1976	35% of all children gone
Central Africa			
Cameroon	Lifetime, region	1976	27% of total population
	To Yaounde	1976	66% of Yaounde pop.

Table 7.1 continued

Country	Migration type	Dates	Migration level
Cameroon	Children out-mig.	1982–83	45% of children in West Cameroon
	Rural out-mig.	1974–75	36% of males in South Cameroon
Congo	Lifetime migs	1984	30% of total population
	To Brazzaville	1984	47% of Brazzaville's pop.
Zaire	Lifetime, Kinsh.	1984	23% of Kinshasa 1985 pop.
	To Kinshasa	1970–84	29% of Kinshasa 1980 pop.
East Africa			
Ethiopia	To Addis Ababa	1967	56% in-mig.
	To Addis Ababa	1978	53% in-mig.
Kenya	Rural households	1980s	30–40% households with head absent
Southern Africa			
Botswana	Rural absentees	1979	34% rural adult males absent
	Rural absentees	1979	24% rural adult females absent
	Mig. to towns	1979	36% in-mig.
	Mig. to S. Africa	1983	2% of Botswana 1980 pop.
Lesotho	Mig. to S. Africa	1983	8% of Lesotho 1980 pop.
	Absentees	1976	15% of Lesotho 1976 pop.
	Absentees	1986	13% of Lesotho 1986 pop.
Malawi	Mig. to S. Africa	1983	0.2% of Malawi 1980 pop.
Mozambique	Mig. to S. Africa	1983	0.3% of Mozambique 1980 pop.
South Africa	Internatl migs.	1983	0.7% of South Africa 1980 pop.
Swaziland	Mig. to S. Africa	1983	2.1% of Swaziland 1980 pop.

Sources: Burkina Faso: Sawadogo, 1990; Ouedraogo, 1990; Mfoulou, 1989. Gambia: Yamuah, 1990. Ghana: Opoko, 1990. Ivory Coast: Koffi and Zanou, 1990. Ivory Coast 1978–79: Dubresson, 1990. Ivory Coast, 1970–79: Dupont, 1989. Liberia: Klu, 1990. Mali: République du Mali, 1990; Findley and Ouedraogo, 1993. Nigeria: Makinwa, 1981. Senegal: Mfoulou, 1989; Ndiaye, 1990; Badiane, 1990. Sierra Leone: Seasay, 1990. Togo: Marguerat 1989; Locoh 1988. Congo: Mfoulou, 1989; Toto, 1990. Cameroon: Mfoulou, 1989; Ngwe, 1990; Franqueville, 1987. Zaire: Lututula, 1990. Zaire to Kinshasa: Uchudi Masudi, 1990. Ethiopia: Mulugeta, 1990. Kenya: Nelson, 1992. Botswana: Izzard, 1992. Botswana: Kurubally, 1990. Lesotho: Sembajwe, 1990. Malawi, Mozambique, Swaziland: Kurubally, 1990. Percentages not given by cited author were calculated for this table by dividing the numbers of migrants reported by the appropriate population given in UN, World Urbanization Prospects 1991.

Trend towards more international migration International migration in Africa is on the rise, with Sub-Saharan Africans accounting for almost half of the world's estimated 80 million international migrants. By the late 1980s approximately 35 million Africans lived outside their native countries (Russell, 1993). An estimated 5.3 million of these international migrants were living in other Sub-Saharan African countries. The greatest numbers came from the landlocked sahelian countries of Burkina Faso (about 1 million) and Mali (about 400,000). Together these two countries accounted for one-quarter of total international African migrants. High levels of international, intra-African migration (more than 100,000 each) were also reported from Guinea, Kenya, Lesotho, Nigeria, Rwanda, Togo and Zimbabwe. These countries contributed an additional 1.4 million migrants (Russell, 1993).

Half of all intra-African migrants were concentrated in the two countries of Ivory Coast and South Africa. Ghana, Uganda and Tanzania absorbed another quarter of the over 5 million African migrants. Two countries, Burkina Faso and Senegal, ranked among the top ten African nations for both sending and receiving intra-African migrants. Burkina Faso sent almost 10 times more migrants than it received, and Senegal sent and received almost equal numbers.

Over the last decades, Sub-Saharan African migrants have been more active in migration to northern countries. In 1960–74 only 17,259 Sub-Saharan African migrants were registered in Western Europe, North America, or Oceania. This figure had risen to 65,085 by 1970–74, and it rose further in the late 1980s to 77,636 (Zlotnik, 1993).

Data from Sub-Saharan African countries suggest that international migration will continue to rise in the 1990s and beyond. Despite political pressures to reduce immigration to Europe, persistent economic differentials between Africa and Europe will continue to induce international migration. Unequal development trends coupled with agreements for greater intra-African economic integration likewise will foster continued intra-African migration. Additional political unrest in the region will further increase the pressure on Africans to seek livelihoods elsewhere, either as voluntary migrants or refugees.

Shift to circular or temporary migration Circularity has long been documented, particularly in long-term labour migrations to South Africa's mines (Mitchell, 1969; Murray, 1981; Oucho and Gould, 1993) or to central or eastern African railroads and plantations (Stichter, 1985). In the Sahel region, circulation began with labour migration to the peanut plantations (Gregory and Piche, 1993).

In recent years, African migrations have become more varied and spontaneous; many who go no longer adhere to the classical labour migration patterns (Mfoulou, 1989). For example, youths may leave to go

Table 7.2 Circulators or temporary migrants as a proportion of total migrants, selected African countries, circa 1980 (ranked by the highest proportion reported)

Country	Proportion of total migrants
Botswana	34% of rural males temporarily absent
Burkina Faso	67% of in-migs to two largest cities 60% of total rural population of sample villages 60% of all rural out-migrants, nationwide
Cameroon	53% of migrants from S. Cameroon have returned 38% of migs to Yaounde plan to stay only temporarily
Ghana	43–69% of urban migrants return annually (1963)
Ivory Coast	20–27% of rural pop. have circulated to urban areas 73% of migs to three cities left again after 6 years
Kenya	57–81% in four high-circulation districts 33%-66% of Nairobi residents circulate 25–41% of Western and Nyanza province out-migration 13% of migrants to 8 cities 79% of migrants expect to retire in home villages
Mali, Senegal and Mauritania	41% of all rural migrants from 100 villages
Niger	63% of migrants to Maradi will return to village 29% of migrants to Maradi continue to farm in village
Nigeria	39–50% of railway workers in eastern Nigeria 52% of Lagos industrial workers return once a year 78% rural out-migrants in south-west Nigeria return yearly 34% of migrants in Benin come during the dry season
Lesotho	18% of total rural population in 5 villages 13% of total national population
Senegal	71% of industrial workers return each year (1964–5)
Togo	97% of rural migrants from Kabye have moved 2+ times
Zambia	30% of males in Masaiti keep rural plot at home

Sources: Adapted from Findley, 1993. Data for Ghana, Nigeria, Senegal, and the last Kenya item are from Oucho, 1990. Dates for his items are circa 1960–70, except for Kenya which is 1981–2. Data for Botswana are 1977–8 from Izzard, 1992; for Cameroon for 1974–5 from Franqueville, 1987; for Ivory Coast for 1991 from Dubresson, 1990 and Dureau, 1989 for 1979–84; for Niger for 1991 from Herry, 1989; for Togo in 1985 from Marguerat 1987; for Nigeria in 1977, from Makinwa, 1981.

to the cities during the dry season and remain there well past the start of the rainy season. Additionally, they may go to a much wider set of destinations than those where 'seasonal' work can be found. This burgeoning of a variety of patterns is seen in rising levels of temporary and long-term circulation, both rural–urban and rural–rural (Findley, 1993; Afolayan, 1991; Hart, 1987; Herry, 1989; Oucho, 1990). As shown in Table 7.2, in many cities or regions circular migrants account for more than one-third of all migrants.

Some circular migrants follow the traditional seasonal nomadic pattern, bringing animals to water or labour to seasonal crops. But many more migrants are labour migrants who leave their own crops during the off-season to look for wage labour to supplement farm income. Another common pattern of circular migrations includes traders – well-known in Lomé, Dakar, and Abidjan – who sell goods such as printed textiles in the destination city and return home with manufactured goods to sell in their home regions.

Some of the circulation is related to the frequent droughts which plague the continent (Oucho and Gould, 1993). For example, during the 1983–5 drought, circulation from the Kayes region of Mali more than doubled, with drought-period circulation accounting for 63 per cent of all migrations, up from 25 per cent just prior to the drought (Findley, 1991). Others are related to the economic downturn in the biggest cities and the increasing difficulty of finding stable, remunerative work there.

The rise in circular migration also is linked to a deterioration in wage-labour employment opportunities on plantations or in industries. In Tanzania, for example, a combination of changes has made seasonal work on tobacco or sisal plantations much less attractive to men (Lwoga, 1985). As in other countries, the net effect is to shift migrant labour away from the plantation zones to a more diversified set of rural and urban sites (Stichter, 1985; Pilon and Pontie, 1991). Similarly, African mines have experienced significant declines in prices for their output, forcing them to cut back on employment and on wages. As a result, men in the South African region are seeking other migration destinations. In Malawi, younger men who used to go abroad for extended periods are increasingly migrating for short periods to nearby zones in Malawi. This enables them to return and assist with cultivation (Hirschmann and Vaughan, 1984). In Zambia, the fall in copper prices shifted migrants away from the copper belt toward Lusaka and other towns (Pottier, 1988).

With economic success not necessarily guaranteed, even with circulation between two places, more migrants find that they must move among several places in order to patch together a living. Migrant itineraries are thus becoming more complex. In Burkina Faso, Cameroon, Ghana, Ivory Coast, Togo and Zambia there have been reports of migrants who move either stepwise to a large city or the reverse, or directly to a metropolitan area (Ouedraogo, 1989; Franqueville, 1987).

Increasing numbers of female migrants In Africa, migration has traditionally been viewed as a male phenomenon. Men moved while women stayed behind. Indeed, migration surveys simply did not ask women about their migration experiences. Where women did move, it was assumed that this was only for marriage or to join family members (Makinwa-Adebusoye, 1990). Thus, even though there have been high rates of female migration throughout Africa, these have been viewed as merely associational and therefore discounted in discussions of migration, urbanization and development.

In the 1980s, studies from western and eastern Africa showed rising numbers of women moving to cities and questioned whether women moved merely as dependants (Chant and Radcliffe, 1992). More recent surveys confirm that economic concerns play an important role in female migration decisions, even when joining a spouse (Findley, 1989; Makinwa-Adebusoye, 1990). On closer examination, it is evident that significant proportions of female migrants are autonomous migrants, moving independently to fulfil their own economic needs. In 62 separate African study populations, 52 per cent of the women cited economic reasons for their moves, and only 35 per cent gave marital or familial reasons (Findley, 1989).

Why have economically motivated female migrations increased in the last decade? In much of Africa, women play key roles in subsistence farming activities. Before the advent of the economic crises, women could raise enough food so that, together with a husband's migration earnings, the family could get by. But as jobs became tighter during the 1980s and men began to be less successful in remitting, many families increasingly have relied on women and their farming activities. However, due to rising costs of farm inputs and declining terms of trade, farm productivity and income have declined. Thus women, like men, are increasingly turning to migration to meet their economic obligations. By the early 1980s the ratio of men to women was close to 1:1 in cities of Botswana, Egypt, Guinea, Gambia, Ghana, Malawi, Tunisia, Zaire and Zimbabwe, suggesting a more even gender balance among urban in-migrants (Chant and Radcliffe, 1992: 6).

Future prospects In a world buffeted by economic, political and meteorological crises, migration holds out possibilities for Africans who otherwise find their worlds severely constrained. Where they go – and for how long – depends on many factors, but especially on their assessment of where there are specific opportunities for them. Although the largest cities will continue to attract millions of migrants, the challenges of everyday urban life undoubtedly will encourage many to try alternative destinations. Whether the migrants stay in their own countries or go elsewhere in Africa will depend in part upon possibilities within the country and in part on political and economic constraints on international migration. Mounting pressures to restrict migration to Europe or the United States, will surely provoke rises in intracontinental migration. The unstable economic situation in the cities added to the continued weakness of the agricultural sector will draw more into circular or temporary migration. For those who do obtain stable jobs, the fear of losing the job may reduce the frequency of return visits. The variety of situations and job constraints will continue to elicit a varied migrant response. The greater involvement of women and children as migrants is likely to provoke changes to African families, as will be discussed below.

African family structures and migration patterns

While many have claimed that migration is a family matter (Harbison, 1981; Mincer, 1978; Wood, 1981; Findley, 1987), nowhere does this seem to be more true than in Africa. At virtually every step, non-migrant family members are intimately involved with migration. This does not mean that the interactions and impacts of the migration are uniformly supportive. Indeed, some studies highlight the tension between individual and family needs. None the less, African families do make claims on their migrants, claims which generally influence the migration, though not always in the directions wished for by the family head. Conversely, migrations may have a profound effect on the family.

In order to understand the ways that family and migration interact, it is important to identify the features of African families most likely to influence the process. According to Locoh (1988b), the key features of African family structure are:

1. preference for an extended family structure;
2. high degree of separation of male and female roles and responsibilities;
3. integration of reproductive and productive functions at all generational levels of the family;
4. stronger lineage than conjugal solidarity;
5. propensity to polygamy; and
6. dominance by elders.

This section of the chapter will outline how each of these six factors conditions migration patterns and vice versa.

Extended family structures   Extended family structures have been shown to facilitate migration in both India (Kothari, 1982) and Mexico (Weist, 1973). Africa is no exception: extended households, especially those vertically extended, are more likely to have migrant members (McDaniel, 1990; Traore, 1991; Piche et al., 1980). In the Senegal River Valley, 42 per cent of the households with children and grandchildren present had migrant members (Traore, 1991). One detailed study of Benin showed that among rural households with a nuclear structure only 7–9 per cent had an absent household head, as compared to between 7 and 26 per cent for families with various extended family structures (Guinguido, 1992). In the Ebira district of Nigeria, a study showed that 49 per cent of the family members left behind by migrants were extended members of the household, especially grandchildren but also siblings or married children of the absent household head (Afolayan, 1991).

Extended family structures also facilitate spatial subdivisions of the family into two or more separate units, a form of 'multipolarity' (Courgeau, 1988). They continue to function as an economic whole, but the units are separated by distance. Migration can be important in holding together complex family structures separated by great distance (see, for example, Locoh, 1991; Guinguido, 1992; Makinwa, 1981; Trincaz, 1989). Contrary to the standard hypothesis that migration and urbanization lead to fragmented families and nucleation, Vimard (1991) suggests that the dual-residence strategy enables families to maintain their extended structure in the face of losses due to migration.

Most evidence about the relation between extended family structures and migration considers how migration leads to larger and more extended families in the city. It is well known that migrants usually start their new life with a visit to a family member (Ouedraogo, 1992b). The already resident family member provides food and shelter until the migrant has established him or herself. In Yaounde, for example, 76 per cent of all migrants had been received by kin (Franqueville, 1987); in Benin City, Nigeria, 82 per cent had stayed first with kin (Makinwa, 1981); and in Abidjan, 90 per cent of migrants live with relatives (Herry, 1991). In some cases, the duration spent with kin is short, until the migrant has found a job and alternative housing. More commonly, the migrant is 'permanently' absorbed into the urban family, spending years living and working with his or her kin (Herry, 1991; Locoh, 1990; Vimard, 1991; Franqueville, 1987). Not surprisingly, the additional migrant members increase the average urban household size. Even though fertility did not rise, data from several African countries showed an increase in average household size from 4.98 to 5.34 between the 1960s and the 1980s (Locoh, 1991).

Very often, already resident family members help the migrant find a job or provide capital so that the migrant can start a business. Thus, families are vital to the success of the migration enterprise. Only a minority of migrants are able to get jobs on their own, and migrants agree that without family connections jobs would be difficult to obtain (Makinwa, 1981). Most migrants report that they obtained their first job only with the help of family (Findley and Williams, 1991). Family connections also play a positive role in establishing and maintaining economic enterprises. Among the Yoruba, family connections are built into the trading and migration partnerships, thereby assuring high degrees of social integration and potential market dominance (Eades, 1987). Similar family-based trading is reported for Zambia (Pottier, 1988).

In Africa, aid passed between family members is usually reciprocal. A gift received is transformed into an obligation to give, and vice versa (Vaa et al., 1989). The new migrants who at first receive help are later called upon to give help – most give help to other family members. One of the most common forms of help is financial, and there are strong obligations for migrants to remit as much and as often as they can. Approximately two-thirds of all migrants send money home to their families (Oucho, 1991).

Just as the aid given to the migrant comes from the larger, extended family, the migrant's remittances may be transmitted over a wide network of kin. In the Senegal River Valley, remittances are sent to the clan head, to be distributed as needed to lineage members (Conde and Diagne, 1986). In Cameroon, migrants send back gifts of money to their lineage as a way of expressing their solidarity and support for the family (Franqueville, 1987). In this way, the extended family also becomes the vehicle for spreading the benefits of migration. The spread of benefits will obviously be more limited if the migrant is not successful in earning money. A migrant with unstable or low income may simply not make return visits, thereby avoiding having to refuse the family possible assistance.

Extended family obligations can become burdensome to the migrant. When a migrant in the city does earn a regular salary, his or her family obligations have a way of expanding to encompass the entire salary. Family members who feel they have a claim on migrants call on them for help, and they may not feel able to refuse. Thus, even though the migrant earns a significant amount, he or she may save or remit very little. In fact, migrants may even be forced to go into debt to meet their urban expenses (Franqueville, 1987).

Male–female segregation of roles Separation of the male and female worlds is particularly prominent in African life (Oppong, 1988; Makinwa-Adebusoye, 1990). Men and women have socially differentiated access to productive resources, to control over the labour process in both domestic and market spheres, to modes of remuneration, and to consciousness about gender and social inequities in power (Tienda and Booth, 1988).

Such separation is reflected in many aspects of life: age difference between spouses, the agricultural division of labour, social interaction patterns and so on. An average difference in spousal age of seven to ten years reinforces male dominance. The subdivision of agricultural responsibilities generally allocates different crops to men and women. When women work on male fields (and vice versa), it is usually to carry out specially designated tasks, and they do not work together. There is also subdivision with regard to household economic responsibilities, with men assigned cash-related obligations (for example major cereal grains, housing, medicines) and women responsibilities associated with childrearing (for example school fees, clothing, supplemental food for her own children). In much of Africa men and women take their meals separately, rarely socialize together, and have marriages where the level of conjugal interaction is quite low.

All this makes it rather unremarkable for men and women to migrate and establish separate residences. When men have the major responsibility as cash providers they are obliged to migrate, but their wives are not. Similarly, when women have major childrearing and food-raising responsibilities, they may prefer to stay behind. The more independent men and women are in their fulfilment of their responsibilities, the less serious will be the consequences of migration by only one spouse. If it is the woman who migrates, having independent responsibilities 'frees' her to go. Yet she may also find it difficult to fulfil these needs on her own.

If certain gender-specific roles are spatially defined (for example, access to village land), the partner whose obligations are more bound to a place will be less able to move. For instance, where women can only gain access to land through the husband's family, it will be difficult for the woman to move away from her affinal relatives. Similarly, gender-specific responsibilities may reduce flexibility and ability to migrate. Because women tend to experience more constraints on land access, the separation of roles tends to handicap women relative to men as far as independent migration is concerned.

When men migrate and leave their wives behind, this may or may not alter the woman's responsibilities and access to resources. If the man leaves but still fulfils his share of household production, albeit from a distant location, then the woman may be able to continue her own activities without serious consequences. If his departure negatively affects the woman's access to resources, then she is likely to suffer unless she can gain access to other production means. The consequences of separation thus depend on whether the woman's roles are seriously jeopardized by the absence of her spouse, whether he continues to fulfil his responsibility to the household support structure, and, if not, how the couple and other family members adapt to enable the wife to continue to fulfil her roles in the absence of the man's support.

Integration of reproduction and production The integration of reproduction and production is characteristic of the rural economy: women combine childrearing with farm work, family members share in child education responsibilities, and children become productive members of the household at an early age. Such integration may be less visible in the urban economy, but it is none the less present. As in the rural economy, the urban family may find it advantageous to maintain a large and flexible labour force that can be deployed as opportunities change. The cost of maintaining a household labour force may be greater in the urban area, but the benefits are the same: ability to mount economic operations quickly (for example, switching to a new trade activity), availability of a free labour force, ease of covering training costs simply by membership in the family.

The 'grand' family will be advantageous to urban migrants to the extent that their income is derived from petty production or trade. In the city, however, the family can be expanded either by maintaining high fertility, by absorbing foster children, or by taking in migrant extended family members – with or without their children. Theoretically, these last two methods of maintaining family size could facilitate urban fertility reductions. In neither case would there be pressure on the household to reduce its size and complexity.

The integration of reproduction and production is also seen in the investments families make in small-scale enterprises. While urban informal sector enterprises may not be family-controlled to the same large degree as in the past, families still dominate the field. Much of the capital used by migrants to establish small-scale enterprises or trade operations still comes from kin (Berry, 1985; Makinwa, 1981; Franqueville 1987; Obbo, 1980). Without the family 'bank' many migrants simply would not be able to launch new endeavours. When urban incomes fall in times of economic crisis, more migrants have difficulty obtaining loans from family members and are thus less likely to succeed in starting businesses (e.g., Lootvoet, 1989).

The urban housing compound has replaced the village compound as the locus for the integration of reproduction and production. Surveys show that women use the compound as a space for both household tasks and market-oriented activities such as grilling meats, producing ginger drinks, tie-dyeing fabrics, or making soap (Rondeau, 1989; Vaa et al., 1989). As in traditional rural areas, children often assist in these undertakings, and both women and children may move freely between market-oriented production and household tasks. This integration appears to work better for women migrants than for men, as men do not seem to conduct their economic activities from their home base.

The integration of the reproductive and productive functions of the family shapes the response of migrants to the economic crises in the cities. Many migrants do not find well-paid jobs, and others do not find any jobs at all. Families may be the only recourse for hard-pressed migrants. Women and children may return to the village to help with harvests, but primarily to have something to eat (Vaa et al., 1989; Obbo, 1980). Men may double up with other kin in a further effort to reduce their costs of living in urban areas.

Most importantly, the family becomes the means by which the group can diffuse its risks of failure in economically precarious times. Migration enables the family to dispatch members to a variety of labour markets. In the Senegal River Valley, single households may often have one or two members in France and another two or three in nearby locations (Findley and Ouedraogo, 1993). As the economy worsens, migrants go to a broader range of locations, minimizing the chance that a single calamitous event will wipe out all their efforts. Some members may seek work on farms in other regions, while others may look for work overseas. It is the family that both supports the diversification of activities and benefits from it.

The high cost of living in the cities can force greater intra-familial separation of reproductive and productive functions. Specifically, if couples can no longer afford to keep their children in the city, they must either separate (dual-residence strategy) or send their children to be raised by relatives in the village or elsewhere. If the former occurs, reproduction and production remain integrated, but only partially, since part of the production now occurs independently of the reproductive functions. If the latter, there is a clear separation of functions. Since the work or help contributions of children are often mentioned as justifications for high fertility, increased fostering of children out of urban households may lead to reductions in fertility. Although the connection to fostering was not explicitly tested, rural–urban migrants to Togo and Kenya both have relatively smaller average numbers of children ever born (Findley and Williams, 1991) – and both societies practice this form of child fosterage.

Stronger lineage than conjugal control   Many facets of migration reflect the dominance of lineage over conjugal relations. Migration decisions tend to be made in conjunction with the head of the household or clan. While there is evidence of individual or 'loner' migration decisions, the majority of migrants indicate that other members of the family, particularly parents or aunts and uncles, had a large say in the decision.

The weakness of the conjugal bond is reflected in the high proportion of spouses separated by migration. When migrants send back money they usually send it to the lineage head, not to their wives. Studies in Kenya and Nigeria (Oucho, 1990) indicate that wives were less likely to receive the remittance sums than were parents, siblings or other kin. This practice further reinforces the lineage tie relative to the conjugal tie. Remittances directed towards the husband's lineage group may destabilize a marital relationship if the wife does not feel that she has received her share of the remittance. Indeed, high rates of marital disruption are found in some settings with high degrees of migration-related spousal separation, such as in Lesotho (Murray, 1981) and Malawi (Chilivumbo, 1985).

On the other hand, the strong affiliation with the lineage favours alternative childrearing patterns. Much child fostering is along lineage lines, and it is sometimes vital for the migrants' economic survival. Without grandparents or aunts, young women migrants would find it difficult to cope with childrearing. Conversely, parents wishing to help their children get a start in the urban area might find it impossible to find a willing urban foster parent were it not for the obligations of kinship.

The strong orientation to the lineage also reinforces the pull on migrants to return to their village of origin. Because the lineage may control access to village land, the migrant has a strong incentive to remain in good standing. Thus, strong lineage bonds reinforce patterns of circular migration, whether of seasonal, irregular or working-life duration.

Propensity to polygamy   Polygamy is both a carrot and a stick with respect to migration. In many polygamous societies the man must pay a bride price in order to marry another wife; migration is often the means by which the man earns the necessary sum. At the same time, extra wives and children increase the family's food requirements and this can spur polygamously married men to migrate.

Polygamy has been associated with male migration. In eastern Senegal, men with two or more wives are more likely to migrate (Sow, 1990). In Lomé, 22 per cent of the women had co-wives living outside Lomé, suggesting that in some cases males use the occasion of migration to the city to take additional wives (Locoh, 1991). At the same time, being in a polygamous union may facilitate migration for the co-wives. Polygamy provides wives with ready help during a husband's absence, and with a co-wife to help with the farming that the husband is abandoning, the senior wife may be less likely to oppose his migration.

Dominance by elders   The gerontocratic structure found in most African families affects migration, inasmuch as elders dominate the decision to migrate. But they also dominate the discussion regarding family economic and social activities. Studies have shown that some men leave simply to get away from the excessive authority of the elders.

When a youth migrates, the ensuing distance from the elder reduces the elder's control of the youth. As a result, youths growing up in the city are likely to be less traditional in outlook and less dominated by elders' decisions. Some women use migration deliberately to seek a more independent life out from under the thumb of the clan elder (Locoh, 1991). In this way, migration may weaken the authority of elders. On the other hand, clan elders at the destination may control access to jobs, housing, or other urban necessities. Having escaped control by one elder, the migrant may find him or herself subject to another's authority.

Migration–family interactions

It is difficult to grasp exactly how these family features are implicated in specific migration patterns and what the migrations will mean for family long term. The next two sections of the chapter illustrate some of the complexities of interactions, specifically with regard to circulation and to female migration.

Circulation, dual-residence and wives left behind The high cost of supporting family members in the cities increases the odds that men will leave family behind in the village or smaller towns where they have their home base (Nelson, 1992; Findley and Williams, 1991). The advantages of leaving a family in the village are magnified when we consider the opportunity cost of the family migrating. If they do not stay in the rural area and the migrant fails to earn sufficiently or loses his employment, the family would have no ready fall-back option (Standing, 1985). These considerations take on added force in the context of high unemployment rates, instability of employment and potential for early dismissal (especially among international migrants). Because migration is no longer viewed as a 'quasi-permanent' solution to a problem, men appear even more likely to leave family behind, and indeed, the separation of spouses in Sub-Saharan Africa is widespread (Table 7.3). In areas where this pattern is found, around one-third of wives stay behind while their husbands go to cities or other rural areas to work.

Spouses give many different reasons for not accompanying each other on their migrant journeys. While economic concerns figure prominently in the list of reasons, familial obligations also play a role. Separated spouses interviewed in rural Bendel State, Nigeria, reported the following reasons for not accompanying their husbands (listed according to frequency of response):

1. Lower cost of living at home.
2. Need to maintain property and supervision of farm activities.
3. Wives' employment and economic activities in the home village.
4. Care for ageing parents.
5. Difficulties in changing children's schools or in finding new ones.
6. Proximity to relatives and friends.

Southern Africa is the region most affected by the lengthy separation of spouses. Farm productivity there has declined steadily since 1950, while the cost of living has rocketed. Families completely dependent on farm work can no longer survive, and men from the region have gone to work in South Africa or Zambia's mines. Whether in Botswana (Izzard, 1992), Lesotho, Malawi or Zambia, women live difficult lives while their spouses are absent. Women depend on men for cash with which to purchase agricultural inputs, while men depend on women for basic survival functions, including childrearing and raising food. When men cannot fulfil their share, women's production either adapts or suffers.

Women left behind adapt their farming practices in a number of ways

Table 7.3 Prevalence of wives left behind in Africa – selected countries

Country, region	Husband absent (%)
Benin	34
Botswana	34
Cameroon	28
Ghana, Avatime	30
Kenya, Abaluyia	39
Kenya, rural	30–40
Lesotho	38–44
Malawi, Zomba	46
Nigeria, Bendel	14
Nigeria, Ebira	33
Nigeria, Yoruba	31
Senegal	43–68

Sources: Benin: Guinguido, 1992; Botswana: Izzard, 1992; Cameroon (only women under 50 years included): Gubry, 1989; Ghana: Brydon, 1985; Kenya, rural: Nelson, 1992; Kenya, Abaluyia: Kilbride and Kilbride, 1990; Lesotho: Murray, 1981; Malawi (includes divorced and abandoned wives): Hirschmann and Vaughan, 1984; Nigeria: Osirike, 1990; Nigeria: Afolayan, 1991; Nigeria, Yoruba: Berry, 1985; Senegal: Minvielle, 1985.

designed to maintain output. Though already overburdened, women may take on the agricultural production roles left by their husbands. In Malawi, 45 per cent of women now perform tasks once handled by men: soil preparation and tilling, seed selection, and crop protection (Hirschmann and Vaughan, 1984). Sometimes they can use remittance income to hire labour, but the low level of urban incomes means they must usually do it themselves. In Cameroon, Beti women work on average 52 hours per week, as against the 35 hours' work performed by men. Women spend 25 hours per week on food cultivation, and when men leave they must increase this by the 5 hours that the men had formerly put in. As in Malawi, even if the husband sends money the wife often cannot afford to hire labour so she must usually do the work herself. Overall rural family income goes down, as the family no longer has the time to raise the cash crops (cocoa) that the men produced prior to departure (Henn, 1985). If the woman cannot manage to do the additional work involved in her husband's tasks, she must cut back on her cultivated area, resulting in a decline in overall food production. This was found to be the case for over half of women left behind in Malawi and Zambia (Hirschmann and Vaughan, 1984; Cliffe, 1978).

In some communities, women left behind have maintained production with the help of family or in a mutual exchange system with other women in the community. Among the Mambwe women of Zimbabwe and the

Luo of Kenya, for example, women have joined together to perform virtually all the agricultural tasks themselves (Findley and Williams, 1991). In Lesotho, Malawi and Senegal, some women report that major tasks formerly done by husbands are now done by the husband's relatives, keeping farm productivity at about the same level (Murray, 1981; Hirschmann and Vaughan, 1984). Women also may shift their energies from farming to non-farming occupations less dependent on timely male inputs. In Lesotho, for example, one woman shifted into grain trading when she found that her husband was consistently unable to remit (Murray, 1981). In Niger, a group of women have developed a pottery cooperative (Arnould, 1984), and women in Senegal have also established cooperatives to strengthen agriculture in the absence of their husbands (Ouedraogo, 1992a).

There is widespread evidence that women farmers tend not to receive agricultural extension assistance. Nor can they easily negotiate loans for fertilizers or other inputs, in part because the women themselves have low incomes and face uncertain economic futures. Thus, even if the husband wishes his remittances to go to improved farming, it is unlikely that the wives left behind can do this independently. Farming improvements in such situations generally come in the context of remittances to the husband's kin, or when he himself returns (Findley and Williams, 1991).

Because men's absences are lengthy, the consequences for the integrity of the family are not trivial. The average separation is from three to seven years, according to several studies (Findley and Williams, 1991). Even if the migration serves the economic needs of the family (and not all do, as studies of returned migrants show), spouses may be separated for periods of years rather than months (Makinwa, 1981). Ironically, while the spouses may initially believe that migration will help maintain the family and traditional lifestyles, the lengthy separations together with low remittance levels have led to significant changes in gender-role expectations, in patterns of childraising, and even in basic strategies of survival for the women left behind.

Aside from the economic consequences, wives left behind have mixed feelings about the lengthy separations from their spouses. In rural Bendel State, Nigeria, most (87 per cent) welcomed their greater autonomy in decision making but disliked the separation and its negative effects on childrearing. They cited lack of control over children and difficulties in caring for young children, particularly where the wife is a trader or has no education. Only half the husbands (53 per cent) were able to visit monthly, despite the fact that most husbands lived less than 100 kilometres from home (Osirike, 1990). In Lesotho, infrequent visits have also contributed to a sense of inadequacy in dealing with childrearing tasks, especially in disciplining children. In Kenya, family separation is thought to contribute to rising problems of child abuse (Kilbride and Kilbride, 1990). In some cases, separation ultimately leads to divorce, due in part to the woman left behind feeling both economically and emotionally abandoned (Ouedraogo, 1992a).

Despite the sometimes high social costs, the separation of spouses does not appear to enable the families to make major improvements in their standards of living. Except in the case of international migrants, the actual remittance level may be significantly lower than expected or, even, relied on. Throughout Africa, males struggling to send home money to their families report difficulties in doing much more than covering their own costs. In addition, men living in the cities have more attractive alternatives to sending money back home; many women find that the family's food needs have taken a lower priority, following rent, beer, other women and electronic equipment (Findley and Williams, 1991). However, if women receive remittance incomes, they appear to spend most of it on food and basic needs. In rural Bendel State, Nigeria, two-thirds (63 per cent) of the wives used the remittance income for food or basic needs; only 37 per cent were able to make any capital investments, including construction of a home (Osirike, 1990). This pattern is very similar to that found in other settings where women left behind report using the bulk of the remittance income for food (Chilivumbo, 1985; Conde and Diagne, 1986; Findley and Williams, 1991; Nelson, 1992; Oucho, 1990).

Because of uncertainty about when and for how long spouses may return, distinctions between definitive 'permanent' migration and temporary migration have become blurred. Perhaps because the 'permanent' migrant seems to be continually at risk of suffering an upset which sends him or her home, migrants continue to view their home village as their real home. Even migrants who have lived in a city for a decade or more may continue to view their natal village as home. They plan their retirement in the village and continue throughout their working life to invest in preparations for it – a home, land, agricultural improvements, and continued participation in village customs and rituals. In virtually all African settings where urban–rural links between migrants have been studied, there is evidence of commitment by both rural and urban kin to maintaining linkages. The intensity of exchanges (human, monetary, substantive) between rural and urban homes has led some to describe the resultant pattern as a dual-residence family (Weisner, 1976) or a multipolar residence (Courgeau, 1988).

The theme of return to the home village is common throughout Africa, whether from the sending or the receiving household perspective. In the city, urban migrants envision their eventual return to the village; in the village, migrants are seen as 'prodigal sons', as 'real' household members who will someday return. The belief that migrants are still part of the family household reinforces the perception that migration has not drastically altered family structure.

Yet, the numbers absent are often so significant that the *de facto* household has a substantially different size and composition. Although not without methodological difficulties (see Gregory, 1989), studies of Botswana (Izzard, 1992) and Senegal (Traore, 1991) have distinguished households as *de jure* (actual and absent residents) or *de facto* (actual residents only). The differences in household size often range from two up to five or more. Almost one-fifth (18 per cent) of the putative population of five Lesotho villages was found to be absent at work in South Africa (Murray, 1981). A 1977–8 survey in Botswana found that 34 per cent of all men and 24 per cent of all women in the rural districts were absent for six months or more and were absent at the survey time.

If the absent male has been the household head, his departure increases the chances that the woman will assume headship. However, if his absence is viewed as temporary, the female headship likewise may be discounted as only temporary (see, for example, Izzard, 1992). As months turn into years, the female 'temporary' heads of household and their families may find the situation increasingly difficult to tolerate (Murray, 1981; Henn, 1985). Social definitions of headship and family structure can thus complicate the transition to practices that would be more functional for the women.

The economic situation is precarious in most cities and, compared to the more settled residents, new migrants have very little security. They do not know when a job may be withdrawn, when a current trading partner may vanish, or when some other calamity may strike, leaving them without any means of support in the city. It is thus common practice to maintain active contact with rural kin. Even if the migrant does not need to return when he or she experiences a setback, the villagers are a resource pool that can help the migrant pull through bad times. For example, he or she may be able to sell enough on a visit to the village to re-start an urban enterprise (Pottier, 1988; N'Sangou, 1985).

The linkages between city and town are continually reinforced by the migrants and their exchanges with co-villagers. Migrants who wish to stay in contact with their home village engage in a wide range of activities and exchanges: sending money, visits, continuation of farm activities or establishment of new cash crops, trading with the village. Among the most important practices is the maintenance of economic activities in the village. Many maintain their farming activities while absent in the city. In Maradi, Niger, 47 per cent of migrants continue to own land in the village, and 30 per cent continue to work their fields throughout their urban sojourn (Herry, 1991). High proportions maintain rural agricultural activities in Cameroon (Franqueville, 1987), Nigeria (Osirike, 1991) and Togo (Vimard, 1991).

Whether or not they maintain farm activities, men try to send back money to their families as often as possible. Table 7.4 shows that between

Table 7.4 Proportion of migrants sending money back to family

Migrant residence	Proportion remitting (%)
Cameroon	90
Ghana, urban areas	63
Kenya, 1977	50
Kenya, 1983	73
Liberia, urban	94
Niger, Maradi	31
Nigeria, Bendel	63
Nigeria, Ife	62
Nigeria, urban, 1986	46
Senegal, Dakar	34
Senegal, Dakar (female)	90+

Sources: Cameroon: Franqueville, 1987: 207; Kenya: Oucho, 1990 for 1977 and 1983; Liberia: Klu, 1990; Niger: Herry, 1989; Nigeria: Adepoju, 1974 and 1986, Osirike, 1991 for Bendel; Senegal, Dakar (female): Diop, 1989; Ghana, Nigeria (Ife), Senegal (Dakar): Gugler and Flanagan, 1978.

one-third and two-thirds of internal migrants remit regularly to their families. Often, the migrant remits regularly to help with food needs and for special ceremonies. For example, 32 per cent of the migrants in Maradi, Niger send home money regularly, and another 29 per cent send money for important celebrations and rites (Herry, 1991).

Migrants who remit regularly send substantial sums, between 5 and 15 per cent of their own income (Rempel and Lobdell, 1978; Oucho, 1990). Families with international migrants have the greatest opportunities to receive major remittances, as more international migrants remit and the sums they send tend to be relatively large. Virtually all migrants (98 per cent) from the Senegal River Valley living in France send money back to family, at least occasionally, and on average they send 19 per cent of their French incomes (Conde and Diagne, 1986).

On return visits (perhaps monthly but usually much less often), the husband not only brings material and emotional support to his family, he also maintains contact with the village elders, thereby reminding them of his eventual return. Even when migrants have not left a spouse behind, they make frequent visits and provide much help to their families and villages. Visits are more frequent if the migrant is close to home, but other factors – such as intra-familial conflict and insufficient funds to bring back to waiting villagers – may inhibit visits. (For discussions of the variety of support provided by migrants on visits, see Adepoju, 1974; Afolayan, 1991; Franqueville, 1987; Makinwa, 1981; Herry, 1989; Nelson, 1992; Osirike, 1990).

For their part, villagers value strong ties with migrants because they may need to call on the migrant for help. For example, when villagers fall ill, they often go to the city and stay with migrant kin while obtaining health care. Just as the migrant may depend on the villager for help in times of crisis, the villager may likewise go to the city for help in raising money to pay a debt or to sell agricultural produce (Pottier, 1988). Migrants in town often have one, two, or three visitors staying with them for various reasons. And, of course, the villager could one day become a migrant, in which case earlier migrants will help by providing shelter and assistance in getting established in town.

Though the stereotypical image is of migrants sending food and money back to the village, current studies of exchanges show much more reciprocal or bi-directional exchanges of food and money than had previously been thought (Oucho, 1990). In both Kenya and Nigeria, one-quarter of the migrants in the city receive money from rural kin (Oucho, 1990), and reciprocal exchanges of goods and money are also reported from Cameroon (Franqueville, 1987), Mali (Vaa et al., 1989) and Zambia (Pottier, 1988). In Liberia, adults, children, food, money and other goods go back and forth between towns and villages (Klu, 1990). In Abidjan, some children are fostered from the city to the village, while others are fostered from the village to the city (Vimard and Guillaume, 1991).

The need to maintain strong migrant–village ties is reinforced further by economic crisis, which has caused major losses in purchasing power (Ouedraogo, 1990; Dureau, 1989; Dubresson, 1990; Demble and Hugon, 1982). Depending on the exact nature of the crisis, urban migrants may have to call on rural kin for help, or vice versa. Women and children from Burkina Faso, for example, were returned home because their husbands could no longer support them in Ivory Coast after the 30 per cent drop in purchasing power sustained there between 1979 and 1985 (Dubresson, 1990). Several other African governments have restricted jobs or benefits to their own citizens, forcing many migrants to return to their home countries (Ngongko, 1990).

The frequent visits back and forth take on added significance in the context of the epidemic of acquired immune deficiency syndrome (AIDS). Men who have been living in the city may have been exposed to the AIDS virus, and when they return on visits they may bring more than just money or gifts. There is evidence that patterns of AIDS and HIV transmission conform to patterns of migrant labour movements in east, central and southern Africa (Hunt, 1989). Unless migrants are seriously engaged in AIDS-prevention activities, they can spread the virus throughout their home regions. The rising volume of circular migration and of spouses left behind underscore the significance of this potentially fatal impact of migration.

Female migration and African families Female migrants in Africa share some of the standard characteristics found among all migrants: young, often entering the labour force at the time of the move, better educated than non-migrant women, and economically active after the move, often as traders of food or home-produced goods (Findley and Williams, 1991).

The exact nature of African female migration, like its counterpart male migration, varies with the sub-region, culture, particular socio-economic situation of the family and so on. Yet certain interesting features distinguish African female from male migration.

Childhood fostering in the cities Large numbers of female migrants start their migration careers as very young children, being fostered to aunts, grand-mothers or other foster mothers. Child fostering is more common in west than in east Africa. Analysis of the World Fertility Survey data shows that in both Ghana and Ivory Coast the proportions of children not residing with their mothers ranges from 13 to 28 per cent. Girls are slightly more likely to be fostered than boys, particularly in regions nearer to the coast (Page, 1989). Although many children are fostered for social reasons (for example, the obligation to foster a daughter with a maternal grandmother or a paternal aunt), others are sent for financial reasons, often to help kin but also as a way to reduce economic pressures for the natal parents (Findley and Diallo, 1988). These economic reasons may tend to select more girls than boys as foster children. From an early age young girls are expected to help with housework and, in the city, foster daughters often end up as unpaid domestic labour. Though their natal parents may expect them to go to school, urban foster parents may not fulfil this obligation, particularly for girls who can bestow immediate benefits by staying at home (Nelson, 1987).

Land rights Where women do not have independent rights to land, their migration away from the village may deprive them of land to farm. Female urban migrants in such situations will be more committed to urban occupations than male counterparts who can go back and forth from farm to city. While men may circulate or migrate seasonally, the female migrant tends to be a permanent migrant. This pattern has a major exception in matrilineal societies where women own land. In Kenya, for example, women migrants have used their earnings to buy land and build homes on a scale much larger than they could have done had they not migrated (Nelson, 1987).

Educational disadvantage While women migrants to cities are better educated than rural non-migrant women, they still have very low levels of educa-tional attainment. The rural–urban migrant may be one of a handful who attended primary school in her home village, but she may be surrounded in the city by many women who grew up with educational opportunities and are likely to have gone to school at least for a few years. Though there are exceptions (see, for example, Benin City, Nigeria (Makinwa, 1981), the female migrant is likely to have a lower educational attainment than the female native citizen. In Monrovia in the 1980s, for example, 54 per cent of female migrants had at least attended primary school, but their average educational attainment was still below that found for native urban women or for male migrants (Duza and Conteh, 1984). Compared to male migrants, female migrants were found to have an educational disadvantage in Botswana, Cameroon, Kenya and Sierra Leone (Findley and Williams, 1991). Although some women do come to the city to study, these are a minority among all female migrants. The educational disadvantage of the female migrant is one which she is likely to bear throughout her new life at the destination.

Entry to the paid labour force Unlike their male counterparts, migration to the city often triggers female migrants' first entry into the paid labour force. For example, in Nigeria, the proportion of women not in the labour force dropped from 50 to 20 per cent after migration, and in Kenya only 29 per cent of female migrants had worked for pay prior to moving (Findley and Williams, 1991).

Low paid, low skilled labour Women's relatively low educational attainment as compared to males' makes them fairly uncompetitive in the modern sector. Female migrants are concentrated in the occupations with the lowest pay and skill levels. In the labour market, women migrants occupy positions which incorporate the traditional skills of mother and housewife. Though they have moved to the city, they continue to do the same kinds of tasks they did in the village. As domestics, they care for children and households, and as traders they use their home production skills in product transformation and small-scale merchandising (Findley and Williams, 1991; Brydon, 1992).

Childrearing and informal sector work Migration occurs for most women at the time when they are marrying and starting to bear children. More female than male migrants are already married and/or parents at the time of their first migration (Findley, 1989). Somehow, they must juggle work with childraising and homemaking responsibilities. This makes it difficult for women to take full-time jobs that take them out of the home, unless it is possible to take children with them or find or hire others to care for young children. Unless the migrant is a member of the professional elite who can afford domestic help, the newly arrived female migrant may have little choice but to start a home-based enterprise. Alternatively, she will find work in the informal sector where she has flexibility in working hours and can bring along young children. As the children grow, they may be able to help the mother with her work by running errands and so on, as in the rural area. The occupations held by migrant women cluster in the trade and sales sector, which offers the kind of flexibility that women migrants seek (Bjeren, 1985; Findley and Williams, 1991). Very few women are in the industrial or productive sectors, where the jobs require either skills or time commitments that they lack (Lacey, 1986; Franqueville, 1987; Findley and Williams, 1991).

What do female migrants do in the informal sector? A recent study in Abidjan showed that migrants (like non-migrants) sell a variety of perishable and non-perishable items, own and operate food stalls, offer beauty and hairdressing services, work as seamstresses, or work as domestics. Women from other nations specialize in particular trade goods: Malian women in kola nuts, brochettes, peanut soap; Guinean women in indigo tie-dye fabric; Ghanaians in food and sexual services; and Nigerian women in itinerant trade (Toure, 1985). Studies show similar patterns of specialization in activities or goods by women from different zones in Yaounde (N'Sangou, 1985) and Lusaka (Jules-Rosette, 1985).

Fear that the desperate female migrant will turn to prostitution has long been an argument clan elders used against female migration. While there is evidence that some female migrants become prostitutes (Bjeren, 1985; Nelson, 1992), most female migrants avoid this activity. Prostitution is more attractive to women who want to earn large sums of money, as in societies where women with enough cash can buy land and build houses. Like target migrants elsewhere, the female migrant may find prostitution the quickest and most lucrative means to earn money for such purposes (Findley and Williams, 1991). Thus, prostitution seems to be a more likely occupation for women in matrilineal societies. More commonly, female migrants in towns seek 'sugar daddies' or steady male friends who will contribute regularly to their support (Mainet, 1985; Obbo, 1980b; Vaa et al., 1989). As awareness of HIV and AIDS transmission grows among women living in African cities, the fear of infection may reduce the numbers of women who exchange sexual favours for money.

Fostering of children back to villages For a variety of reasons, women migrants with children may send their children to live with relatives in the village or elsewhere. The principal reason reported for this is that they cannot look after the young child while working and prefer to send the child back to grandparents or siblings rather than seek alternative (and expensive) child care arrangements (Brydon, 1992). Others send their children back to the village because they feel that only a traditional upbringing is proper for their children. Still others send children to live with grandparents simply because they cannot afford to house, feed and school their children in the city. This is particularly a problem for single women, who may be completely on their own in the city and unable to obtain any help from the children's father. Usually, children are fostered with the grandparents or siblings of the head of household, but a minority may be fostered to non-relatives (Vimard and Guillaume, 1991). The level of fostering appears to be highest in west Africa, where various studies show that 10 to 46 per cent of all migrants have sent children to live with relatives in the village (Bledsoe and Isiugo-Abanihe, 1989; Findley and Diallo, 1988; Herry, 1991), but fostering is also reported in east Africa (Nelson, 1987; Obbo, 1980b).

Female urban support networks While migrants generally report becoming involved in a social world extending beyond the family, female migrants appear to be more inclined in this direction. Perhaps because their social world prior to migration revolved around family and kin, women migrants in the city join savings clubs, develop fictive kinship links with friends, and establish close, supportive relations with neighbours. Though these various relations do not replace family interactions in the village, they give women a network of people upon whom they can depend in time of need (Vaa et al., 1989). These support networks actually appear to be better placed to help female migrants cope with adversity than are kin networks. As Fall (1991) discovered in his work among Dakar residents, the 'other family' of the neighbourhood encompasses all types of exchanges: social, economic, tasks. The most common form for women is the rotating savings club or tontine, which helps them save their meagre earnings towards major ceremonial expenses or debt repayment. In addition, clubs may name 'mothers' for each other, to help the newcomers get established. If there are fights between co-wives or neighbours, the club or association mediates the conflict, just as a senior wife might do in the village. Finally, club members help each other make contact with resource persons, helping newcomers establish themselves economically, just as kin would do. This multiple dimensionality of the network makes it invaluable as a support network for the migrant, whose needs likewise vary.

Family and migration in the development process

In one way or another, migration touches the lives of millions of Africans. Many millions are migrants themselves, and through their movements and interactions these millions bring the realities of migration to their families, friends and neighbours. Whether, where, and when a migrant goes is very much influenced by the migrant's family, and the migration in turn can have significant consequences for the family's structure and livelihood. These interactions between families and migrants do not cease at the moment of departure; on the contrary, under most circumstances they persist throughout the migrant's life, repeatedly underscoring for both the families and the migrant the interdependence of their worlds.

Based on the trends reviewed in this chapter, the following stand out as salient features of these interactions.

1. Greater geographical extension: more migrants are entering international migration circuits. Although transportation systems have improved in recent decades, travel is still difficult and time-consuming in most of the region. Because migrants interact more frequently when they are close to their family and village, greater migrant dispersion will reduce face-to-face interactions between families and migrants. This, in turn, may lessen social ties and solidarity, ultimately affecting commitments to help each other and to retain close financial ties. For international migrants who return only every two to three years, the resulting sense of distance may produce conflicts regarding the migrant's role in the family.

   If the distant migrant members remain committed to their families of origin, the greater geographic extension can lead to significant economic changes for the latter. Through his or her activities, the distant migrant extends the family economic activities into a new region and possibly a new sector. For many regions, migrants are the vehicle by which the family economy becomes semi-proletarianized, combining peasant and wage-labour activities. More critically, distance increases the chances that the migrant will bring back skills, money, and new ideas which will help the family establish themselves in new economic activities in the village. Thus, migrant dispersion fosters both economic diversification and greater integration with the monetary economy.

2. More frequent moves: the greater economic instability of the region means that fewer migrants can count on finding stable and remunerative work at the selected destination. As a result, circulation and repeat or 'chronic' migration is on the rise. If the migrant returns often to his family of origin, this can reinforce family solidarity, particularly if the migrant brings home contributions to family financial reserves. At the same time, frequent returns will pressure the family to adapt to the on–off presence of the migrant member. Some families may end up assigning the migrant to a new role (for example, trader, or broker with the system) that can be fulfilled at all points of the itinerary, while others may simply adjust the current division of labour. If the migrant is less successful and continually moves on in search of better opportunities, the frequent moves may weaken family ties and lessen the chance that migration can remain an integral dimension of family life.

3. More multipolar residences: throughout Africa, members of a family may end up living in different towns or regions yet continue to function as an economic unit, assuring the support of elderly, women and children family members in the home base. As a result of this dispersion, the definitions of family and household are becoming blurred.

No longer is permanent residence a criterion for household member-ship; households may include absent members who come back only once a month or seasonally. Likewise, families may count in their membership foster children sent from town to be raised in the village.

In the past, the migrant town residence may have functioned as a separate entity. The migrant had his town wife and a life apart from the village wife, to whom he returned only periodically with money or much later to retire. Mounting economic and social pressures in both the urban and rural areas stimulate much greater interchange between the town and village family units. Wives go back and forth carrying out trade activities; children may be fostered in either direction; the rural household may send food to town; and the urban and rural units may collaborate in launching an enterprise. These flows reinforce the complex, extended nature of African families.

4. More female migrants: perhaps the greatest migration-related pressure on African families comes from the increased prominence of female migration. No longer are women moving only for marriage and family reasons. Like their brothers, their survival strategy may incorporate economic and social activities at different locations. It is expected that these activities will be more openly recognized and that women will be accorded a stronger role in the family's participation in the monetary economy.

Where female mobility has long been a part of their trading activities, families and the women themselves have evolved an intrinsic understanding of the utility of migration for the entire family. In this case, the migration merely extends existing patterns to more women and more families. Where such traditions do not exist, women must adapt or modify social practices to enable them to integrate migration into the life of the family. For example, the adaptations may include long-distance child fostering, increased reliance on urban kin for assistance and support, or adopting a uxorilocal rather than patrilocal residence. As yet, most of the adaptations reinforce the extended family structure preferred in many settings. In fact, migrant women may be more favourable to polygyny because a co-wife can assist the family in coping with an absent wife. The category of women most likely to break with tradition are the more educated female migrants who view their migration as a departure from tradition and an entry into a different world. But even here, the evidence suggests that these elite women continue to rely on traditional structures for assistance in coping with migration.

Rather than being a brake on progress, families throughout Africa are helping their migrant members establish themselves in new places. By retaining close and supportive relations with the migrant, the family ensures it will share in whatever benefits the migrant attains by his or her mobility. All too often, the benefits are smaller, later, and more infrequent than either the migrant or the family envisioned. None the less, both parties remain basically pro-migration and optimistic that the various adaptations they make to stay connected will be worth it in the long run.

This does not mean that migration does not bring problems to the families. It is not easy for families to 'launch' members, and not all agree on who should go, where and when. Not all migrants remain financially committed to their families of origin, and they may not help their families even if they are able. The situation is more likely to be that they cannot help the family, but rather have to call on family to help them cope with the latest economic reversal.

Although migrants do rely on friends and on wider sets of contacts for assistance in settling into the city or in coping with setbacks, the family remains at the heart of migrants' lives. While not always a close partnership, thus far it is one of the few partnerships that has facilitated family survival, albeit in an adapted, spatially dispersed form.

CHAPTER 8

The African family and the status of women's health

Wariara Mbugua

Introduction

The African family is under severe stress, from both within and from without: environmental degradation threatens the livelihood of families; structural adjustment programmes (SAP) are leading to a suspension of familial aspirations in health, education and employment; rapid rates of urbanization, closely associated with migration, are giving rise to the adoption of new familial arrangements; civil strife in many parts of Africa is bringing about the disintegration of families and producing large numbers of refugees; and gross mismanagement of many African economies precipitates waste of resources, capital flight, and low levels of investment – all of which deny families the opportunity to be fully productive members of society.

While entire families are suffering the negative consequences of these many factors and conditions, the African woman is in a particularly vulnerable position because by both definition and default she bears the brunt of all these ill effects. Within the African context the overwhelming majority of women, who mainly reside in rural areas and are largely uneducated and unskilled, still derive their status from the family. Being culturally mute themselves, the family articulates their wants and desires, and ascribes their roles and functions. It thus defines their status, on the basis of which communities and the society at large – including all of the society's institutions – base their perceptions and expectations of what women are. When structural changes occur within the family – for example, as a result of migration of young men from rural communities – women are by default prescribed additional roles and functions within the family. The consequence of such structural and dynamic processes is that the health of African women, and therefore the African family, is in serious jeopardy.

A conceptual framework for women's health An understanding of the health status of women in Africa can be approached conceptually from two interrelated perspectives. First of all, the roles that women play have

Women as bearers of children
The physical environment
The socio-cultural economic environment

Health status of women
Women as providers of health care
Women as producers of health inputs
The health of the community and nation

Figure 8.1 Conceptual framework for women and health.
Source: Developed by the Centre for African Family Studies (CAFS),
Nairobi, Kenya.

a direct consequence on their health; second, the environments within which they operate either aggravate or reduce risks to their health. Schematically these interrelated factors are shown in Figure 8.1.

Within this conceptual framework, women are perceived both as actors in the overall realm of health provision and as acted-upon, either negatively or positively, with respect to their health. As actors, African women have the potential to change for the better their own and their families' health situation – a potential that is largely untapped and unrealized, although this is where the greatest promise for the future lies. The conceptual framework also highlights the way that women's varied roles in their separate realms are all closely linked: addressing one role invariably means addressing another. Many programmes that purport to address aspects of women's health fail to operationalize this linkage. Population programmes, for example, have tended to overemphasize fertility regulation and demographic change by focusing primarily on contraceptive usage. This approach tends to underplay the health concerns of women associated with pregnancy, childbearing and childrearing.

There are two principal environments to which women's health can be related: the physical environment and the socio-cultural and economic environment. Both are perceived to affect women's health status directly, as well as indirectly through women's roles as health actors.

In reviewing the status of the family and women's health in Africa, this chapter will apply this conceptual framework to examine analytically how women's roles impinge generally on their health status. The environments in which African women and their families are operating and how these affect women's health will then be discussed. Finally, the chapter will assess how policies and programmes can be brought to bear on the deteriorating situation of women and their families in Africa.

Women as bearers of children

Childbirth, rather than being a happy occasion, is now increasingly seen by large numbers of women in Africa as a time of consternation and anxiety owing to the circumstances in which pregnancy may have occurred or the conditions under which the baby will be born. Bearing children is perhaps the greatest health risk in the lives of many African women. Women who become pregnant in Africa face a risk of death due to pregnancy that is 80 to 600 times higher than that for women in developed countries (UN, 1990). The health risks of childbearing are particularly pronounced for those who bear children at too early an age, for those whose births are too many and too close together, and for those who continue to bear children too late in life.

It is estimated that each year between 500,000 and one million women around the world die from maternity-related causes (UN, 1990). Using the conservative figure of 500,000, Africa alone is estimated to contribute 150,000 deaths every year, which amounts to between 500 and 1,000 deaths per 100,000 live births.

Adolescent childbearing   Recent findings from the series of Demographic Health Surveys (DHS) show that at least half of African teenagers between the ages of 15 and 19 have already had one or more children; countries such as Kenya, Liberia and Mali have the highest rates (Macro International, 1992). These data do not include terminated pregnancies. In Sub-Saharan Africa, between 20 and 30 per cent of total fertility is attributable to teenagers; indications are that this may be rising, particularly caused by low contraceptive usage among this age group.

Serious health risks accompany this level of fertility. Adolescents who give birth constitute a large population that is in need of prenatal, maternal and child health services. A large number of these young women are also exposed to the much higher risks associated with first births. From a health perspective, unwanted pregnancy rather than fertility is the real problem among adolescents. It has been observed that menarche, or the onset of the ability to conceive, is occurring earlier and earlier among adolescents in Africa. Furthermore, given the cultural encouragement of early age at marriage, pregnancy among adolescents may occur either within marriage or premaritally – but the health consequences for the mother are the same. When a pregnancy is carried to its full term, the provision of proper prenatal services is critical. In the absence of such care, complications such as high blood pressure and anaemia are unlikely to be recognized and dealt with in a timely fashion, leading to obstructed labour. Thus for the African teenage mother the probability of the baby dying in the womb, of experiencing vesical or rectal vaginal fistula, of premature labour, or of puerperal sepsis is quite high. A complication such as vesical or rectal vaginal fistula is particularly serious because it often leads to social ostracism – the adolescent can become a social outcast at a very early age. In west African countries such as Mali, Chad and parts of northern Nigeria, where the Islamic religion has a stronghold and where very early age at marriage is encouraged, social ostracism as a result of childbirth complications is a serious problem.

In many cases, adolescent pregnancies are unplanned and unintended. Thus many teenagers, afraid of interrupting their studies or fearing the wrath of their families, resort to intentional miscarriage or induced abortion. Studies have shown that adolescent girls resort to abortion using methods such as herbs, chloroquine, ink, knitting needles, coat hangers, and other sharp instruments. There is invariably excessive bleeding or haemorrhage, infection, and injury to the genital tract, and often death. The combination of the African teenager's ignorance about her own reproductive biology, the lack of effective family-life education programmes, and the high expectations that are increasingly being placed on the adolescent, mean that more and more are resorting to induced abortion as the solution to unintended pregnancies. The result is that in many hospitals in Sub-Saharan Africa the most common emergency admissions at present are related to complications arising from induced abortions.

Frequency of childbirth   In comparison to other parts of the world, the average number of children per woman is quite high in Africa. Despite loss of births through intended and unintended miscarriages, African mothers have had an average of five or six children by the time they are 30 years old. The tempo of childbearing is so fast in order to achieve the expected number of children as soon as possible. Although educational campaigns emphasize the importance of child spacing, there are tremendous pressures at the family and community level that impel women to maintain a high rate of childbearing, despite the problems it poses to their health. For the majority of African women who reside in rural areas, the role of mother remains a primary one. Their status in the family and community, and the benefits and resources they derive from it, remain contingent on their successful enactment of this role for the simple reason that other alternative roles either do not exist or have not been found acceptable.

A high tempo of childbearing causes health problems for women, both because of what it does to their bodies physically and the environmental pressures in terms of work and competition for resources. Besides the increasing likelihood of both maternal and child mortality with higher parity, a fast rate of childbearing contributes significantly to maternal depletion syndrome – a result of poor nutrition. Women's nutrition in Africa is not simply a function of a lack of resources with which to obtain a balanced diet, but is also a result of fatigue and lack of time to feed themselves properly – a tendency to subordinate their own health. In Africa many mothers are malnourished, as measured by the incidence of anaemia. Anaemia increases susceptibility to illness, pregnancy complications, and maternal death, and also contributes to overall death rates. Women in their reproductive years require three times as much iron per day as do men. Because anaemia starves the body of oxygen, it makes women tired and listless. It also increases the danger of haemorrhaging and other complications. Nearly two-thirds of pregnant women in Africa are clinically anaemic.

Iron deficiency is also very common in parts of Africa. In parts of Ethiopia, the Sudan and Nigeria, for example, cultural taboos sustained by the family discourage pregnant women from eating fruits, vegetables, rice and other high-calorie foods, thus endangering the mother and her unborn child. In many African societies, it is still the custom for adult women and young children to eat after the men have had their fill, leaving them less of the more nutritious foods. The tendency for girls and women to eat less food (or food with less nutritional value) is part of what diminishes the otherwise longer life expectancy of infant girls at birth as compared to boys.

Older mothers   As a result of familial pressures to keep having children as long as possible (often until their own children start bearing children), and also as a function of their expected roles as nurturers of their own kin (and sometimes of their non-kin's children), few African mothers enjoy the relative leisure associated with the 'empty-nest syndrome' – that is, the time when parents no longer have pre-school or young school-age children to look after. For many African women there is no distinction between biological motherhood and social motherhood; when the former is terminated by menopause or cultural taboos, the latter function is immediately substituted.

The biggest health hazard facing older mothers in Africa is mental stress. At a time when their physical strength is dwindling, mothers in their mid-40s and older are being faced with unabating, and in some instances increasing, responsibilities. Women in these higher-age categories often find themselves divorced or widowed. In light of prevailing customs in most of Africa, they thus also suddenly find themselves destitute – disinherited from their matrimonial wealth by their husbands' families, mostly brothers, and unprotected by weak national inheritance laws and legal provisions.

The frequency of marital dissolution in Africa is such that by their fiftieth birthday approximately half of women are no longer in their first union – two-thirds because of separation or divorce, and one-third because of the death of their spouse (Locoh, 1988b). Remarriage in this higher age group means highly unequal relationships that may create further stress (as in the case of leviratic unions, where widows are 'inherited' by their husbands' brothers).

Marital dissolution also means that older mothers often become the heads of their own households at a time when their resource base is dwindling, and their own strength and stamina are fast declining. In countries such as Kenya – where the proportion of female-headed households has reached 45 per cent in some areas – a large proportion of such households are headed by women in their 40s, 50s or 60s. They are characterized by extreme poverty and a large proportion of very young children under their care. The resultant mental stress experienced by such women as they try to cope with their circumstances is progressively harder to bear, especially as both the traditional familial support systems and their economic resources disintegrate. Africa is thus beginning to witness a rise in mental disturbances among older women; extreme cases are manifested in urban areas in geriatric delinquency such as begging in the streets and alcoholism.

Morbidity associated with old age is also being found more commonly among older women because they survive longer than their husbands. Physical disabilities through accidents; health impairments as a result of prolonged childbearing, hard physical labour and chronic malnutrition; diabetes; and breast and cervical cancer are all evidence of the increasing health vulnerability of African women who have passed their reproductive age. Their health problems are aggravated by the fact that they are either too busy, too poor or too weak to seek medical assistance when they should, and their health conditions then deteriorate into life-threatening ones.

Sexually transmitted disease   Whether young or middle-aged, the role of women as childbearers exposes them to the risk of HIV and other sexually transmitted diseases. Every sexually active woman in Africa runs the risk of contracting these, whether she is married or not. Some estimates consider that the HIV pandemic has the potential to erase all the gains that have been achieved in women's health over the past decade. World Health Organization (WHO) figures suggest that during the 1990s AIDS will kill one and a half to three million women of reproductive age in central and eastern Africa, producing several million orphans (WHO, 1990). Such large-scale social disruption will put unprecedented strain on families and social services alike. Some communities are already finding the sheer number of AIDS orphans completely overwhelming, even where the extended family is still strong, as in many rural parts of Africa, and even where relatives are ready and willing to offer assistance.

Although the condom is seen at present as the only effective preventive measure against the sexual transmission of HIV, for the majority of African women (as indeed for those in some other cultural settings) the suggestion that their partners or husbands use a condom is either seen as evidence of the woman's infidelity or perceived as defiance or insolence. At best, this may result in a breach of the relationship; at worst, in the woman being beaten or abandoned. In the cultures prevailing in Africa, where women are traditionally expected to bear many children, the woman's insistence on safer sex or her refusal to engage in a sexual relationship is an invitation to marital dissolution and is, therefore, in most cases impracticable.

Other less-dramatic sexually transmitted diseases continue to affect women. Each of the more than 20 disease agents that are transmitted sexually has serious repercussions for women's health, as well as for the health of their children, their partners and, ultimately, their entire families. Ulcerative conditions of the genitals, often associated with sexually transmitted diseases such as herpes, facilitate the transmission of the AIDS virus. Other types of sexually transmitted diseases such as syphilis or gonorrhoea contribute to the incidence of blindness, brain damage, pelvic inflammation, spontaneous abortions, ectopic pregnancies and cervical cancer, and are a major cause of infertility. One of the more serious sexually transmitted diseases is chlamydial infection. Evidently a single episode of chlamydial tubal infection can cause tubal blockage in 17 per cent of women, leading to infertility. The figure rises to more than 60 per cent following three or more episodes. Yet chlamydial genital infection remains asymptomatic in 30 to 50 per cent of men (WHO, 1990; Carael, 1992). In Sub-Saharan Africa, up to 85 per cent of primary infertility in women and 20 per cent of infertility in men can be attributed to previous genital tract infection. The rate of tubal occlusion among women in Sub-Saharan Africa is three times that in developed countries (WHO, 1990). Infertility of the female spouse is in turn one of the major causes of marital dissolution in Africa (Pebly and Mbugua, 1989; WHO, 1990; Carael, 1992).

Women as providers of health care

The role of women as providers of health care to their families, the community and society at large is one which is deeply rooted and one which makes them viewed as nurturers *par excellence*. Little girls are taught from early childhood that it is their responsibility to look after their older or younger siblings, particularly the male siblings, who are often portrayed as incapable of taking proper care of themselves. At the family level, therefore, a strong gender distinction is made as to who should be 'given' health care and who should be the 'giver' of such care. This gendering of health provision continues throughout life and is reflected in policies, programmes and institutions that address women's health issues in Africa.

Some important points of reference should be kept in mind. First, the major focus for women as providers of health care is in the first instance on children and in the second on other women. Beyond their immediate spouse, health care provision by women to other male kin or community members is much less pronounced, although clearly still present. Secondly, for women and children the first contact in the chain of health provision is usually a woman. For children such contact is usually the mother, sister, aunt or other close female relative; for women a first point of health contact is a sister, a co-wife, a step-sister, a daughter, a traditional birth attendant or a female herbalist. These channels of communication are often prescribed by the prevailing cultural practices and sustained by the family. This may be the case because a significant proportion of health care is related to reproduction and childbearing, areas which traditionally were never the man's domain (Oppong, 1988, 1992b).

This role of African women has health consequences, both for themselves as providers as well as for the receivers of such care – mainly other women and children. In the best of circumstances many women depend upon their own skills or those of a compatriot to diagnose and then make a prognosis on the health condition that they are dealing with. Being largely illiterate, their success will depend to a great extent on the proven abilities of their mentors, who could be their own mothers or other female kin. Many traditional birth attendants (TBAs) in Africa, for example, are expert midwives, having obtained practical knowledge through long experience; they are capable of delivering even the most complicated pregnancies.

In many instances, however, the first point of contact in the chain of health provision is a trial and error affair which may worsen the course of the disease. Traditional beliefs about the cause of disease persist in many areas of Africa. Consequently, although some of the practices that relate to prevention may be consistent with scientifically acknowledged causes and treatments, others make the control of preventable diseases difficult because the perceived etiology has no scientific base whatsoever. In many parts of Kenya, for example, the tendency to attribute illnesses to non-medical socio-cultural and supernatural factors remains strong. Thus infertility is associated with witchcraft; cancer with the evil eye; malnutrition and diarrhoea with a breach of taboo; malaria, tuberculosis and acute respiratory infection with the wind; frequent child deaths with a curse; dysentery with a new harvest; and polio with fate (UN, 1989; Ajayi et al., 1991). Thus in the absence of a proper understanding of the scientific causes of disease, well-meaning health provision by women can actually contribute to a worsening of the situation. It is perhaps, therefore, not surprising that infant and child deaths as well as maternal deaths continue to remain quite high in those areas where health provision, at the family level, is still significantly under the control of women and little or no efforts have been made to improve their knowledge of the etiology of common diseases or the simple skills that are needed to prevent or treat such ailments. Interventions that enable women to achieve such improvements, for example teaching them oral rehydration therapy (ORT), hold great potential for success and appear to be relatively cost effective.

Even so, African women as health providers are increasingly being put into circumstances with which they can barely cope. A major concern now is how women can deal with the large number of AIDS orphans, who in countries such as Uganda have lost not only their parents but their uncles, aunts and other close relatives as well. It is mostly older women, who have already terminated their childbearing, who are left behind to provide all the nurturing that such children require. In some cases, the children are themselves HIV positive. Other children are also under the care of these older women as a result of parents' migration or of having been born out of wedlock and then repatriated to live with their grandmothers. Besides the fact that the capabilities of women looking after so many children are stretched to the breaking point – and often do break – another important question is the sociological ramifications of large numbers of Africa's future generations being brought up by grandmothers as primary parents.

Women as producers of health inputs

African women are still primarily responsible for producing all the major health inputs for their families, their communities and society at large. These inputs range from breastfeeding, food and nutrition, water and fuel, to sanitation and a domestic environment safe from health hazards.

Prolonged breastfeeding is the norm rather than the exception in many parts of Africa. Exceptions arise as a function of the role changes women undergo, such as entering the formal wage sector. Normally, however, almost all children are breastfed for periods ranging from two months to two years. Since breastfeeding provides a level of immunity against diseases for the infant and also suppresses ovulation, it serves to promote the health of both mothers and children. Although breastfeeding has been on the decline in many parts of Africa, concerted efforts are underway to encourage women not to abandon it altogether (*Network/Family Health International*, 1992, 13[2]). These efforts can only succeed, however, if they respond to some of the fundamental factors that lead women to abandon breastfeeding, such as being required to take on an ever-increasing share of income-generating activity for the family.

The role of African women in food production and nutrition is now widely recognized. Many studies suggest that this has become even more important as a result of men's increased migration to cities and towns (FAO, 1987; Palmer, 1992). None the less, African women are grossly disadvantaged as they strive to provide food and nutrition to their families and communities. While up to 80 per cent of food producers in some

African countries are women, they receive only between 2 and 10 per cent of the extension contacts (Palmer, 1991). This means that they are unable to obtain sufficient skills to improve land productivity, storage and processing of food; this leads in turn to low and poor yields, and to massive food loss in storage. Secondly, changes in agriculture have also tended to undermine women's security. The widespread shift from production of subsistence food, mostly grown by women, to the growing of cash crops has often meant that control of the crop passes to men because agricultural training, credit and technology are routinely provided to men rather than women. Women farmers thereby lose a major source of income but, more importantly they lose an important source of nutrition for themselves as well as their families (Palmer, 1991; Makinwa-Adebusoye and Olawoye, 1992).

The relative neglect of women as key players in the provision of food and nutrition in Africa has major repercussions for women's own health as well as for that of their families and communities – indeed for African nations in general. A case in point is Ethiopia. Although it was widely known that 84 per cent of Ethiopian women are involved in agriculture, the famine was never portrayed in the mass media as a disaster for women as farmers – and this despite the fact that any aid aimed at rebuilding agriculture in Ethiopia would have had to be directed as much at women as prime actors, as at men. Such lost opportunities condemn Africa to recurrent famines by failing to empower women to do whatever they are doing, better. If they are to provide better food and nutrition to their families, African women must be assured access to land and credit, as well as training and appropriate woman-friendly technology to make their work easier, more productive and less time-consuming (Goldschmidt, 1987; 1994).

Water and fuel are further essential health inputs that are provided mostly by women. Both are necessary for food processing and preparation as well as for sanitation. However, while it appears that considerable though still insufficient progress has been made toward the provision of access to improved water supplies (as a result of the impetus given by the International Drinking Water Supply and Sanitation Decade, 1981–90), less can be said of efforts to improve access to sources of cheap fuel. Electrification is expensive, solar energy has not been exploited, and energy obtained from other sources such as gas provide an insignificant proportion of total energy needs. For most African households, then, the main source of energy remains firewood.

In many African countries, the search for firewood has become a full-time occupation as the sources have declined more and more. Women have to trek long distances to obtain firewood because of the deforestation, desertification and environmental degradation that are now commonplace everywhere. Inadequacy of firewood means poor food preparation, which has serious implications for health. The time spent in search of firewood means that women have to forgo doing other essential tasks at home and also contributes to their fatigue and attendant problems.

Despite the progress that has been made globally in providing access to improved water supply, Africa as a continent still lags far behind. A large proportion of African households are still without easy access to good water, and many live with inadequate sanitation. The implications for women's health are serious. In countries where water-borne or water-related diseases – such as river blindness and bilharzia in many parts of western Africa – are endemic, women are more exposed to them than are men because so many of women's tasks require them to be around water. These include fetching water, washing clothes, bathing, and working in irrigated fields. Irrigated fields added to improper drainage create fertile breeding grounds for mosquitoes and consequently for malaria, which is now endemic in many parts of Africa. This leads in turn to the use of pesticides, giving rise to resistance in mosquitoes. For those living in urban areas, the effects of inadequate water supply and lack of proper sanitation are compounded by overcrowding and the makeshift nature of slum dwellings.

African women are also primarily responsible for ensuring that the family enjoys domestic conditions that are safe and conducive to healthy living. They are responsible for cleaning the compound so that dangerous objects which can cause accidents are out of reach, especially from children; they strive to ensure that proper sanitary practices are observed in and around the compound; and they dispose of household waste. Because of widespread ignorance of disease transmission and/or a lack of resources and proper technology, women often endanger their own health as well as that of their families in the course of managing their environment. Lack of understanding, particularly of water-borne diseases, may aggravate the situation when waste disposal is upstream of water sources; similarly, the perimeters of wells may remain unprotected from contamination by domestic animals.

The physical environment

The health of women in Africa is also endangered by the physical environment in which they perform their familial roles and tasks. Given that the majority of women are involved in agriculture and that they spend long periods of time fetching water, looking for firewood and washing clothes, a substantial part of their lives is spent exposed to the harshness of the climate – be it excessive heat, heavy rainfalls or severely low temperatures. The vagaries of the weather take their toll in many ways. In their often malnourished and debilitated states, women find themselves easily susceptible to pneumonia. They are exposed to a variety of injuries that can expose them to tetanus (when collecting firewood, for example).

Having to depend on less than clean water for drinking when they are far away from home exposes them to a variety of water-borne and water-related diseases. They must also constantly forgo proper nutrition in an effort to fulfil all their multiple tasks on time. This harsh physical environment is made worse by the lack of labour-saving devices that are women-friendly. Appropriate technology in agriculture is normally more amenable to use by men than by women. Grain mills, for example, are huge machines whose technology is beyond what most women, with the overwhelming demands on their time, can learn and understand. Likewise, the operation of tractors for land preparation is geared more towards men than women. Increasingly also, African women in agriculture are faced with new health hazards because of exposure to harmful pesticides. Although global figures on the effects of pesticides on agricultural workers are available (Makinwa-Adebusoye, 1990; Palmer, 1991), more information on their short-term and long-term effects on African women needs to be compiled.

In summary, then, there is a synergistic relationship between the health of women and the kinds of work they do. As water carriers, firewood carriers, cooks, sweepers, washers of clothes – in all the tasks they must perform for their families – African women work extremely long hours doing heavy, dirty and monotonous work, work that has a high risk of injury and which involves prolonged standing, stooping, bending and carrying of heavy loads. Regardless of their physical condition, this work must go on. The physical and mental stress from the amount of time spent working as well as from the types of work done is associated with the rising incidence of high blood pressure, stillbirths, and premature births and deaths – especially during peak periods in harvesting, weeding or planting.

Socio-cultural and economic environment

A major cause and consequence of African women's deteriorating health conditions can be located in the socio-cultural and economic context in which the African family finds itself today (see Chapter 3). Harmful traditional health practices persist at a time when the viability of the African family as an economic unit is being challenged. Prolonged socio-political conflicts add their share to the health burden of the family and to that of women in particular.

Socio-cultural factors   It is common in Africa to invoke 'tradition' as the major reason why various cultural practices, be they useful or harmful, persist. African newspapers are replete with such pronouncements from political and opinion leaders, administrators and community leaders. But careful examination of such pronouncements shows that 'tradition' is mostly resorted to as an explanatory variable when issues of the gender allocation of power and resources are raised, particularly within the context of the African family. In considering how women's health is affected by their social and cultural environment, it is important to recognize a contradiction: women's importance to society for their various productive, reproductive, familial and communal roles is belied by the self-same society's denial of virtually all the resources that would enable them to perform those roles better. This contradiction is captured in Boubacar Diallo's summary of how African women are viewed by their own societies:

> The paradox is that spiritually the African woman is a superior being, a kind of intermediary between God and men. In practice however, she uncomplainingly bears the weights of traditions which make of her a sacrificial victim. Many popular songs and sayings state that woman gives birth to prophets, savants, great warriors and rich men, but that a woman may never herself be a prophet, a savant, a warrior or a rich person. In these societies a woman can never act or state her opinions freely, and the work she does, although a tremendous burden, is never paid for. She is guaranteed no property rights whatsoever, neither in her home nor in the community, neither by law nor custom. Her social status is always inferior to the man's. (Diallo, 1985: 26)

The expectation that African women will remain mute, passive and powerless, as is dictated by cultural prescriptions and traditional practices, is one of the strongest supports to the continued existence of practices that are detrimental to women's lives and health. Both the bridewealth and dowry traditions, for example, as well as the need for certainty about virginity, lead to early marriage for most of Africa's adolescent girls and thus to the health risks that accompany early pregnancy (as discussed above). Girls as young as eight, nine or ten years of age are given in marriage, invariably to a much older man. Because of the high probability of their husband's death within a few years of marriage, many of these girls are immediately condemned to having multiple sex partners and thus to the health hazards this brings – not least of which is HIV infection.

Female circumcision or excision, also commonly now referred to as female genital mutilation (FGM), is a harmful practice that tenaciously persists in most of Africa. Estimates by the Inter-African Committee on Traditional Practices Affecting the Health of Women and Children (IAC), established in 1984, indicate that female circumcision is still widely practised in some 26 African countries. FGM involves the removal or mutilation of an otherwise healthy sexual organ. It is performed at a time when the girl is vulnerable and powerless, and therefore often occurs against her will. There are three types of FGM in Africa:

- *Clitoridectomy* (or 'sunna') – removal of the skin over the clitoris or the tip of the clitoris;
- *Excision* – removal of the entire clitoris and the labia minora, but without closing up the vulva; and

- *Infibulation* – removal of the clitoris, the labia minora and parts of the labia majora, stitching together the sides and leaving just a small opening for urine and menstrual fluid to pass through.

The 'operation' is carried out in various settings. Among rural traditional birth attendants a razor blade, knife or piece of broken glass is used, while the labia are held in place and stitched together with thorns. Well-to-do parents may resort to modern health facilities, where the operation is done by skilled health professionals under anaesthesia (a practice strongly disapproved of by the World Health Organization, medical associations and health ministries).

Regardless of how it is done, female circumcision contributes to poor health among women. Immediate effects include pain, shock, haemorrhage, retention of urine, infections, fever and tetanus; death is not uncommon, especially if access to proper medical care is some distance away. Over time, however, African women who have been subjected to the custom suffer from one or several of the following negative health conditions: difficulty in penile penetration, pelvic infections which can be severe enough to block the fallopian tubes, urinary tract infections, formation of cysts and hard scars, obstructed labour, urinary or rectal fistula and, eventually, prolapsed uterus. Heightened risk of AIDS infection has now become part of the picture.

Although it is difficult to quantify the health problems posed by female circumcision, most service providers in Africa attest that it constitutes a major public health dilemma. One study in Sierra Leone, for example, estimated that 83 per cent of circumcised women had had a circumcision-related condition requiring medical attention at some point in their lives.

Violence against women – especially wife battery and other forms of domestic violence – is extremely widespread in Africa but remains largely unquantified and undocumented. Wife battery in countries where the status of women is low is defended on the ground that husbands have the right to 'discipline' their wives. Indeed, when an act that would have protected women from all sorts of injustices and which included protection for women within marriage was introduced into the Kenyan parliament in 1986, it failed to be passed by the predominantly male body because it was seen as interfering with husbands' God-given disciplinary authority over their wives, among other things. Some of the most heated discussions centred on the proposed act's purported incursions into areas considered by tradition to be the strict prerogative of husbands. Perhaps as a consequence of knowledge that lawmakers are tolerant of wife battering, the incidence of such violence against women has been on the increase in Kenya. A growing number of such cases end in death, and others result in various disabilities for women such as blindness, amputated legs or arms, and paralysis of various limbs (Kenyan newspaper reports, 1986–

93). Such physical damage to women's bodies masks the psychological injuries that contribute further to women's mental distress. Given that African women have not been empowered to speak out against the domestic violence in which they are the chief victims, this threat to women's health remains largely confined to the family in both cause and effect.

Besides wife battery, sexual violence – which includes sexual harassment, rape and incest – is a serious threat to African women's lives which has neither been exposed nor begun to be addressed in any systematic way. Except for newspaper reports, which in turn derive their information from proceedings in court cases, there is almost no information on the extent of sexual violence in Africa. However, if lessons are to be learnt from other parts of the world, the chances are that what is currently being observed is but the tip of the iceberg.

In the context of African traditional practices, and, by extension, in the prevailing policy environment and legal framework, violence is yet to be recognized as an exercise of power – as a violation by force of the integrity of a woman's body, a violation of the basic human right to the security of the person. Rather, sexual violence, especially against minors, is still viewed primarily as an assault on the honour of the family. In many court proceedings rape is defended on the grounds of extreme provocation of the defendant by the victim, by the way she either dressed, talked, danced or behaved. In other circumstances, it is explained in terms of lust or uncontrollable sexual urges brought about, more often than not, by alcohol. Legal sanctions are extremely mild, reflecting the dominance of cultural precepts which aim to preserve these expressions of perceived male supremacy. Sexual violence is therefore likely to remain a source of serious health dangers to African women until such time as a reconstruction of gender relations in Africa takes place.

The pursuit of beauty and desirability to males also presents some serious potential health problems for African women. In some cultures female circumcision is defended on aesthetic grounds, as making women more sexually desirable to their husbands. Practices such as ear-piercing are probably less of a health hazard than those that require large body part scarification or those that measure a woman's desirability by her waistline. The latter contribute to obesity, with all its attendant problems.

Economic environment The economic situation of the African woman is getting worse, not better, given the current African economic crisis. Her economic status can be summed up as the poorest of the poor. Structural adjustment programmes (SAP) have reduced her family's resource base, shifted a larger share of income-generating activities onto her shoulders, added more family health-provision and health-care responsibilities for the family to her burden, and reduced her and her family's access to health, education and employment still further. Structural adjustment programmes have locked women even more tightly into survival strategies that emphasize their childbearing roles. Old sources of insecurity are aggravated and the hope of providing for old age with economic resources has receded further. As family resources become scarcer, so discrimination against girls increases in nutrition, health and educational expenditure (Sadik, 1989).

Women's increasing poverty operates on several fronts with respect to health: not having enough food or the right kind of food; not having decent housing, sanitation or water supply; not being able to get health care when needed (because if health care is free, money for transport is insufficient, or because the alternative of forgoing an opportunity to generate income and thus depriving the family in favour of going to seek medical attention is not acceptable); not being able to take advantage of educational and training opportunities for self and/or children; adopting short-term survival strategies and plans so as to respond only to current crises; and not being accorded dignity as human beings (Cleland, 1989; Oppong, 1992a). A recent survey in Namibia, for example, concluded that poverty and unhealthy living environments are the major factors pre-disposing people to illness and poor health. Further, the interactive combination of moderately inadequate food intake with disease is one of the most important explanatory factors in the death of young children and contributes to morbidity among both adults and children, particularly among pregnant women and those of childbearing age (UN, 1989). Other evidence from Namibia indicates that while illness among children under five years old was common, it was most frequently reported in female-headed households, which are the poorest.

Prostitution in Africa is driven by the shrinking of opportunities to pursue economically viable occupations for the proportion of mainly young women who practise it. Family disruption through divorce, death of husbands, parents or other guardians, and sanctions against premarital childbearing are some of the factors that lead African girls and women to resort to prostitution. In the majority of instances it is an urban phenomenon.

Because of the already disempowered position in which prostitutes find themselves, they are particularly susceptible to all sorts of health problems. They frequently encounter physical violence. They may contract any of the sexually transmitted diseases, including AIDS, because most of them are not in a position to insist that their clients use a condom. Extremely high rates of HIV infection have been found among prostitutes in cities such as Nairobi and Kampala. Prostitutes also run a high risk of becoming pregnant and resorting to unsafe abortion, with the consequent problems. Data are scanty on the specific health problems that prostitutes in Africa face, but it is clear that their way of life adds an additional dimension to their already precarious health as women (Bledsoe, 1989).

As the economic situation in Africa worsens, families are forced to adopt a variety of survival strategies. These strategies often lead inadvertently to the adoption of lifestyles which can be detrimental to women's health. Migration into the cities in Africa is thus associated with alcohol consumption as well as with smoking among an increasing number of women. Changes in diet also lead to the consumption of too many saturated fats. All these will eventually contribute to an increase in non-communicable diseases such as heart disease, lung cancer and cirrhosis of the liver among African women. Most of these diseases have a cohort effect, so they only begin to manifest themselves among the survivors of the cohorts exposed to the risk after a long span of time, maybe 10 to 20 years. It should be expected therefore that future generations of African women who survive to their old age will correspondingly be afflicted with many of these diseases; the mortality patterns by cause of death will be distinctly different to those exhibited in the 1990s.

Socio-political conflict and full-scale wars in Africa result when different political factions demand more equitable shares and usage of available economic resources. They affect the health of women at several levels. In some countries, such as Ethiopia, Somalia, Zimbabwe and Mozambique, women have participated extensively as fighters alongside the men. In that context they have suffered all the mortality and morbidity associated with war, as well as the psychological trauma. However, the number of women who become actively involved in warfare as soldiers remains relatively quite small in Africa, as fighting is still considered a male occupation. None the less, women still bear the brunt of armed conflict. They constitute the largest proportion of the fatalities recorded among non-combatants. Their physical helplessness makes them easy targets for political repression and for revenge against the unseen male opponent. In times of conflict women and young girls are the victims of rape, torture and other forms of physical violence. They are widowed when young but are still expected to keep the family together. In the deprivations that surround the hostilities, such as famine and lack of shelter, food, clothing and services, assuring the survival of the family rests primarily with women. This causes untold stress on both their bodies and their psyches. Often women have to strive to create a semblance of family life in refugee conditions – the most deprived conditions of all. Currently there are small-scale or large-scale conflicts underway in the following countries: Burundi, Chad, Ethiopia, Kenya, Liberia, Mozambique, Rwanda, Sierra Leone, Somalia, South Africa, Sudan, Togo, Uganda, Western Sahara and Zaire.

Policy and programme interventions

The precarious situation of the health of African women persists in spite
of national health policies. Existing health policies and programmes need
to be reviewed in light of the accumulating evidence that the strategies
adopted are either not reaching women at all or are addressing health
issues which are not a priority to women themselves. At the heart of the
matter has been the failure to acknowledge that, at both the macro
(national) and at the micro (family or individual) levels, the productive
and reproductive activities of women are inextricably linked and therefore
cannot be addressed in isolation from one another. Unhappily, however,
such separation has been the norm rather than the exception. Thus while
most health programmes promote better nutrition for both women and
their children, they do not consider the more fundamental question of
how such women will gain access to and sustain good nutrition. At the
policy level this is reflected most clearly by the failure of many governments to guarantee gender equity, even if only in terms of constitutional
rights, in all sectors of the economy. While an emergent nation such as
Namibia may have a Bill of Rights, the inherited colonial laws which are
still operative make such a Bill an empty legal instrument.

Thus a major weakness of current health policies and programmes,
especially as they pertain to women, is that health indicators have been
treated in isolation without any accompanying policy on the underlying
determinants of health. A good example is family planning. As a health
measure that is primarily focused on women, family planning is partly one
of practical containment, but it can be and is defeated by other more
primary influences such as women's illiteracy. Such primary influences
cannot be addressed in like fashion; rather they must be given a more
central place on the overall agenda of each country's economic planning.
In essence this means that the prevailing separation between economic
and social planning, whereby the latter is always being seen as laying claim
to the former, needs to re-evaluated.

With reference to the health of women and to the vast untapped
resources for promoting their own and their families' health that they
represent, it is imperative to address the question of the impact of gender
on economic and health policies. This goes beyond the current dialogue
concerning the impact of economic and other policies on women. The
adoption of such a framework must utilize gender analytically as a variable,
in at least five stages of the planning process:

1. identification of the problem which planning aims to solve;
2. clarification of the development objectives;
3. selection of indicators;

4. adoption of strategies to be utilized; and
5. consequent policy packaging, that is, development of 'programmes'.

This approach is likely to produce vastly different results than currently exist because gender inequities in health – the underlying determinants of which are located in many other sectors – will be dealt with as an integral part of development planning rather than as special projects. Given the critical role of women in the economies of African countries, their health concerns will be ignored at the peril of future generations.

Conclusions

This chapter has discussed the situation of African women's health within the context of the family. Utilizing a conceptual framework for women and health that relates the multiple roles of women as providers of health care and health inputs for their families and communities to the socio-cultural, economic and physical environments in which they live, this chapter has shown the precarious and deteriorating health situation of women. While women's health concerns that are linked to their repro-ductive roles have been the main focus of most government interventions, it has been postulated here that even these concerns have been addressed from a macro perspective that largely ignores the real and more strategic health concerns of women.

Health problems that women face as a function of their productive activities are still not being addressed in a systematic manner. Even more serious are those health conditions and problems which emanate from suppressive and life-threatening traditional practices perpetuated by the prevailing patriarchal systems, in the face of which operational legal frameworks remain mute. A condition for improving women's health is the tapping of the vast resources that lie within the women themselves by involving them in a participatory process at all stages of health planning. This can be accomplished by adopting a gender perspective, within which women are not treated as a residual category but where their central but different needs are taken into account in a situation of equity.

CHAPTER 9

African family systems and socio-economic crisis

Christine Oppong

Introduction

During the past three decades the majority of Sub-Saharan African countries have simultaneously experienced rapid population growth, increasing youthfulness of the population, and high levels of spatial mobility and dislocation. There has been a marked shift of people from rural to rapidly growing urban conglomerations. These demographic changes have occurred within a context of economic stagnation, recurrent crises, spiralling debt burdens and the introduction under international pressure of structural adjustment programmes (SAP).

Such programmes are characterized by in-built gender biases (for example, Elson, 1987). Adjustment policies have put both women and men out of paid work and have cut back social programmes in health and social welfare. Accordingly, people have less money and time to care for their families. Living standards and nutrition have been declining across the board. The net result of such policies has been that larger proportions of incomes are now being devoted to food and to the fuel for cooking it. Chronic malnutrition rates among children have risen still higher, providing stark evidence of the harsh impacts of these policies. Subsequent programmes to alleviate such effects have tended to treat women merely as victims, rather than taking into account their very real contributions.

The employment crisis deepened during the 1980s, and employment problems fall disproportionately on young people and women (OAU, 1991). Besides exploring faster expansion of the urban formal sector, African states are seeking to expand employment in rural agro- and cottage industries and are making an intensified effort to increase productivity and incomes in the urban informal sector. Of great concern is the unemployment of the most energetic section of the population, the young men. There is, therefore, emphasis on gearing education and training policies to the promotion of self-employment and thus of family-based micro-enterprises.

The demographic facts   For the past several decades, the chief demographic factors that have fashioned population profiles in the region have been persistent high mortality and fertility, and widespread mobility of populations in the search for the means of survival – if not employment – in increasingly harsh economic and ecological environments. The latter has involved labour migration of women, men and children, as well as the dislocation of increasingly large numbers of refugees, who have fled regions stricken by drought or internecine warfare.

Continuing high fertility is considered the result of a combination of socio-cultural and economic factors: very early marriage for girls, erosion of traditionally prolonged breastfeeding periods and post-partum sexual abstinence, and the limited use of modern contraception. The position of women relative to men in society is legally, economically and socially unequal. Indeed, in many countries in the region the statutory law affecting women is often overridden by the customary law, especially with respect to marriage and family spheres, where women are still treated as minors and subordinate to men. Women's legal status is thus recognized as a major stumbling block to their achievement of equality.

In view of the comparative youthfulness of populations, dependency burdens are high, affecting overall economic performance, consumption patterns, capital formation, indebtedness, the quality of the labour force, and household composition and needs. In view of the labour-intensive nature of most work, including subsistence labour and the lack of mechanization and infrastructure, there is a heavy dependence upon child labour. This affects levels of schooling and training achieved by the young, and particularly by girls, who are especially deprived since they early take on the double burdens of productive and reproductive activities. Dependence upon child labour in communities and households lacking modern labour-saving machinery also provides continuing pressure for high fertility.

Population policies   A consensus is developing among governments that population factors play an important part in planning processes, marked by shifts from a *laissez-faire* approach to expressions of need for compatibility between economic and population growth (Locoh, 1988a). A majority of governments now perceive growth rates as too high, and there is increasing dissatisfaction with the persistently high levels of fertility.

The Economic Commission for Africa has found that a majority of countries responding to inquiries perceive the status of women as having a significant influence on demographic trends, and many have accordingly formulated policies with a view to ensuring equal opportunities for women with their male counterparts. A major concern in many cases is raising the age at marriage so as to enable women to postpone the first birth and undergo longer periods of training for employment.

Recent studies on the subject have also stressed that the design of an effective population policy requires the dynamics of family systems and, within them, women's roles, to be taken into account. On the one hand, traditional family norms and practices may favour high fertility and thus present obstacles to the use of contraception; on the other, women's more modern roles in higher education and employment are identified with demographic and contraceptive innovation. Thus it has been advised that, in designing family planning programmes, governments should take more effective account of existing family structures and gender roles. The failure of past population programmes in the region to attain their object-ives has been blamed in part upon the lack of understanding of the dynamic nature of the socio-economic and demographic systems within which they are located.

Economic policy making   These concerns have been paralleled by a similar realization in the economic sphere that current attempts to restructure economies that are actually based largely upon family-run agricultural units and other micro-enterprises are also likely to be doomed to failure if the nature of the underlying family systems is systematically ignored (Palmer, 1991). Neglect of the complexity, diversity and change in the region's principal economic units – including female and male roles, and sexual divisions of labour and resources – is likely to seriously hamper economic planning and progress. Moreover, given the intricate connections between economic and demographic change, at both the micro and macro level, the two need to be dealt with simultaneously.

These are themes which need to be taken up and addressed in the context of regional and national policy debates on economic and demographic issues. This chapter focuses on some shifting aspects of conjugal, parental and kin roles, and their significance within the context of economic crisis and demographic change.

Family solidarity: crisis and change

Africa is without doubt the region of the world where women engage in a life-long struggle to combine reproductive and productive tasks and responsibilities within the family context. Their levels of both fertility and economic activity are higher than for any other region, and they initiate both sorts of activities at an earlier age than do women elsewhere. At the same time, their conjugal roles are often characterized by greater autonomy than are the roles of women in other regions. Thus they depend to a great extent upon support from kin in carrying out these heavy and frequently conflicting tasks.

Sharing and delegation of economic activities and child care tasks among female kin, especially mothers and daughters, is crucial to the viability of domestic groups. Descent groups control most rights in land and immovable property. Family systems have accordingly been character-ized by solidarity and substitutability of kin in all domains: parenthood; fostering and delegation of child care; marriage (polygyny, polycoity, delegation and sharing of sexual and procreative rights); and sharing and delegation of household maintenance tasks (Oppong, 1992a). But at the present time the migration of people to seek employment and to escape political and ecological crises means that increasingly large numbers of women no longer have the support from female kin and affines that they once enjoyed.

Investment in children A strategy that long served to promote allocation of material resources, and female and male energy to productive success and to long-term investment in children was the strict control exercised by the older generation over the sexuality and reproductive powers of the young (Lesthaeghe, 1989). This was ensured through the strict upholding of puberty ceremonies and the involvement in marriage transactions of relatives from the two sets of kin. In many cases these involved the passing to the bride's family of considerable sums of wealth, often in the form of cattle or manual labour. Moreover, nubile girls were carefully protected from the untoward advances of young men by strict segregation of the sexes or by precise monitoring of sexual intercourse, even after marriage.

These patterns of control and protection, focusing upon young girls and women during the reproductive span, often involved the grandparental generation, who played a significant part in the rearing and training of the young. Relationships have been traditionally very close between alternate generations of grandparents and grandchildren, lacking the ambivalence which often typifies parent–child interactions. Given residential patterns and the likelihood that births to young women would occur in the house-holds of the mother's or father's parents, as well as fostering practices, grandmothers have frequently been the main caregivers for the young. Indeed, in contexts where women have been noted for a combination of high fertility and heavy work schedules, the cooperation of kin (including older siblings) in child care has been essential.

Impact of social and spatial mobility Evidence is now mounting that these traditional systems of controlling, monitoring, protecting, and sup-porting the young, and pregnant and lactating mothers are breaking down. This collapse is occurring amid massive spatial dislocation of people seeking new sources of security and support. Mothers increasingly lack the needed support from husbands, kin or affines, as they try with declining success both to earn incomes and produce goods and services for subsist-ence needs and to breastfeed, rear and socialize their young. Maternal resources are increasingly jeopardized.

Spatial separation of siblings, of parents and children, and of husbands and wives – through labour migration and the constraints of urban housing – means that increasing numbers of people are living far from the possibility of customary kin support and care. Moreover, in a growing number of instances, individuals have access to resources, including cash income, which can be privately allocated and controlled, as against family resources managed on behalf of kin groups (human labour, crops, cattle and land). Thus the economic basis of sibling solidarity is being whittled away and private property, individual incomes or personal penury are taking its place.

In such contexts questions are being posed as to whether traditional solidarities can survive: whether descent groups will disintegrate; whether rampant individualism will prevail; whether the vulnerable, the old, the young, and pregnant and nursing mothers will be abandoned; and which categories of the population will suffer most as changes of different kinds unfold.

Another important line of questioning involves the kinds of economic initiatives being taken by families in order to survive the economic, political and ecological catastrophes now engulfing entire nations. What evidence is there of different sectors of the population, including women or children, having to work harder? What evidence is there of new means of maintenance and novel forms of livelihood?

In some communities there is indeed evidence that traditional kinship solidarities are breaking down in urban areas, as the flows of rural–urban migration increase and urban residents are unable to extend the hospitality traditional in former times. In other instances, there is evidence that maintenance of kinship solidarities is preventing untold numbers from sinking into destitution.

Demographic data provide at least some evidence that the decline in the size of co-resident domestic groups is widespread, except in northern Africa. Kin co-residence remains common, however. What is new is the increasing number of households headed or maintained by women; these now make up as many as 20 or 30 per cent or more of households in some regions. Many such household heads are elderly women; others are mothers who have been separated from their partners by labour migration or simply abandoned. Many of the household heads are widows. Some evidence indicates that a comparatively greater share of the resources in female-controlled households is allocated directly to dependent children; evidence from Ghana at least shows that children may be better served when there are several adult females co-residing.

In view of the erosion of traditional kinship solidarities there is need to take a more dynamic perspective on the family and to examine fertility, mortality and mobility simultaneously within the context of changing family relationships. This would be preferable to the past common practice of allowing one topic to take centre stage to the exclusion of the rest (Oucho,

Table 9.1 Africa in the late 1980s (orders of magnitude, millions)

Total population	600
Rural population	360
Rural to urban migrants, per year	4
Children under 15 years of age	300
Live births, per year	28
Infant and child births, per year	4
Children of primary-school age (6 to 11)	100
(of whom not in school)	50
Boys in primary school	35
Girls in primary school	25
Youth (15 to 24 years)	120
Labour force	250
(of whom disabled)	25
Labour force entrants, per year	15
Wage employment in modern sector	25
Additional waged jobs, per year	0
Refugees	5

Source: ILO, 1988.

1991). To date, however, there has been a painful lack of studies indicating the effects of migration on family life and vice versa.

The economic base: family survival

Only one-tenth of recognized labour force participants in Africa are in wage employment in the modern sector. Agriculture still employs about two-thirds of the region's labour force, providing not only food but raw materials for agro-based industries and the bulk of commodity exports. Most other people are engaged in non-agricultural activities such as trade, crafts, and services (see Table 9.1).

Petty trades occupy an estimated one-quarter to three-quarters of the labour force in towns and cities. This so-called informal sector is increasingly providing an economic arena for rural migrants, the unemployed from the modern sector, and school-leavers (Maldonado, 1989). This sector is of increasing importance for the survival of women and their families, as well as for men (UNDP, 1991).

In spite of over two decades of work on the informal sector, however, remarkably little is generally known about women's position in it. Nor has sufficient attention been paid to the fact that such firms are embedded in family systems (Greenhalgh, 1991). Women's and men's roles as spouses, parents and kin tangibly affect their access to and demand for resources critical to business establishment and expansion (ibid.). Women entrepreneurs in the region are especially hampered by a number of pervasive barriers to advancement, including familial constraints and pressures (Karlin, 1992). Participation in informal sector enterprises does not necessarily empower women in some larger way but may be the main means to ensuring child survival and development.[1]

Domestic work   Unpaid, undocumented, and unevaluated household work drains much of the time and energy of women and children but is basic to the subsistence and survival of most families in the region (Goldschmidt-Clermont, 1987, 1990, 1994). Such work and the way it is performed are highly relevant to a range of population, development and labour policies in the region, inasmuch as it prevents labour from being allocated to other activities such as breastfeeding, child care, agriculture, and income-generating work. Domestic work has as-yet unmeasured effects upon maternal and infant mortality and exerts continuing pressure for high fertility.

Women's time and energy crisis   A useful way to analyse the conflicts and changes occurring in women's roles is the method of documenting time allocation (see, for example, Popkin and Doan, 1990). Major demands on women's time include domestic work, child care and feeding, plus work outside the home. In periods of environmental stress the hours spent on tasks such as water fetching and fuel gathering may multiply to unmanageable proportions. Numerous studies of time allocation in different cultural settings have also indicated that women's work is often done for longer hours than that of male counterparts, and that child care is mainly carried out simultaneously with a variety of other tasks and often delegated to siblings and others. Since women in poor countries typically work so hard and for so long their time is a major constraint that may prevent the introduction of new agricultural techniques. Time constraints may also prevent the introduction of health initiatives, since women have no spare time to walk miles to clinics or to visit health workers. Likewise, lack of time may obstruct sanitary procedures and maintenance of household cleanliness, and the prolongation of breastfeeding needed both to prevent diarrhoeal diseases and to promote child survival and child spacing. Yet the women so affected are the same ones who are typically classified in official statistics as unemployed, non-working 'housewives'.

   Health studies have shown that even small changes in women's household and child care practices can have marked impacts upon children's health and survival by improving sanitation, and quality of water, food and hygiene. Similarly, prolongation of exclusive breastfeeding diminishes the likelihood of infant sickness. But the time costs of health initiatives such as immunization and family planning clinics may be so prohibitive that they prevent the use of available services – even when the services themselves are free. The policy importance of the time women spend in back-breaking, subsistence and non-market (as well as market) work is increasingly being realized. If the time needed for some of these activities can be decreased then time allocated to child care, productive work and health needs can be increased.

Training The economic crisis has brought growing realization that existing training systems are for the most part inappropriate. They need to be reoriented away from preparation for non-existent wage employment and towards preparation for self-employment and entrepreneurship. They must also be directed towards those who in the past have suffered neglect, including women (ILO, 1989).

Just as many find their livelihoods outside the modern wage sector, in the same way the majority acquire their skills outside the public training system. Informal training methods include traditional apprenticeship systems, particularly in West Africa, where these systems are often in the guise of fostering arrangements; transfers of people and skills are marked by appropriate rituals and rites of passage.

Training activities are also organized by youth cooperatives or by associations of informal-sector artisans. Private vocational training schools also play a part. Despite the importance of the rural sector, skill training for rural workers is a modest affair in some countries and negligible in most others. Rural women, who represent the single most important group of producers in Africa, are also the least trained for their multiple tasks. Formal agricultural training in special schools at the secondary or tertiary level is largely confined to men, who represent a minute fraction of the people engaged in farming and who, more often than not, are reluctant to go back to farming.

Illiteracy is especially acute among women. Not only do fewer girls than boys attend school, but far more drop out because of early marriage and teenage pregnancy. This low educational base limits their higher level training, which is in any case biased towards traditional female skills. The nature of women's employment reflects their limited participation in training. The few in the modern sector are usually channelled into low-status, poorly paid, traditional female occupations. Beyond the modern sector, women of all ages, from childhood onwards, take part in rural subsistence production and in a wide variety of informal sector activities such as trading, food and beverage production, pottery, sewing and handicrafts. These are almost always characterized by low levels of productivity (ILO, 1988).

Youth: productive and reproductive role transitions

The number and proportion of young people in the population have been increasing rapidly and will continue to do so into the twenty-first century (see Table 9.2). The proportion in school has also been advancing. Between 1960 and 1983, the number of primary and secondary students increased from about 13 million to some 63 million, leading to a massive rise in the literacy level of the adult workforce and to a sharp increase in the number of job seekers with some schooling. However, half of African children of primary-school age are not in school, instead they are helping parents and relatives in survival tasks on farms, in markets and in craft workshops.

Girls in particular are kept out of school in times of labour scarcity. In addition, their vulnerability to teenage pregnancy causes them to drop out of school in disproportionate numbers. Parents also more frequently withdraw girls from school than boys and set them to domestic tasks and trading to ensure family survival when mothers are hard pressed to make ends meet. Such sex inequalities in access to schooling have profound demographic and economic consequences, and increase and perpetuate systems of sexual inequality of resources and opportunities.

Growing numbers of the youth population are encountering serious problems as they enter the transition to adulthood. Whereas in a former era these transitions were facilitated and controlled within the contexts of kin groups and community institutions, now girls and boys, young men and women, who have been drafted into schools are found to be in many cases without the skills and resources needed to become either responsible parents or productive workers.

Traditional knowledge and customary modes of training the young have been marginalized, but modern knowledge and resources have not effectively taken their place, leaving a serious hiatus in which growing numbers of youths are both unemployed and unproductive. They lack useful skills – especially for farming – and also lack the parenting resources and skills to become successful mothers and fathers of the next generation.

Traditional socialization   Traditionally children grew up and were trained in familial contexts to become adult workers in homes, markets, farms and crafts. Young men remained dependants in the households of their seniors; having little or no personal resources, they would work for many years under the supervision of senior kinsmen, on whom they often depended for payment of bridewealth, without which it was often impossible to marry. Girls learned wifely and maternal skills in the home until marriage, which occurred soon after puberty. Often these processes of socialization took place under the tutelage of kin, inasmuch as fostering of children until adulthood and marriage was a pervasive norm in many societies.

Table 9.2 Urban and rural youth population, world and regions, 1970–2000 (millions)

	World			More developed regions			Less developed regions			Africa		
	1970	1984	2000	1970	1984	2000	1970	1984	2000	1970	1984	2000
Urban	264.8	409.9	565.2	125.3	145.9	145.4	139.6	264.0	419.8	17.2	36.7	80.7
Rural	396.2	511.8	496.3	49.5	41.4	28.6	346.6	470.4	467.7	48.5	65.5	89.4
Urban (%)	40.1	44.5	53.2	71.7	77.9	83.6	28.7	35.9	47.3	26.2	35.9	47.4

Rites of passage of various kinds, frequently combining symbolic dramas and practical training, often marked the beginning of the reproductive span for girls or the initiation into manhood for boys. Genital mutilation soon after birth or later was a common component of ritualized practices for both sexes. Serious kin and community sanctions constrained sexual behaviour to adhere to culturally accepted norms, which varied between ethnic groups. Often full adulthood was only achieved after the demise of all parental figures in the kin group, which might mean the period now designated middle age. In their elder years the authority of the ancestors and their spiritual dictates still held sway.

These processes of socialization and training in specialist skills were complex and continuous in nature. They also served to augment the familial labour force and to inculcate filial respect, obedience and diligence. In addition, they ensured the inter-generational transmission of the patrimony. Parents were accordingly often loath to send their children to school, for school attendance truncated these processes and the outcomes of such changes were uncertain. Among a host of imponderables, sexual protection of girls and their good marriage prospects could not be guaranteed (see, for example, Oppong, 1973).

Certainly many parental fears have been substantiated by massive school attendance, for while some youths have gone on to take up well-paid jobs in the modern sector, others have fallen by the wayside economically. Traditional constraints to sexual relations and childbearing among teenagers have clearly been flouted, both rules concerning births outside marriage and also the tempo of pregnancies. In a number of cases curves of fertility by education show a U-shape, with girls having little schooling neither maintaining traditional birth spacing practices nor adopting the innovations assumed by the more highly educated. This has led observers of fertility rates in the region to note upward tendencies rather than a lowering of rates.

The truth is that the processes of rural–urban migration, schooling and the search for jobs have split many of the youths from their elders and the sources of traditional socialization, customary knowledge, experience and control. Almost half of African young people will be in urban areas by the year 2000, and many of these will be beyond the control or support of kin.

Sexual relations For well-nourished girls menarche appears earlier than in former times. Meanwhile, marriage is tending to be postponed. Teenage sexual relations are common, and in the case of girls many such contacts are with older men. Data from the Demographic and Health Surveys (DHS) conducted in 11 countries indicated that at least 50 per cent of teenage girls aged 15–19 had had sexual relations. In a number of countries more than half of these were not married[2] (Population Reference Bureau,

1992). Some studies have shown that while large numbers of teenagers do not approve of such behaviour, they still engage in it, indicating considerable confusion and ambivalence about a topic on which there is often little relevant information from any knowledgeable source – not from parents, school teachers, peers or community groups.

While contraceptive use is low for women and men, it is even lower among girls and boys in their teens.[3] Lack of access is a major barrier to use. In some countries, reluctance to provide information and services on family planning to the youth has led to an outright ban on contraceptives for young people. A recent UN survey indicated that six out of eighteen countries would not provide contraceptives to unmarried teenagers, and only one in five countries indicated that family life education was included in the school curriculum. Such unprotected sexual intercourse among young people has a number of serious and unintended consequences – economic demographic and social. A high proportion of all births are to teenage mothers, many of whom are ill-equipped and lack the social support from kin or husbands to be mothers. Fifteen to twenty per cent of all births in Africa occur to teenagers, a proportion that is far higher than in any other region of the world. The usually insurmountable difficulties of continuing education while pregnant or nursing mean that unsafe and illegal abortions are often the mode chosen to resolve the impasse.[4]

A region-wide waste of serious proportions is the extent to which schoolgirls continue to have to drop out of school as a result of pregnancy. Other serious outcomes include rejection by the fathers of their children and their own relatives, baby dumping, poverty and prostitution. Children born in such circumstances often perpetuate a cycle of deprivation. The heavy costs to education programmes in terms of the wastage of pupils may be enormous. The tolls of morbidity and mortality from sexually transmitted diseases may increase rapidly in future, given present trends which indicate in several countries that the incidence of HIV is significantly higher among teenage girls than boys.

Marriage

Age at marriage The age at which females become mothers or marry is a critical lifecycle event which not only affects female chances for maturation, social development and economic autonomy, but also by and large marks the end of the formal learning process. Given the unique role of women in childrearing, their cycle of learning is quite fundamental to the progress and development of the younger generation. So it is not surprising that one of the clearest and best documented demographic correlations of the past decade has been the link between female education and child survival, health and development (Cleland, 1989; Caldwell, 1990; Hobcraft, 1992). Higher levels of female education have also been associated with demographic and contraceptive innovation – lower family size and adoption of modern family planning methods.

Africa continues to be characterized by both the lowest levels of schooling found globally for girls as well as the lowest ages at first birth and marriage. Given the profound demographic, economic, medical and social impacts of these continuing trends, the importance of raising the age at marriage both in law and in reality continues to be stressed in many fora (see, for example, Mensa-Bonsu, 1991).

Type of union Recent studies have shown that traditional marriage practices – cousin marriage, bridewealth payments, arrangement of marriages by senior kin – still persist in Africa to a large extent. It is in fact quite usual for a variety of different marriage forms and types of conjugal relationships to coexist in the same community. There is frequently a plurality of laws, with new forms of marital unions emerging. Indeed, at the present time there is evidence that marital relationships are becoming even more fluid and diverse than in the past, especially as conjugal forms diversify in the wake of rapid societal transformations (Bledsoe, 1990; Agounke, 1991, Donadje, 1991). A 'state of flux' is not uncommon in urban areas, where many diverse factors are influencing behaviour (Burnham, 1987; Isiugo-Abanihe et al., 1991).

The sophistication, complexity and variety in African systems of marriage means that their documentation requires more than the simplistic marital status attributes collected in standard demographic surveys. While there is a dearth of systematic, cross-cultural evidence on conjugal roles and relationships, either within or across countries, there is clear evidence that at least in some countries there is an increasing tendency for marriage to lack formality and to be increasingly fragile and unstable.

Sub-Saharan Africa remains the only major world region in which polygyny is still widely practised, despite modern religious and legal attempts to constrain its incidence. Current economic and social changes might be expected to alter the balance of economic, sexual, social and demographic advantages to be gained by either men or women from polygynous marriage, but there is insufficient evidence to show whether the incidence is decreasing or increasing in different communities and social strata. A recent attempt to show trends over time in three countries using WFS and DHS data for Kenya, Senegal and Ghana indicated that trends in polygynous marriages may be decreasing. Higher levels of polygyny are found among illiterates, especially illiterate men. However, there still remain substantial minorities of polygynous marriages among literates, including those with higher education. Variations between countries are substantial.

Problems in the definition of work status for women make it difficult to examine differences in marital status among working women. Women's religious affiliation is not associated with higher or lower levels of polygyny. Economic changes may force a decline, despite the continuity of social and cultural values approving or stimulating polygyny. In fact, there are signs from various sources that while formal polygyny may be declining in some contexts, it is in many cases being replaced – especially in urban areas – by *de facto* polygyny, '*deuxième bureaux*', outside marriage, and 'sugar daddy' relations (Dinan, 1983; Bledsoe, 1990). This permutation of forms obviously makes it even more difficult to observe or deduce linkages with fertility levels.

Not only does polygyny die hard, but aspects of polyandry may be reinforced or appear, leading to what Guyer has termed 'polyandrous motherhood', whereby a woman may manage ties with several men at once so as to maximize her children's advantage, thus making marriage almost incidental to her reproductive career (Bledsoe, 1990: 119).

Migration has potentially profound impacts upon conjugal relations, providing opportunities and incentives for men to have more than one wife located in urban and/or rural areas. There are growing numbers of mother–child units visited by husbands – a modern adaptation of polygyny and one which may give educated wives a greater degree of freedom and autonomy. Traditional control by the kin group and the husband over these mother-centred units is said to be looser; in the event of conflict, separation is more frequent (Locoh, 1988b).

Women alone The proportion of women and children alone and of female-headed and maintained households is increasing. In some countries as many as a third or more of households are in this situation. In some countries, such as Ghana and Senegal, growing numbers of monogamously married women are living separately from their husbands (Gandaho, 1992). For some women this is a status forced upon them by male migration and abandonment. For others it is a conscious choice, a strategy for survival until other options become available. For women alone in either urban or rural areas there are problems to be faced, unknown a generation ago, as they struggle to ensure survival for themselves and their children.

Female-headed or maintained households are not necessarily poorer. Indeed, data from a variety of studies suggest that they can in fact be better off and children better nourished if a larger proportion of resources are channelled directly to them. But the potential vulnerability of these households means there may be a strong case for specifically targeting them with different types of aid resources.

Sexuality and disease transmission

Women traditionally spent many of their reproductive years abstaining from conjugal sexual relations and at menopause or as grandmothers often had the option of retiring from the rigours of marital sexuality and other chores, to concentrate on the valued pleasures of child care. During marriage the presence of co-wives is recognized as reducing the fatigue commonly experienced by monogamous wives. In contrast, men have had the option of officially marrying more than one wife at a time and of being constantly in a courting mode *vis-à-vis* other women. This has been the case even for men physically past their prime, since in a number of societies wives may take lovers in order to conceive – with or without their husbands' knowledge and consent.

Sexual intercourse is not only a core element of the conjugal bond and the source of precious procreation, it is also increasingly a mode of action whereby disease and death are spread. Urban residence, mobility, migration, and lack of cohabitation with a regular partner have been found to be predisposing factors for sexually transmitted diseases (STDs) (Carael, 1992). Both abandonment of customary rules or a new environment may be conducive to disease transmission. Crises such as war, labour migration or economic catastrophe can sharply increase the spread of STDs.[5] Such events break down social structures and systems of control, protection and restraint affecting human behaviour.

Thus the vast sexual markets existing in certain African cities may be less a response culturally determined by tradition than the result of massive disruptions of social relations resulting from multiple society-wide misfortunes and the subsequent efforts of individuals to cope. The massive misfortunes and lack of coping mechanisms include widespread unemployment, poverty, and increasing streams of labour migrants seeking a means of survival and family maintenance. For women these include the lack of opportunities for gainful employment and economic security, especially after divorce or abandonment in pregnancy, and also the lack of the traditional kin support and conjugal protection formerly enjoyed. They also include the poverty and insecurity of women in workplaces, who may be subject to severe forms of sexual harassment.

Prostitution is a key factor in the epidemiology of STDs in the region. However, few studies have related prostitution patterns to either local kinship organization or to the relative economic position and power of women. In eastern Africa the majority of prostitutes are divorcees, widows or women abandoned with young children (Carael, 1992). In western Africa, female autonomy and matriliny have been implicated (see Adomako, 1993).

Recent WHO findings indicate that, despite widespread awareness of AIDS, knowledge and use of condoms remains quite low. Surveys of responses regarding sexual behaviour indicate that the frequency of casual sexual relations increases with urban residence and levels of schooling, particularly for men. Being single, separated, divorced, or in free or cohabiting unions are also associated with a higher frequency of casual sex (Carael et al., 1990). On the basis of eastern African evidence the hypothesis was proposed that the greater the imbalance in sexual freedom between men and women, the more rapid the progress of the HIV/STD epidemic. There is growing recognition that wives are at risk as a result of their husbands' sexual exploits.

The potential demographic effects over the next two decades of the AIDS epidemic are admittedly hard to discern. But AIDS is likely to wipe out gains made in the fight against mortality and in the longer term to have profound impacts upon the age structure of populations. Mother-to-child transmission will have a marked effect upon infant mortality. It took some years during the 1980s before it was realized that women are particularly affected by the HIV epidemic because of biological, socio-cultural, economic and status factors. Certainly, as Carael (1992) has stressed, 'any long-term projection of socio-demographic impact on AIDS depends on a greater understanding of sexual behaviour and on the assumptions of behavioural change.'

Global AIDS prevention programmes currently depend on condom promotion. It is clear that the ability of women to negotiate their use depends upon women's relative levels of sexual equality with their male partners. But little is known or understood regarding influences on sexual behaviour and decision making among women of various social classes and ethnic groups. Knowledge is lacking about relationships between cultural values (including gender roles and behaviour), sexual norms and actual sexual behaviour in communities where AIDS is having a serious impact.

Parenthood

Unprecedented economic, ecological, and political crises are affecting the daily lives of most African families. In particular, they are inhibiting the ability of parents to feed, maintain, educate and care for their offspring. Levels of malnutrition are high and rising. There is widespread evidence of attempts to prevent births through abortion and other traditional means. There is even evidence of child abandonment and street children – desperate phenomena unheard of in previous decades. For some unfortunate children traditional systems of familial support have completely broken down. For many children, fathers have proved incapable or irresponsible and mothers have been left alone to care for them, often with the help of their own mothers and other female kin. Increasing numbers of such mothers are unable to cope.

The total fertility rate (TFR) remains unremittingly high in most areas, with persistent averages of over six children. A widespread observation is that girls with a little schooling may have higher fertility than either those illiterate and subject to continuing customary constraints on sexual congress and conception, or those with higher levels of education, who have more ready access to the modern forms of contraception.

The difficulties faced by African families in bearing and raising children to adulthood have been recognized for some time. On the one hand increases in schooling and rural–urban migration have raised the costs of child maintenance and rearing and have dispersed the kin, including siblings, who would normally have cared for them. Meanwhile, rural–urban migrations have decreased children's utility as farm labour; parents now require cash to support children. Women, however, still remain in subsistence production, self-employment, and informal-sector work in which children's assistance can play a crucial part. Indeed recent evidence on desertification and pauperization has indicated that child labour for some is becoming increasingly necessary for survival, given the labour and time intensity of most forms of subsistence work.

Costs of maternity   When babies are born, mothers often pay with their health. Maternal malnutrition, chronic iron deficiency, anaemia, and low infant birth weights and death form terrible sources of suffering for many women. Iron deficiency affects at least half of all African women of reproductive age, more than 60 per cent of pregnant women, and about half of children under 12 years of age.

In 12 out of 29 countries for which data are available, the maternal mortality rate is higher than 500 for every 100,000 live births. Moreover, it has been estimated that each year about 150,000 mothers in Africa die from pregnancy or childbirth complications and roughly the same number suffer permanent disability. At the same time, the infant mortality rate for most of Sub-Saharan Africa ranges from 100 to 170 for every 1,000 live births. Rates of disability and death are particularly high among teenage mothers.

If maternal mortality is to be reduced, comprehensive systems of health care must provide both preventive and curative medicine. Attention will also have to be paid to family planning and prenatal care, as well as to a system of access to immediate referral and emergency care, especially during the critical time of labour and delivery. Many countries are adopting safe motherhood strategies, a set of programmes for which needed technical assistance has been forthcoming. Strategies for 'Health for All by the Year 2000' also give high priority to safe motherhood initiatives.

Over the past decade and more, it has become much easier – at least potentially – for both women and men to control the timing and spacing of births. Reliance upon traditional methods of long-term abstinence remains prevalent, however, and acceptance and availability of modern forms of contraception remains uneven. Prolonged breastfeeding is still a widely used mechanism for spacing births. It is estimated that 90 per cent of mothers are still at least partially breastfeeding their infants at six months of age. For the many women who have little or no access to means of birth postponement other than post-partum sexual abstinence, which remains important, frequent and prolonged breastfeeding is a preferred means not only to feed their babies, but to space the next birth through post-partum amenorrhoea and suppressed ovulation. In fact, it has been calculated that in many countries more births are averted by this means than by any other single family planning method. (WHO, 1990) Even though lactational amenorrhoea is not completely reliable for protection against pregnancy for the individual mother, the overall effectiveness of breastfeeding as a birth-spacing mechanism has important health policy implications.

But among the educated, urban dwellers, and women in formal-sector employment, breastfeeding tends to be truncated. There is accumulating evidence of the erosion of the intensity and duration of nursing practices, especially among mothers whose work separates them from their children. There is a need for more studies of women's working conditions and of child feeding and care practices in different types of environments (Oppong, 1991a). Among other things, this would demonstrate the relevance and effectiveness of the maternity protection that exists and would also highlight the types of support required, such as child care facilities and nursing breaks, which are now demanded by working women in both rural and urban areas.

Infant and child mortality African parents face the terrible prospect of losing one in five or more of the children born to them. Levels of infant and child mortality were observed to be declining three or more decades ago, but more recently harsh economic programmes have been associated with evidence of new increases in infant mortality. Differences are apparent not only between countries, but between different ethnic groups and localities. Rates for Africa as a whole remain among the highest in the world.

In a third or more of child deaths, malnutrition is implicated – due to the inability of mothers and other caregivers to provide adequate food. This failure is partially linked to too closely spaced births and too high parities. Mothers' resources are under too great a strain. The strain is greatest in cases where traditional mechanisms for control and support have broken down but modern mechanisms of control and assistance have not been put into place.

Contraception and birth spacing UNICEF's report, *The State of the World's Children*, recently stressed the importance for child survival and well-being of maintaining a balance between births and maternal resources available for care, through responsible planning of births. The report emphasized that alternative practical methods available for ensuring responsible parenthood are sufficiently numerous and varied as to meet the needs of different cultural and religious groups (UNICEF, 1992).

A major finding of demographers and health specialists of the past decade has been the fact that there are potentially huge gains to be made in terms of human lives and well-being of mothers and children from more appropriate adequate spacing and timing of births. Not only can such practices avert deaths and physical suffering, but they can help to avert the stresses and conflicts suffered by mothers who are otherwise unable to cope with the responsibilities that child care and maintenance involve.

The majority of countries in the region have the lowest contraceptive prevalence in the world (less than 20 per cent). At the same time, demand is growing for child-spacing methods other than sexual abstinence by the mother. Indeed, one-quarter to one-half of maternity-related deaths are associated with abortion. Recent analysis of the data from the Demographic and Health Surveys has shown that in all Sub-Saharan countries except Kenya the demand for family planning for spacing purposes still exceeds that for limiting births; the main need is for methods to delay the next birth. Meanwhile, contraceptive use is increasing where it is available – that present rates of contraceptive prevalence could be increased to 25 per cent in most countries. Changes in reproductive behaviour are seen most clearly when both education and community-based family planning services reach women. In the recent past women's own organizations have increasingly become involved in this aspect of family welfare provision. The potential of women's income-earning groups in this regard is quite significant.

Sympathetic recorders of women's situation have noted how women may easily become the scapegoats for persisting high fertility, for the failure of family planning programmes, and for malnutrition of children and poor feeding practices. But the fact is that most individual women lack the knowledge, resources or food supplies to take action. Solutions for these widespread problems clearly require more than individual approaches. Fortunately, socio-political action is being taken by a variety of women's organizations, trade unions, cooperatives and others, through programmes of education and primary health care.

Paternal responsibilities   Men typically give different degrees of recognition to children from different relationships, allocating to them differential resources and care. Likewise, fathers vary tremendously in the proportion of overall attention, resources, and care that they devote to their paternal roles. The issue of differential investment by fathers in their children is one over which there has been considerable discussion in legal and social welfare circles, as attempts are made to close gaps between modern laws, traditional norms and stark realities with regard to children, their legitimacy, and the allocation of responsibilities for their maintenance and rights of inheritance (Mensa-Bonsu, 1991). As observed in other regions, the costs of fatherhood and motherhood may be diminished and controlled by selective investments in parenthood. Fathers' opportunities for reneging on responsibilities to offspring are usually greater than those of mothers.

Research attention has generally focused on the impact of women's work outside the home, rather than on male resource allocations and activities within the home. Paternal roles in child care, domestic work, and child maintenance have been poorly researched. Still, there is a fragmentary but growing body of evidence from different sources to support three contentions. First, a greater proportion of women's than men's resources are likely to be allocated directly to children and their needs. Second, so long as males are 'free riders' as fathers and in the home, they are unlikely to carefully restrain their own procreative activities (see Oppong and Bleek, 1982). And third, to the extent that fathers take personal responsibility for the children they beget and are actively involved in their care and related domestic work, they are likely to become contraceptive and demographic innovators, wanting and begetting fewer offspring than their fathers did (Oppong, 1987). Pressures towards personal action and responsibility by fathers, leading to role strain and triggering innovation, may result from decreasing delegation of parental responsibilities to siblings, parents, and others (that is, diminishing the propensity to the fostering of one's own children), and from the increasing equality and jointness observed in some conjugal role relationships (Oppong, 1987). Such household-level changes are linked to both increasing social and spatial mobility, as well as to the relative equality of spouses, the latter being associated with comparative levels of resources (education, income and so on).

Of course if fathers are irresponsible, paternal neglect of children, who may also lack kin to care for them, will be the result. Indeed, there is now more and more evidence that the balance of parental responsibility is shifting further onto women: the most rapidly growing type of domestic group in this region, as elsewhere, is that of mothers alone with their children. This type of 'headship' is not simply a residential phenomenon. In many cases it is a clear indication of the extent to which fathers have diverted not only their presence but their material resources away from the children they have begotten. Female household heads may enjoy more decision-making power than those who live with adult males, as well as a more equitable distribution of resources within the household. But they pay a very high price in loss of access to male market income, and they almost certainly bear an even larger share of the costs of children than do women in traditional male-headed households (see, for example, Lloyd and Brandon, 1993). Such redefinitions of family responsibilities are taking place globally, as men everywhere gain and take advantage of greater scope for rejecting paternal responsibilities so as to lower the costs to themselves of parenthood.

Community-wide exertion of pressure on all fathers to allocate sufficient time and material resources to the care of each and every child they beget might be the most effective strategy, both for lowering family-size desires and outcomes, and simultaneously for raising the quality of care and resources currently available to all children. This point is being hotly debated in richer regions of the world, where paternal negligence has the same result – inadequate care for children (Oppong, 1988).

Demographic and contraceptive innovation

With regard to demographic and contraceptive innovation, the correlations most often stressed by demographers have been women's education and women's work. In the case of the former it is only when girls have secondary schooling and higher that differences are noted. Postponement of the *first* birth is what enables girls to stay in school; spacing and limiting births enables women with higher education to pursue opportunities for formal-sector employment. But a more crucial question for most women is whether they are able and willing to delegate child care or not (Oppong and Abu, 1987). Attempts to correlate work with either fertility or contraception have been hampered by the vague definition of work in the major comparative survey sets available (Lloyd, 1991), as well as by the fact that nine out of ten women in the region are subsistence or own account workers in the 'informal sector'.

Data from various parts of the world indicate that fertility declines do not simply follow changes in such indices of modernization as literacy, women's work, or female autonomy. Rather, macro-level socio-economic changes affect different sectors of the population in different ways, and fertility declines occur according to changes in the value of children within the context of class-specific family economies and costs (Oppong, 1985; Greenhalgh, 1990). All kinds of political, legal, social and economic changes can have profound impacts on the family economy. These include such changes as child labour laws and their enforcement, or changes in employment opportunities.

Social and spatial mobility are linked to demographic and contraceptive innovation. Mobility sets people apart from the conservative values and pressures pervasive in customary kin and community networks and places them in more differentiated, looser-knit social networks in which new ideas are pervasive and new practices possible. Innovation results occur readily when new aspirations and values are adopted, strains and stresses make the achievement of traditional goals more problematic, and the means to innovate are available and socially sanctioned. In other cases where strain is less intense, innovative resources and practices are adopted merely in order to achieve traditionally held values, such as a large number of well-spaced births (see, for example, Caldwell, 1990).

But for the majority the only readily available means of birth postponement or avoidance remain the traditional ones. Contraception is still
seldom used, except in Botswana, Kenya and Zimbabwe (Demographic
and Health Survey data). Relatively widespread migration and access to
education are implicated in the latter cases, as well as greater access to
modern means of family planning (Mhloyi, 1991; Hammerslogh, 1991).

The importance of gossip and information transfer via informal
women's networks has been highlighted (for example, Watkins, 1991).
Women's participation in women's organizations, trade unions and so on
is likely to provide access to new knowledge and new ways of doing
things. Such groups provide women with new ideas and support for
innovation. Market women's associations are among the most common
such groups in western Africa and have already become vehicles for the
sale and spread of information on health and family planning products.
Church groups also play an important part in spreading the word on
family life, marriage and responsible parenthood. Where women's networks
are extensive and socially heterogeneous, there is likely to be a more rapid
decline in fertility than where women's networks are more local and socially
homogeneous. (Watkins, 1991)

Conclusions

Recognition is now spreading in Africa and elsewhere that if the economic
and demographic goals of both nation-states and households are to be
reached, there will have to be a fairer allocation of resources between
boys and girls, and women and men. Such resources include places in
primary schools, secondary schools, and non-traditional areas of vocational
and technical training, as well as the resources required for farming and
employment opportunities. Women will also need a more adequate allocation of health care to help them undergo pregnancies and childbirths
with lower levels of morbidity and mortality.

International agencies are working together with national governments
in the region to promote greater equality of treatment and opportunities
in workplaces and in all realms of education, health and employment. A
watchword now is to 'mainstream' women in policies and programmes so
as to engender adjustment policies (Commonwealth Secretariat, 1989). A
number of current changes that have been identified point to immediate
needs for intensified policy and programme initiatives. These include the
following macro-economic and demographic changes, which will have
significant implications at the family and household level and will face all
governments in the region during the 1990s and beyond.

Role transitions The numbers of vulnerable girls entering the post-
pubertal teenage years and at-risk of motherhood in social and economically

unsupported and deprived circumstances must be assessed. Programmes and services of many kinds are needed, including education, vocational training, counselling and social services; family welfare and planning; and maternal and child health. Grave consequences for the upcoming generations will be the outcome of failure to heed these calculations. For vulnerable girls, the loss of kin protection and control are serious, as they become prey to sexual coercion and exploitation in a variety of situations.

Productive and reproductive conflicts For growing numbers of workers there is serious conflict between domestic, parental, and occupational activities and responsibilities. Home and work are increasingly separate and ever greater numbers of children are suffering the effects of maternal and paternal deprivation. Increasing social and spatial mobility is having insidious effects upon kin solidarity, which in a former era ensured survival in time of crisis or disaster. Individual parents are increasingly being left to shoulder parental responsibilities alone, or grandmothers alone are looking after children. Indeed, increasing numbers of children are being separated from both parents, in contexts in which fostering has become a form of child service or labour. For growing numbers of women it is necessary to combine breastfeeding, child care and gainful employment, inasmuch as kin who would have shared responsibilities are being dispersed and modern workplaces are not providing the infant-friendly environments of more informal workplaces. The intensity and duration of breastfeeding are affected, along with the quality of weaning care, with serious implications for child spacing, child development and survival.

Women alone A phenomenon of increasing proportions is that of women alone without husbands or kin, either to assist, control or protect them. Such women are subject to the vagaries of labour markets and of informal-sector work, as well as to the advances of single male migrants. Such migratory patterns are now recognized as putting individuals at increased risk of sexually transmitted diseases, especially in contexts in which gender inequalities are rife (Carael, 1992). Migrant workers now form up to one-quarter of the population of some African countries, short-term seasonal movements of workers are also common, and mobility has been linked critically to reproductive morbidity and mortality. Likewise, evidence is accumulating from a variety of sources that women's share of parental responsibilities and maintenance has been growing more quickly than that of their male counterparts. Relevant data include escalations in out-of-wedlock births, increasing numbers of women and their children living separately from the fathers of the children, and the growing numbers of female-headed households.

Unequal spouses Women in general have less schooling, fewer material assets, and fewer opportunities for well-paid jobs than men. They are often legal minors. In addition, given their physiological burdens as wives and their much greater burdens of domestic work, they are at a distinct disadvantage *vis-à-vis* their husbands and are frequently unable to establish intimate egalitarian relationships within which planning and goal sharing in the most intimate areas of conjugal life are possible. They are thus at a serious disadvantage in negotiating sexual relations and reproductive outcomes.

Dependence upon children In the context of kin dispersal, ecological pressures, environmental stress and economic disasters, and growing burdens of labour-intensive work, an increasing number of women depend upon their children for current survival and future security. Failure to adopt and disseminate appropriate technologies to decrease the burdens of household drudgery, subsistence work and the escalating environmental stresses means that domestic activities are taking up more time and energy of mothers and their children, at the expense of other activities. This has serious policy implications, both economic and demographic.

As was clearly enunciated in Gaborone at the UN Expert Group Meeting on Population and Women, official discourse on population issues has been largely *de-gendered* and detached from actual relations between real-life women and men. It continues to be dominated by demographic projections rather than by a commitment to women's interests (Postel, 1992). Similarly, discussions on family planning are rarely embedded in a holistic consideration of family systems and how these are changing as a result of macro-political, economic and demographic forces. The aim of this chapter, then, has been to help to put 'gender issues' and family systems squarely at the centre of such future discourse on population and development in Sub-Saharan Africa.

Notes

1. Intensive micro-level anthropological research is required to learn how such small businesses operate. Few such studies have been done to date (Greenhalgh, 1991). The close interconnectedness of the family and business organization is, however, relatively well-established, even though few studies in the development literature focus on the family/firm connection.

2. In Botswana, Ghana, Kenya, Liberia and Togo more than half of the teenagers with sexual experience were not married. In contrast, in Burundi and Mali sexual activity was found to take place mainly within marriage.

3. Data from the DHS indicate that contraceptive use among currently married teenage girls ranges from 25 per cent in Zimbabwe to 1 per cent in Nigeria. For unmarried teenagers, however, contraceptive use ranges from 25 per cent to less than 5 per cent (in Kenya).

4. Data from 13 African countries show that adolescents in the teenage years represent between 39 and 72 per cent of all women presenting with abortion-related complications in major hospitals in the region. Recent evidence has indicated that adolescents are more likely to seek abortions from a non-medical person or to seek abortions later in their pregnancies, and are slower to seek medical help if abortion complications develop. These delays lead to still greater complications, more expensive medical treatment, longer stays in hospital, and greater morbidity and mortality.

5. Lesotho presents an extreme labour-migration situation where massive out-migration of males has resulted in a long-term sex imbalance producing late marriage, decline of polygyny, increase in marital dissolution, and frequent extramarital sexual relations associated with high levels of prevalence of sexually transmitted diseases.

CHAPTER 10

Law and the family in Southern Africa

Alice Armstrong

In order to discuss law and the family in Africa, it is necessary first of all to discuss what is meant by 'law' and what is meant by the 'family' and the functions of each, both in traditional society and today. Thus we will begin by setting forth a conceptual framework for dealing with legal issues regarding the family, based on perspectives developed by Women and Law in Southern Africa (WLSA), a multi-disciplinary group of researchers in Zimbabwe, Zambia, Swaziland, Mozambique, Lesotho and Botswana.

Law and the family – a conceptual framework

What is the law? Most states in southern Africa recognize both customary law and Western-based, general law – composed of common law and/or statutes. The only exception is Mozambique, where although the state does not recognize customary law the latter does influence community courts' interpretations of their mandate to apply 'good sense and justice' (Welsh, Dagnino and Sachs, 1987).

The customary law recognized by the state is that which is applied in the court systems. It is a product of the social and economic transformations of African societies that occurred as a consequence of the penetration of capitalism and colonialism. Before colonialism, customary law was a system which favoured the negotiation and settlement of disputes rather than the strict application of rules. Family-centred rather than state-centred, it was a system which evolved spontaneously to meet new conditions as decisions were made by the family and the community. However, the colonial state and post-independence governments constructed a new kind of customary law within which 'customs' were reduced to rules to be applied in formal courts. The outcome of this process, the official customary law of many African states, is a rigid, skewed and sometimes distorted version of the original customary law and often has little to do with the lives of the people in whose name it has been applied.

The creation of such official customary law occurred in different ways in different states (Woodman, 1983). In Zimbabwe and Zambia, official customary law was created largely by the courts themselves as they struggled to apply customary law to the disputes before them. Customary law was fitted (at times forced) into the mould of English law and legal remedies, and tempered by the 'repugnancy clause', which provided that African customs which were 'repugnant' to colonial judges did not have to be applied. The great variety of customary laws of various ethnic groups was reduced to a single customary law of the 'African'. An example of this is the Zimbabwean customary law that the heir of a deceased man inherits all his property; this has been shown never to have been a part of Ndebele customary law yet has been applied by the courts for the entire country (WLSA-Zimbabwe, 1994). As the courts applied the doctrine of precedent, customary laws became fixed in time rather than being allowed to evolve.

In other countries, official customary law was created in the form of codifications or restatements. In Lesotho in 1903, a commission set out to record the customary laws of the Basotho in the form of the Laws of Lerotholi (Letuka et al., 1994; Poulter, 1979). This document is today used in the courts of Lesotho as the final word on 'customary law'. Even if they may have been accurate reflections of the customs of the Basotho in 1903, the Laws of Lerotholi are hardly accurate reflections of the customs of the Basotho in the 1990s. Similarly, the reduction of the customary law to rules in a written document neglects the spirit of negotiation and compromise which allows disputes to be settled peacefully within the context of the community and the family.

Moreover, the Laws of Lerotholi and other semi-codifications of customary law – such as the Restatement of Tswana Family Law (Roberts, 1972) – may not have actually represented the customs of the people even at the time they were drawn up. First, the sources used for these written documents were invariably oral evidence given by *men* thought to be knowledgeable about custom. This fact alone shows that the testimony of half the population, women, was left out, thus skewing the evidence in favour of male rights. Second, most of the expert witnesses were elderly and may have emphasized the rights of the old over the young. Third, the witnesses were mostly those in positions of power in the traditional hierarchy of authority; the results might have been very different if evidence from persons not in authority had been taken. Fourth, the codifiers were white, male Europeans who may have interpreted the evidence in line with their own thinking about law, the family, and other issues such as the rights of women. Finally, the creation of these written documents on customary law must be seen as a political process, influenced by the political agendas of both those taking evidence and of those giving it. As Rwezaura says,

> what the elders and other witnesses gave as evidence of customary law was a distorted and rigid version of customary law designed to express their idea of what the law should be and not what it really was ... Their versions were

greatly influenced by the elders' anger and frustration at their loss of political power and challenges they were facing at the time from women and young men (Rwezaura, 1992; see also Armstrong et al., 1993).

It is important, then, to uncover the actual customary law of the past and the present, and to re-examine the family and family law in that context. If one takes the perspective that the 'official' customary law is a distorted version of the 'real' customary law, then it is possible to identify at least two other forms of customary law. One is what WLSA has called 'traditional law', that is, what individuals assert to have been the customs of their people in times past. Such traditional law has an important influence on the way people think, their expectations and their motivations. It incorporates customary values and principles.

Uncovering the traditional law – the real values and principles of the original customary law – challenges the nature of what is today held forth as 'custom'. We have seen that customary law is sometimes created by people to serve their own political ends. One example of this is its use as a tool to control or to subordinate women. Thus men tell women that their illicit affairs are 'customary' because polygyny is 'customary'. But if traditional law is examined it becomes clear that polygyny was originally a mechanism for ensuring that women were taken care of in a setting where life without a man was extremely precarious. The consent of a first wife was sought before a man took a second wife, and the first wife was not abandoned but remained an integral part of the family, with higher status because of her position of control over younger wives. This is a far cry from modern 'polygyny', where a man abandons his older wife for a young wife in town and uses polygyny as an excuse for sexual freedom.

The values and principles of customary law are family- and relationship-centred. Thus what is called 'customary law' can be interpreted as truly 'customary' if it preserves the family and relationships, rather than tearing them apart. Practices such as 'property-grabbing', whereby relatives of a deceased man or woman step in when the body is still warm to help themselves to the property of the deceased and toss the spouse out to fend for him or herself, cannot be 'customary' because they do not preserve the family and relationships.

A second kind of customary law is what WLSA calls the 'living law'. Customary law was originally unwritten, flexible and capable of evolution to meet new conditions. The living law is thus the customary law as it has evolved today, as embodied in the practices of the people.

The uncovering of the 'real' tradition has important implications for understanding the family. Unlike Western law, which takes the state as its point of departure and focuses on the power of the state to enforce its rules, customary law centres on the family and the community. The family is the primary institution which makes and enforces the customary law on most issues (particularly those which lawyers consider to fall within the ambit of 'family law'). For instance, in Western law there are rules which determine whether a marriage exists, when a divorce can occur, whether a child belongs to a family, who has custody of a child, rights of inheritance, and so on. But in customary law, while there is a framework of guidelines and principles within which decisions are made, it is basically the family which decides when a marriage exists, when a couple is divorced, when a child belongs to a family, and so on.

If the family makes these decisions, then the family must be investigated to determine the evolved and evolving customary law of today. One way of looking at this is to see each family as having its own legal system, as forming what Moore has called a 'semi-autonomous social field' that makes and enforces its own rules and solves its own disputes (Moore, 1978). Thus family law must be investigated not only by looking at court cases or into legal textbooks, but by looking at the customary legal norms of individual families and communities, the practices that have crystallized into 'law' by repetition. This opens up a whole new field of legal study which begins to look more like the work of anthropologists and sociologists. It also incorporates an Afro-centric, rather than a Euro-centric, definition of 'the Law'.

What is the family?   It is commonplace to observe that the organization of the family is changing throughout the world. In Africa, it is necessary to ask (a) What is it changing from? and (b) What is it changing into? It is usually observed that rather than the nuclear family – supposedly the norm in Northern societies – the 'extended family' is the norm in Africa. It is also generally assumed that African societies are undergoing a transition from a focus on the extended family to a focus on the nuclear family. But the WLSA's research suggests that the situation is considerably more complex.

What *was* the family? It is clear that, traditionally, in the past, society was organized around the extended family. However, it is necessary to distinguish between organization for the purposes of rituals and ceremonies, and organization for the purposes of daily living. At the level of rituals and ceremonies, the extended family was composed of a number of descendants of a common male or female ancestor. In southern Africa, these were the people expected to attend and participate in funerals and weddings, for instance. On the other hand, in most polygynous societies, daily life was organized around a unit composed of a mother and her children – a unit smaller than the Northern concept of the 'nuclear family'. The husband/father in such families might have been absent for many weeks hunting, and even when present may not have stayed with his wife but visited other relatives and/or other wives. It was the woman who was responsible for providing for the daily needs of her children.

What *is* the family today, what is it changing into? WLSA research indicates that the organization of the family for the purposes of rituals and ceremonies is changing very little. In the case of inheritance, for example, we have found that the extended family remains the central institution dealing with everything concerning death: funerals, mourning, division of property, and so on, and that this extended family is still defined by 'blood', that is, by descent from a common ancestor.

With regard to the family in the context of day-to-day living, however, WLSA research has found a great variety of forms, all of which must be taken into account when discussing the family today. First, one might talk of the family in terms of *residence*. There are 'extended families' living together on land held in common and farming that land, but these extended families are seldom complete – some members are almost always living apart, performing or seeking paid work. There are men living alone in town while their wives and children live in the rural areas on traditional land. There are women living alone in town, with or without their children. There are sisters living together, nieces living with aunts, and so on. And, of course, there are 'nuclear' families. But there are also people staying together who do not consider themselves a 'family' at all, and there are at the same time people not staying together but who do consider themselves a 'family'. Even the concept of 'staying together' deserves some examination: in one set of interviews we conducted we asked men whom they were 'staying with' and were offered a list of family members, only to learn that the men actually stayed in single hostels in town during the month and went home to family only on payday weekend. But they still considered themselves to be 'staying with' those relatives.

One might also think of 'family' in terms of financial support. WLSA research has found great variety in the obligation of financial support considered appropriate to the family. On the one hand, research on maintenance has shown that, even when it is the operational unit in terms of residence, the 'nuclear family' is not a financial unit. Women and men, in general, keep their finances separate and divide financial responsibility for the household in gendered ways, with women responsible for food and children and men for larger investments such as the house. We also found a variety of other financial units besides the 'nuclear family', including sisters living together and pooling resources so that one could care for the children while the other worked for wages, daughters working in town and supporting mothers who looked after the children, and so on.

If one takes as one's point of departure the obligations of customary law, it may be appropriate to define 'family' in terms of those obligations rather than in terms of residence. Looked at in this way, there is evidence that while family for the purpose of larger obligations such as ceremonies, funerals or bridewealth is still defined by blood, 'family' in terms of support obligations may be moving towards the concept of reciprocity.

There are indications that the criteria for incurring obligations towards an individual today may be more likely to be related to affection and past assistance than to blood alone. For example, a person may feel more obliged to support the cousin he grew up with and called 'brother' than a true blood brother whom he never knew.

Finally, the family in southern Africa today represents a division of aspects that in traditional times went together. Families traditionally lived together and were mutually dependent, but today residence and dependency may be separated. This division has important consequences for the legal functions of the family, as the discussion which follows will show.

The legal functions of the family

In traditional law, the family had productive, reproductive, ceremonial, and other functions. Its legal functions included making and enforcing law, settling disputes within the family, and representing the family's interests in the community. These legal functions depended on three important factors: the co-dependence of family members, power hierarchies within the family, and recognition by the community of the family as legal authority and representative.

Co-dependence The co-dependence of family members was a part of traditional life. The family members who were co-dependent were those who lived together, tilling the same or adjacent fields, participating in rituals together, assisting each other in childbirth, sharing food and labour. In patrilineal societies, these were usually relatives joined by blood descent from a common male ancestor, and in matrilineal societies from a common female ancestor.

Spouses to these blood relatives were also part of this co-dependent community, although of a different status. In patrilineal communities wives were said to 'join a new family' on marriage, but in reality they were part of their husband's family for some purposes but not for others. They seldom, for instance, took part in legal decisions of the family as a whole or in certain rituals.

This co-dependence made it necessary for family members to reach agreement on issues in ways which preserved the peace. Negotiation was made easier because all parties needed a solution that allowed them to continue to live with and depend upon each other. Consensus of values and principles was easier to reach inasmuch as people shared a common way of life and common perspectives on life.

But if the family was once co-dependent, what is it now, and what are the legal implications? In most of southern Africa the family members who once lived and tilled the land together no longer do so on a day-to-day basis. Some family members may live in towns, on commercial farms or at the mines and return 'home' only at weekends. Others may migrate to other countries for work and return home once in two years. Children may be passed from relative to relative, living in different parts of the country (Armstrong, 1994; Russell, 1989). The far-flung family members are no longer dependent on each other from day to day. This weakens the power of the family to produce negotiated settlements of disputes and to enforce these settlements. A family member who does not want to conform can simply leave. This situation also destroys the consensus of values upon which the traditional law was built. Family members who travel to far-off places encounter different ideas and values, and their broader experience may make family-level decisions even more difficult to reach.

On the other hand, co-dependency has not been totally destroyed. In the first place, the family remains a safety net in times of economic hardship. If a family member does not need his family now, he may do so in the future and thus often wants to keep his relationship good against that eventuality – one that is not unlikely in these times of economic hardship and unstable economies. Second, families remain spiritually important. Death, and the rituals concerning death, are central to traditional ideology. WLSA research has established that the extended family is still the central institution in southern Africa dealing with death and inheritance (Noube and Stewart, 1995). Mourning the deceased and other funeral rituals are the obligation of each family member, and each is dependent on his fellow family members to mourn him when the time comes if he is to have a peaceful afterlife.

This situation points to conflicting forces regarding the legal power of the family. On the one hand, the dispersal of family members weakens the day-to-day supervision once wielded by the family; on the other, future material and spiritual needs mean that family members continue to have powerful incentives to conform to family decisions, at least on larger, more important issues.

Power hierarchies The legal functions of the family in traditional law were based on hierarchies of gender, age and position. With regard to the function of representing the family's interests in the community, it is clear that men took the forefront. In many societies, such as the Tswana, women were not supposed even to attend community meetings (*kgotla*). A woman needed a man if she was to acquire legal access to resources, although this practice may have been, and clearly is today, manipulated by women (Rose, 1988). With regard to other legal functions, such as making and enforcing the law and settling disputes, hierarchies of age and position may have been more important than hierarchies of gender. Older men and women traditionally have authority over younger men and women, based in part on the power of the older generation to distribute resources, including land.

One's position in the family is also important. In patrilineal societies women who marry into families have less authority than women born into families, or, to put it another way, women have more authority in their family of birth than in their family of marriage. Similarly, one's position in relation to a particular person is often important – in matrilineal societies, for instance, a brother, by virtue of his position, plays an important role in the life of his sister and his sister's children.

How has the system of hierarchies changed, and with what legal consequences? Access to wage employment has meant that younger family members, and women as well as men (although usually to a lesser extent), have the power that comes with money. As far as access to resources is concerned, this has reversed dependencies, with the old often now dependent on the young for resources rather than the other way around, weakening age hierarchies. It has also meant that women may have access to resources independently of men, weakening gender hierarchies. Again, this means that the legal functions of the family become more problematic. The old have trouble enforcing their decisions on the young, upon whom they may depend. Men have trouble enforcing their decisions on women, who may have independent access to economic resources. With regard to position in the family, family members not living together may have less influence on each other's lives than do family members who live together. This may mean, for instance, that a woman has more influence in her 'nuclear' family, if that is how she is living, than in her family of birth, if the latter is now scattered throughout the country.

Again, however, there are conflicting forces. While age, gender and position hierarchies are weakening, they are reinforced by ideology and by spiritual beliefs. Respect for elders remains one of the key values in southern Africa and is expressed particularly in the way that men and women take seriously their obligation to provide financial support to their parents. Spiritual belief systems also point to respect for elders, both living and dead, as the key to happiness, success and good luck.

Similarly, male dominance is still a key part of customary ideology in southern Africa. One example of this is the power that men have to supervise the behaviour of women in Swaziland, deciding whom they should befriend and what they should wear (Armstrong and Nhlapo, 1985).

Recognition by the community   The legal power of the family in the traditional setting was also dependent on the recognition of its power by the community. When communities were organized traditionally, under chiefs, the family's power to arbitrate most disputes and to speak for its members was assumed.

Today, the 'community' also includes the State. With modern transportation and mobility, a dispute which once had to be resolved within a confined geographic and legal sphere may now move to other geographic and legal spheres. Most importantly, a legal issue may be moved out of the semi-autonomous legal sphere of the family and into the courts or the administrative machinery of the State, thereby moving beyond the reach of the family and the community.

While one might have needed the consent of the family to get married in the past, today a couple may simply approach the Registrar and contract a civil marriage without regard to the family. Even if the marriage is not recognized by the couple's family, it is recognized by the larger community – the State. In the past, if a couple had a problem, they were supposed to discuss it within the family; today, they may independently approach a court for a divorce. In the past, questions of custody of children were decided by the family alone; today, a parent has the option of applying to a State court. The pluralistic legal system under which people operate today, then, has the effect of weakening the power of the family to make and enforce law, as its members have other legal options embodied in other legal systems. Again, however, there are conflicting forces at the level of ideology and spiritual beliefs.

Some family law issues revisited

Marriage   The issue of marriage presents the most fundamental of all problems in 'dual legal systems' and will be discussed here in terms of the conflict in the concepts of civil and customary marriage.

Most contemporary African States allow at least two forms of marriage: civil marriage, which is monogamous, follows Western formalities, confers rights and duties according to Western-based law, and is between two individuals; and customary law marriage. Some States provide for registration of customary law marriages and some do not.[1] The difference between civil and customary marriage is usually said to be that civil marriage is monogamous and customary marriage is potentially polygamous. That, however, is not the fundamental conflict. When a person chooses to enter into a civil or a customary marriage, he or she knows that he or she is implicitly choosing monogamy or polygamy, respectively. Rather, the conflict is rooted in a set of more fundamental distinctions. A civil marriage is conceptualized as one that:

- is between individuals;
- comes into being at a particular point in time;
- is defined by the State; and
- ends upon divorce or death.

On the other hand, a customary marriage is conceptualized as one that:

- is between families;
- may take decades to come into being;

- is defined by the family; and
- does not end, for some purposes, upon divorce or death.

Between families   As discussed above, African society has been and arguably still is organized around families, and marriage according to traditional law establishes a relationship between families. It has been said that

> a marriage relationship in most precapitalist African societies was intended to serve three major functions: the continuation of the lineage group through natural reproduction, the provision of domestic labour by the wife, and as means by which wider political and economic alliances were established between the families of the wife and that of her husband. (Armstrong et al., 1993)

The institution of marriage had objectives which 'went beyond the immediate concerns of the parties' (Armstrong et al., 1993). This conflicts with the civil law concept of marriage between individuals and produces problems for both families and individuals. A family may find it difficult to understand how two individuals can contract a marriage without consulting the family, indeed without even introducing the families to one another. If such a marriage faces a crisis, the families may feel that it is not their responsibility to help the individuals through the crisis because they have not been involved in the formation of the marriage. On the other hand, individuals may find it difficult to understand why the larger concerns of the family should play a role in what they see as an individual choice.

The result of these conflicts is a fusion of family forms in southern Africa into one amalgam which is neither fully civil nor fully customary. Most of those who marry civilly also involve their families and even exchange bridewealth in the customary way. If these formalities are not followed, the family is not likely to recognize a civil marriage. Thus civil marriages, at the level of 'living law', have taken on some of the characteristics of customary marriages. On the other hand, customary marriages have also taken on some of the characteristics of civil marriages. Since registration of marriage is necessary for many modern functions, customary marriages are often registered, and it is the individual parties to the marriage who register. Many States require evidence of consent, and it is the consent of the individual rather than that of the family which is sought. Families are less likely to initiate marriage proceedings themselves, but instead let individuals choose their spouses and then either condone or oppose that choice.

Marriage formation   The formation of a civil marriage is a one-point-in-time event. Individuals go into a church or a registry office and sign some papers and then they are married. Customary marriage is much more fluid and process oriented, reflecting 'the negotiability and flexibility of traditional African social relations' (Armstrong et al., 1993). The formation of such marriages may involve a number of ceremonies conducted over a period of many years. For example, in Swaziland, ceremonies may include (in any order):

- *kucela* (asking for a girl's hand in marriage);
- *bayeni* (the groom's party that goes to negotiate for and pay *emalobolo* (bridewealth) to the bride's family);
- *keteka, umtsimba* (traditional wedding ceremony);
- *kuhlambisa* (giving of gifts by the bride to in-laws); and
- *kuphekisa* giving a single woman to right the 'cook' at her in-laws' place (Aphane et al., 1994).

Along with each of these actions or ceremonies come rights and obligations. For instance, socially approved reproduction may predate the traditional wedding ceremony by many years.

This conflict in concepts of marriage produces several problems. First, the Western law and most Western-styled institutions require specific answers as to whether a couple are married or not. When one fills in a form for medical aid, for instance, the insurance company asks 'Are you married?' and expects a 'yes' or 'no' answer, not 'sort of' or 'somewhere along the way'. Thus, the courts of Swaziland have ruled that Swazi customary marriage exists when a woman is smeared with red ochre,[2] which usually occurs at the traditional wedding ceremonies but could occur in other circumstances. This presents a contradiction in some circumstances between when the State considers a couple to be married and when the couple and/or their family consider them to be married.

Second, the concept of marriage as a process also presents problems because it leaves the existence of marriage open to negotiation:

> it was always possible for one side to deny that a marriage had been concluded if they were unhappy about something. For example if the wife delayed in conceiving her marriage would remain in doubt, while a man who delayed in paying sufficient amount of bridewealth would provoke his wife's family to deny the existence of the marriage. (Aphane et al., 1994)

This gives rise to uncertainty and leaves it open to the stronger, more powerful individual or group to define the existence of a marriage. The negotiability of marriage causes problems for some women, particularly for young widows whose husbands have died, thereby allowing the husband's family to argue that they were never married (Dow and Kidd, 1994). But it also allows women themselves to negotiate and even 'construct' a marriage in certain circumstances.[3]

Defined by the family   The State has its own rules for determining the existence of a marriage. Civil law always requires registration. Different countries arrange customary law marriages differently. For instance, in Zimbabwe, the State recognizes registered customary law marriage, and – for certain purposes only – unregistered customary law marriages (Armstrong and Stewart, 1990). But many customary marriages recognized by the family are not recognized by the State. In Swaziland, the State recognizes 'customary marriages' regardless of registration, but the High Court has decreed that a 'customary marriage' is only valid after the woman has been smeared with red ochre. Thus, again, many customary marriages recognized by the family are not recognized by the State (at least for some purposes). In Mozambique, the concept of *de facto* marriage has been introduced, under which a couple may legally constitute a marriage by merely living together, without the involvement of the families. Thus the State may consider a couple to be married even though the family does not.

In customary law, the family was/is the legal institution that defined marriage, not the State. Numerous problems arise from this. As just mentioned, there may be circumstances where a marriage exists under one system and not under the other. Indeed, the family may decide to deny (or declare) the existence of a marriage to suit its own objectives. WLSA research found that a family might consider a woman 'married' for the purpose of mourning a dead 'husband' but 'not married' when it comes to inheriting his property.

Death and divorce   A marriage under civil law is ended by death or divorce. But some ethnic groups say that under customary law there is no divorce; others have provisions for 'divorce tokens' and other public indications that the spouses no longer intend to live as man and wife. But WLSA research has found that, again, a couple may be considered 'divorced' for some purposes and not for others. For instance, a woman may be considered divorced for purposes of custody of children – and the family may expect the children, in a patrilineal ethnic group, to remain with the husband – but still married if the husband should die and needs a woman to mourn him. This appears to be linked almost always to children. If a woman in a patrilineal ethnic group has children with a man, ties are created between the families which cannot be broken even by death or divorce.

Today, of course, a woman who has been divorced is allowed by the State to remarry. This may cause problems for both her own and her first husband's family, each of which may expect her to remain connected for life with the family of her children's father. Similar problems are not presented for the divorced man, who may marry another woman even if he remains married to his first wife inasmuch as customary marriages are potentially polygynous. This is one among the many reasons that divorced women tend not to remarry.

Similarly, death does not end a marriage, in the sense that marriage is a relationship between families. This is evidenced in the customs of 'widow inheritance',[4] under which a widow is offered a new husband from her deceased husband's lineage, and of 'sororate', under which a widower is offered a new wife from his deceased wife's lineage. The issue of death is also relevant to posthumous marriages which involve marriage to a deceased man in order to produce children to carry on his name (biologically produced for him by a relative).

Polygyny   Polygyny, an institution that allows a man to take more than one wife, is a feature of almost all southern African societies. It is essential to differentiate here between historical polygyny and modern 'polygyny'. Historically, wives were a source of wealth and status, as were the children produced by these wives. Polygyny was thus a class-based indication of wealth and status. Moreover, with each new wife, a man had the right to more fields to enable the wife to support herself and her children. Thus although polygyny was linked to wealth in patrilineal societies – because a man needed to pay bridewealth in order to acquire wives – wealth was not as important in terms of supporting these wives on a day-to-day basis.

Today, however, the situation is reversed. In many societies, bridewealth is no longer necessary for a marriage and thus a man does not need wealth in order to acquire new wives. But acquiring a new wife does not automatically mean acquiring the means to enable her to support herself. A man working in town does not get a salary increase when he marries a second wife, nor does she get a field to enable her to maintain herself and her children. Although it is a mistake to assume that all wives are dependent on their husbands, modern polygyny presents financial problems of day-to-day maintenance. The modern scenario is one of a man leaving his first wife in a rural area, dependent on him for cash for farm inputs, and taking a second wife in town, and neglecting the first wife and her children in favour of the second. Another variant is to neglect the first, urban wife, who is dependent on his income, in favour of a second, younger wife. In modern money economies, polygyny is not necessarily restricted to those who can afford it, and it presents serious financial problems for families.

Historically, when a man took a second or subsequent wife, the other wives were consulted. More senior wives acquired status and control over the labour of the younger wives. Today, this custom is seldom if ever followed. Men take second and subsequent wives without consultation, and sometimes without even the knowledge of senior wives. Second and subsequent wives may also not know of the existence of a senior wife or wives when they enter into marriage. Thus the 'customary' practice that a man may marry more than one wife is still followed, but the customary procedures for doing so are not.

Polygyny served a historical purpose: to provide the protection of marriage to women in conditions where a woman without a man was extremely vulnerable. However, with today's changing conditions and expectations, polygyny serves as a 'customary' excuse for sexual promiscuity and is both physically and emotionally damaging to women. Thus the institution of polygyny, although perhaps justified within the specific social context in which it developed, may currently constitute a source of subordination of women.

Bridewealth The practice of giving bridewealth, usually in cattle, from the groom's family to the bride's family exists in all patrilineal southern African societies. In traditional society it had a number of different functions: to transmit the productive and reproductive capacities of women from one family to another; to involve the entire family in the marriage, thus creating family interest in the survival of the marriage; and to signify the importance of women to the family and the community. The significance of bridewealth

> lay and still lies in being the mode through which certain rights and obligations were acquired, not only by the spouses, but by other members of their families, such as their children and parents. In traditional society, the payment of *lobolo* (bridewealth) secured the position of the woman within marriage and granted her certain rights, claims and guarantees. She could not just be 'expelled' or arbitrarily divorced by the husband without an elaborate process involving both families. (Armstrong et al., 1993)

Although the giving of bridewealth is no longer necessary for marriage in most countries of southern Africa, it is still widely practised. But its use has been perverted into a means of control over women in some circumstances. For instance, whereas in the past bridewealth ideally served to preserve a marriage for the wife and the children, today's laws allow easy divorce. Bridewealth instead serves as a means of enabling the husband's family to keep the children in the event of divorce, on the grounds that they have 'paid' for the reproductive capacity of the woman. Thus if she divorces, the wife is divorcing her children as well. Even in countries such as Zimbabwe, where the formal law applies the principle of 'the best interests of the children' – almost invariably interpreted to mean that the children stay with the mother after divorce – the pull of culture is so strong that in practice most children remain with the father's family (Armstrong, 1994).

Similarly, the notion of bridewealth has sometimes been perverted to chain a woman to a marriage which is not good for her. For instance, a woman who is beaten by her husband and complains to her family may be told that he has every right to beat her because he has 'paid' for her (Maboreke, 1986).

The case of bridewealth again points to how the family continues to make and apply its own laws, regardless of formal State regulation. Even where States do not recognize bridewealth, as in Zimbabwe and Mozambique, the practice continues. Moreover, these and other perversions of bridewealth[5] can be traced to the introduction of cash economies and the disruptions and changes within the African family that this has caused. Whereas women were once valued for their productive and reproductive capacities, the introduction of monetary relations reduces the perceived value of their labour because it is mainly in the subsistence agricultural sector and the home, and thus does not produce cash income. Valuation of the bridewealth in monetary terms also turns women into a commodity. When families are disrupted and the woman's labour is no longer being contributed to the family farm but is individualized, her well-being becomes less important than the money 'paid' for her.

Maintenance All State legal systems in southern Africa provide that, regardless of marriage, biological fathers and mothers are both obliged to maintain their children. Such laws are based on a 'nuclear family' concept and exclude the customary-law obligations of the extended family – the obligation of children to support their parents, and of uncles, aunts, cousins, brothers and sisters towards each other. State legal systems also implicitly view the husband as 'breadwinner' and the wife as 'dependent'. In some countries, this is evidenced in the very title of the maintenance legislation (for example, Lesotho's Deserted Wives and Children's Act, 60, 1959), and in others in the practices of the courts (Armstrong, 1992).

WLSA research has found that most maintenance claims and/or disputes in southern Africa never reach the formal courts; rather, the family is the institution of first resort.[6] Even when the family fails to produce a negotiated solution and the State court system is used, negotiations at family level continue and the two systems are played off against each other (Armstrong 1993).

Under traditional law, the family had two procedures for dealing with disputes: formal and informal. Among the Swazi, for instance, if a wife has a complaint 'she should always speak first to her mother-in-law, who acts as an intermediary between the husband and the wives' (Marwick, 1940: 130–1). Only if this fails is the husband's *lusendvo* (family council) called and consulted. Similarly, among the Tswana, if a wife feels she is being mistreated or neglected, 'she should first complain to [her husband's] parents or other relatives. They will take him to task, reminding him that it was through them that he got her in marriage, and that therefore he is not entitled to treat her as he likes' (Shapera, 1959).

WLSA research found that such informal procedures are still widely practised, although the formal procedure of calling a family council is much less prevalent. Most maintenance is claimed informally, either by approaching family members for assistance in convincing a father to support his children, or by simply asking family members for assistance. Maintenance asked for in this way does not conform to the formal legal concept of maintenance duties arising between married partners or through biological connection to a child. Instead, it conforms more closely to traditional-law obligations of support for extended-family members. Thus we found siblings helping to maintain each other, mothers-in-law helping to maintain daughters-in-law, and so on. Significantly, women maintain as well as men, and a woman's natal family as well as her family of marriage often helps to maintain her and her children. This contrasts with assumptions – based on what is presumed to be customary law – that (a) men maintain and women are maintained, and (b) when a woman marries, the responsibility to maintain her is transferred from her natal family to her family of marriage.

State maintenance laws also assume that maintenance involves monetary payments from one person to another. However, WLSA research found that families also practise 'custody as maintenance' (Armstrong, 1993). If maintenance is reconceptualized to include all ways of 'maintaining' a person (usually a child) rather than the simple provision of financial support, then the transfer of *de facto* custody to different family members can be seen as a form of maintenance. Thus when an unmarried woman gives her child to her mother to look after while she goes to town to engage in wage employment, the mother is 'maintaining' the child. Research shows that fluctuating custody of children is a major way of redistributing both finances and obligations between members of the family (Armstrong, 1994; Russell, 1989).

Thus the family still has an important legal role in terms of maintenance, particularly of children. This takes diverse forms: attempting solutions among nuclear family members, providing financial contributions among extended-family members, and caring for extended-family members. This suggests that the extended family is not 'disintegrating', as some have argued, but rather continues to be central to African society and African law.

Inheritance WLSA research also found that the family plays an important role in inheritance. In all six WLSA countries, although statutes and common-law provisions exist to regulate inheritance, the overwhelming majority of estates are dealt with by the family, under customary law, in two important ways. First, the family determines the status of relevant individuals. When a man dies, the rights of his 'wife' and children depend on the woman's status: is she a 'wife' or not? As discussed above, the existence of a marriage is often open to negotiation and interpretation, and it is the family that negotiates and interprets – in some ethnic groups, by manipulating the mourning process; in others, by manipulating the State court system (Aphane et al., 1994; Dow and Kidd, 1994; Kasonde-N'gandu et al., 1994).

Second, the family controls the distribution of the property of the deceased. Even where the traditional institution of the family council is dying out, the family does this informally (Aphane et al., 1994). Practices appear to differ between ethnic groups. Among the Shona, and to a lesser extent the Swazi and Ndebele, the tendency is for the family to leave a widow or widower alone and allow her or him to remain with the property acquired by the couple during the marriage. But the family also abrogates its obligations to support the widow and her children within the extended family (Dengu-Zvobgo et al., 1994; Aphane et al., 1994). On the other hand, it appears that in Zambia the family often steps in before the body is even cold and helps itself to the property acquired by the spouses during the marriage, leaving the widow (and, less often, the widower) without either property or family support (Kasonde-N'gandu et al., 1994). In Botswana and Lesotho, although the extended family has a role, it appears that once a marriage is determined to be in existence the nuclear family is seen as the controlling institution with regard to property. The widow or widower remains with the marital property, and the major issue is the distribution of property to children of the marriage after the death of both spouses (Dow and Kidd, 1994; Letuka et al., 1994).

Again, the extended family clearly has an important role to play and is not 'disintegrating'. That role, however, is changing. The formality of family meetings and decisions seems to be lessening, and informal solutions appear more prevalent. This is probably necessitated by modern conditions, under which it is difficult to bring together family members who may have had to relocate all over the country or even in neighbouring countries to find work, and by the reduced authority of traditional family leaders, who may now be dependent for support upon the very family members who were once dependent on them. Informality of decision making may allow more opportunities for individual family members to manipulate situations to their own advantage without the mediating role of others to control them. Thus a handful of greedy family members in Zambia may act for 'the family' and take a widow's property for their own use, despite the fact that other family members condemn their actions. The control once exerted by the family as a group is lessening.

Conclusion

In conclusion, we have seen that the family's legal role is still the most important legal role played by any institution in southern Africa: more important even than the State law. This suggests that any study of law must include a study of the law made and applied by the family. We must rethink our concept of law as something that is state centred and re-conceptualize law in its *African* sense as something that is family centred. This should usher in a whole new kind of legal research, one which takes the family as its starting point.

When legal research starts from the family, it is necessary first to examine the changing role of the family. I have suggested that the legal functions of the family depended on three important factors: the co-dependence of family members, power hierarchies within the family, and recognition by the community of the family as legal authority and represen-tative. Each of these is changing as extended families no longer live together in an agricultural economy, as economic and spiritual hierarchies are shuffled between generations and genders, and as the State has acquired legal authority alongside the family and traditional structures. This sets the stage for understanding that, although the family still plays an important legal function, its function is diluted, and less 'customary'.

When examining law and the family, it is also necessary to re-conceptualize 'customary law'. The official 'customary law' which has been applied in the courts, and the 'proclaimed customary law' which is used to justify actions which are contrary to customary *values* must be 'decon-structed' – re-examined and re-thought. The former, 'official customary law', is a product of political struggles during the colonial era and at the State level in the post-colonial era. The latter, 'proclaimed customary law', is a product of a political struggle going on even today, particularly in the attempt to control women and in the attempt by traditional leaders to reclaim some of the powers that were once theirs and have been eroded by the modern State systems.

The 'living law' – the 'customs' of indigenous people today – is neither 'customary' nor 'Western' law; it is a mixture of both, plus other, uniquely African, features. Some aspects of the living law are firmly grounded in the *values* of customary law, such as respect and support for the family. Financial support for extended family members was given as an example of this kind of 'living law'. Other kinds of 'living laws' are grounded in changes in the economic and social order – increased individualism – and are probably inevitable. An example of this is increasing individualization of marriage. Still other aspects of living law, however, can be critiqued as neither 'customary' nor inevitable responses to modern conditions. They are, instead, the reflection of the worst aspects of the hierarchical and patriarchal power relations of customary law coupled with the worst aspects of the individualist and competitive modern world. 'Poverty grab-bing' by relatives of deceased persons was given as an example of this kind of 'living law'.

The analysis of the law and the family in southern Africa contained in this chapter also examined several issues conventionally considered to be part of 'family law'. The first of these was 'marriage' which, although criticized as not always central to the definition of 'family' in southern Africa, is nevertheless an important institution. Marriage presents perhaps the most fundamental of conflicts between the 'customary law' and the Western-based, introduced legal system. I suggested that the conflict arises from the following dichotomies:

Customary	Civil
between families	between individuals
process	one point in time
family-defined	state-defined
potentially un-ending	ends upon death or divorce

However, in the 'living law' we are seeing a movement away from these dichotomies into a third form of marriage, which is neither fully 'customary' nor fully 'civil'. Individuals, for instance, may decide whom to marry, but bridewealth is still paid and the families are still involved in the ceremonies. Many couples complete both the 'one point in time' civil ceremony as well as the customary 'process'. The state definition of marriage is used for some purposes, for example to obtain a housing loan, but the family definition is used for others, for instance in determining family 'member-ship'. A marriage may be considered ended for some purposes, such as custody of children, but not for others, mourning a deceased 'husband' for example. Thus, again, we are seeing a new, vibrant, unique version of 'living law' which mixes rather than rejects elements of both systems.

This chapter reflects on a similar mixture of legal systems in relation to polygyny, bridewealth, maintenance and inheritance. In each, the 'customary' institution has not died, but has been transformed by its contact with Western-based law. In the case of polygyny and bridewealth, this mixture has largely brought problems for women as customary institutions once controlled by the family become individualized, and what may once have been means of protecting and caring for women have become means of controlling them. On the other hand, maintenance has evolved as a mixture of customary obligations to care for one's relatives and Western rights to financial support within marriage – in a way which still emphasizes some of the customary *values* encouraging preservation of the family. Finally, inheritance in the 'living law' exhibits some of the family-centred values of the customary law, but some of the individualistic tendencies of the Western-based, introduced law. Perhaps more than in the other examples, in the case of inheritance the flexibility of the living law allows the powerful to manipulate the law to their advantage while leaving the vulnerable without legal protection. The family, in some countries, becomes an institution which *controls* inheritance, but which often does not provide the *support* which should go hand-in-hand with that control.

Finally, the analysis of southern African law as 'living law' also has important implications for 'development' programmes and strategies, if by 'development' one means not just increased economic production but improving the lives of individuals at the social and personal level as well. The implication is that formal law will have only a limited effect as an instrument of social change, since most legal activity actually goes on within the family, which is notoriously difficult to regulate. Rather we must look at power relations within the family, and the effect of external forces upon the family. We must also look at the interrelationship and interaction between the State formal law and the family's informal law, and devise solutions to problems based on this. Ultimately, we must reconceptualize the family itself: away from both the Western-oriented notion of the nuclear family and the traditional notion of the extended family based exclusively on one's biological relationship, to a concept of family based on its functions, and the rights and duties created by its own system of laws, as they operate in the socio-economic conditions of southern Africa today.

Notes

1. Many states also allow religious marriages, such as Muslim marriages, but these are not common in southern Africa, which is the author's area of expertise. Religious marriages will, therefore, not be discussed in this chapter.

2. R. v. Fakudze 1970 SLR 422.

3. For instance, one woman in the WLSA-Botswana inheritance study constructed a marriage by putting herself into mourning for a deceased 'husband'.

4. We do not like the term 'widow inheritance' since it implies that women are property to be inherited. In fact, in traditional law, a widow could choose not to continue the marriage with the deceased husband's family by accepting a relative in the place of the husband. But, of course, her options were limited, and if she refused she might not be allowed to remain on family land or retain her children.

5. Such as the Zimbabwean practice whereby a family may refuse to bury a deceased woman until her husband's family has completed payment of the bride-wealth, thus leaving her spirit to roam and bewitch the family.

6. Griffiths (1987) finds that women only use the State system when the informal system fails.

Bibliography

Achebe, C. (1958) *Things Fall Apart*, London, Ibadan, Nairobi: Heinemann Educational Books.

Adams, B. N. (1968) *Kinship in an Urban Setting*, New York: Markham Publishing.

Adegboyega, O. (1992) 'Structure and dynamics of family formation', in Union for African Population Studies, *The Structure and Dynamics of Family Formation in Africa*, Dakar, Senegal: UAPS.

Adegboyega, O. (1993) 'Situation of families in East and Southern Africa', Consultation paper, Proceedings of UN Economic Commission for Africa and Economic and Social Commission for West Asia, Joint Preparatory Meeting for the 1994 UN International Year of the Family, Tunis, Tunisia.

Adepoju, A. (1974) 'Migration and socio-economic links between urban migrants and their home communities in Nigeria', *Africa*, 44(4): 383–96.

Adepoju, A. (1977) 'Rationality and fertility in the traditional Yoruba society, South-West Nigeria', in C. Caldwell (ed.), *The Persistence of High Fertility: Population Prospects in the Third World, Volume 1*, Canberra: Australian National University Press.

Adepoju, A. (1979) 'Non-formal training in small-scale industries', in U. G. Damachi and K. Ewusi (eds), *Manpower Supply and Utilization in Ghana, Nigeria and Sierra Leone*, Geneva: International Institute for Labour Studies.

Adepoju, A. (1982) 'The dimension of the refugee problem in Africa', *African Affairs*, 81(322): 21–35.

Adepoju, A. (1983) 'Patterns of migration by sex', in C. Oppong (ed.), *Female and Male in West Africa*, London: George Allen and Unwin.

Adepoju, A. (1984) 'Migration and female employment in South West Nigeria', *African Urban Studies*, 18 (Spring).

Adepoju, A. (1986) *Rural Migration and Development in Nigeria*, Department of Demography and Social Statistics, University of Ife, Ile-Ife, Nigeria.

Adepoju, A. (1988a) 'International migration in Africa south of the Sahara', in R. Appleyard (ed.), *International Migration Today, Vol. 1: Trends and Prospects*, UNESCO, Paris and University of Western Australia.

Adepoju, A. (1988b) 'Migration and urbanization in Africa: issues and policies', in E. Van de Walle et al. (eds), *The State of African Demography*, Liège: IUSSP.

Adepoju, A. (1990) 'State of the art review of migration in Africa', in Union for African Population Studies, *The Role of Migration in African Development: Issues and Policies for the 90s, Commissioned Papers*, UAPS, pp. 3–41.

Adepoju, A. (1991a) 'La Jeunesse et l'avenir de l'Afrique', in *Les enfants martyrs*, Special No. 002, Dakar: Hope Unlimited, pp. 23–6.

Adepoju, A. (1991b) 'Africa's population crisis: formulating effective policies', *Africa Recovery Briefing Paper No. 3*, New York: United Nations.

Adepoju, A. (1991c) 'South–North migration: the African Experience', *International Migration*, 29(2): 205–22.

Adepoju, A. (1992) 'The African family and the survival strategy', keynote address delivered at the Pan African Anthropological Association Conference on the African Family (Yaounde), 24 August.

Adepoju, A. (ed.) (1993) *The Impact of Structural Adjustment on the Population of Africa: The Implications for Education, Health and Employment*, London: James Currey.

Adepoju, A. (1994a) *Population, Poverty, Structural Adjustment Programmes and Quality of Life in Sub-Saharan Africa* (commissioned report to Population and Quality of Life Independent Commission), Paris.

Adepoju, A. (1994b) *Population Growth Prospects in Africa in the Context of Integrated Rural–Urban Development*, Population Policy Paper Series, African Development Bank, Abidjan.

Adepoju, A. (1994c) 'Preliminary analysis of emigration dynamics in sub-Saharan Africa', *International Migration*, 32(2): 197–216.

Adepoju, A. and Mbugua, W. (1994) *Rethinking the Approaches to the Study of Population Dynamics in Africa*, Dakar: Union for African Population Studies.

Adomako A. (1993) 'Women and AIDS in Ghana "I control my body" (or do I?)', in *Women and Demographic Change in Sub-Saharan Africa*, Liège, Belgium: IUSSP.

Afolayan, A. A. (1991) 'Socio-economic consequences of rural migration on source region, especially on women: a case study of Ebira Division, Nigeria', in Union for African Population Studies, *Spontaneous Contributions to the Conference on Women, Family and Population, Volume 2*, Dakar: UAPS, pp. 257–84.

Agnelli, S. (1986) *Street children: a growing urban tragedy.* (A report for the Independent Commission on International Humanitarian Issues), London: Weidenfeld and Nicolson.

Agounke A. (1991) 'Les nouvelles formes d'unions en Afrique de l'Ouest: aspirations et ruptures', in UAPS, *Commissioned Papers, Conference on Women, Family and Population, Volume 1*. Ouagadougou: UAPS.

Ajayi, A. A., Marangu, L. T., Miller, J. and Paxman, J. M. (1991) 'Adolescent sexuality and fertility in Kenya: a survey of knowledge, perceptions and practices', *Studies in Family Planning*, 22(4), July/August.

Ajayi, F. Anza, S., Ephson, B., Morna, C. L. and Seck, K. M. (1990) 'Tools of the trade: do farmers have the right ones?', *African Farmer*, 5: 5–13.

Antoine, P. and Guillaume, A. (1984) 'Une expression de la solidarité familiale à Abidjan: enfants du couples et enfants confiés', in *Les familles d'aujourd'hui*, Colloque international de Genève.

Aphane, D., Dlamini, T., Magwaza, M., Manzini, N., Mkhonta, F., Mthembu, L. and Vilazaki, P. (1994) *Inheritance in Swaziland: Law and Practice*, Mbabane: WLSA.

Armstrong, A. (1992) *Struggling Over Scarce Resources: Women and Maintenance in Southern Africa*, Harare: University of Zimbabwe Press.

Armstrong, A. (1993) 'Different women, different laws', unpublished PhD dissertation, University of Copenhagen.

Armstrong, A. (1994) 'School and sadza: child custody in Zimbabwe', *International Journal of Law and the Family*, 8: 151–70.

Armstrong, A. and Nhlapo, T. (1985) *Law and the Other Sex: The Legal Position of Women in Swaziland*, Mbabane: Webster's.

Armstrong, A. and Stewart (1990) *The Legal Situation of Women in Southern Africa*, Harare: University of Zimbabwe Publications.

Armstrong, A. et al. (1993) 'Uncovering reality: excavating women's rights in African family law', *International Journal of Law and the Family*.

Arnould, E. J. (1984) 'Marketing and social reproduction in Zinder, Niger Republic', in Robert McC. Netting, Richard R. Wilk and Eric J. Arnould (eds), *Households:*

Comparative and Historical Studies of the Domestic Group, Berkeley, CA: University of California Press, pp. 130–62.

Aryee, A. F. (1967) 'Christianity and polygamy in Ghana – the role of the church as an instrument of social change', *Ghana Journal of Sociology*, 3(2): 98–115.

Aryee, A. F. and Gaisie, S. K. (1982) 'Fertility implications of contemporary patterns of nuptiality in Ghana', in L. Ruzicka (ed.), *Nuptiality and Fertility*, Liège, Belgium: IUSSP.

Assogba L., N.-M., (1990) 'Statut de la femme et migration urbaine: le cas du Togo', in UAPS, *Spontaneous Contributions to the Conference on The Role of Migration in African Development*, Union for African Population Studies, Nairobi, Kenya, 24–28 February, pp. 740–7.

Azu, Diana G. (1974) *The Ga Family and Social Change*, African Social Research Documents, Vol. 5, Leiden: African Studies Centre.

Badiane, Wally (1990) 'Migration et mobilité professionelle des jeunes travailleurs de la Medina', in *Spontaneous Contributions to the Conference on the Role of Migration in African Development*, Union for African Population Studies, Dakar/Nairobi, 24–28 February, pp. 247–61.

Barou, J. (1976) 'L'émigration dans un village du Niger', in *Cahiers D'études Africaines*, 16(3): pp. 627–32.

Basden, G. T. (1921) *Among the Igbos of Nigeria*, Philadelphia: J.B. Lippincott.

Baumann, H. (1928) 'The division of work according to sex in African hoe culture', *Africa*, 1(3).

Baylis, C. (1958) *Ethics: The Principles of Wise Choice*, New York: Henry Holt and Company.

Beattie, J. (1964) *Other Cultures*, London: Routledge and Kegan Paul.

Becker, G. S. (1981) *A Treatise on the Family*, Cambridge, MA: Harvard University Press.

Bernardi, B. (1959) *The Mugwe: a family prophet*, Oxford: Oxford University Press.

Berry, S. (1985) *Fathers Work for Their Sons: Accumulation, Mobility and Class Formation in an Extended Yoruba Community*, Berkeley, CA: University of California Press.

Bjeren, G., (1985) *Migration to Shashemene: Ethnicity, Gender and Occupation in Urban Ethiopia*, New York/London: Africana Publishing.

Bledsoe, C. (1989) 'The cultural meaning of AIDS and condoms for stable heterosexual relations in Africa: recent evidence from the local print media', in IUSSP, *Population policy in Sub-Saharan Africa: drawing on international experience*. IUSSP: Liège.

Bledsoe C. (1990) 'Transformations in Sub-Saharan African marriage and fertility', *The Annals of the American Academy of Political and Social Sciences*, 510.

Bledsoe, C. and Isiugo-Abanihe, U. C. (1989) 'Strategies of Child Fosterage among Mende Grannies in Sierra Leone', in Ron Lesthaeghe (ed.), *African Reproduction and Social Organization*, Berkeley, CA: University of California Press.

Bona, A. N. (1990) 'Some lessons from traditional practices for present-day education in Africa', in UNESCO/UNICEF, *African Thoughts on the Prospects of Education for All*, UNESCO, Dakar and UNICEF, Abidjan.

Boohene, Esther et al. (1991) 'Fertility and contraceptive use among young adults in Harare, Zimbabwe', *Studies in Family Planning*, 22(4): 264–71.

Boserup, E. (1985) 'Economic and demographic inter-relationships in sub-Saharan Africa', *Population and Development Review*, 11 (3): 383–97.

Botswana, *Demographic and Health Survey, II (1988)*, Gaborone: Central Statistics Office.

Botswana, *Population and Housing Census Report (1991)*, Gaborone: Central Statistics Office.

Boye, A. K., Hill, K., Isaacs, S. and Gordis, D. (1991) 'Marriage law and practice in the Sahel', *Studies in Family Planning*, 22(6): 343–9.

Bradbury, R. E. (1973) *Benin Studies*, Oxford: Oxford University Press/International African Institute.

Bradley, C. (1992) 'Fertility and the household division of labour among the Maragoli of Western Province Kenya', unpublished paper presented at Inter Faculty Seminar, PSRI, University of Nairobi.

Brass, W., Coale, A. J., Demeny. P., Heisel, D. F., Lorimer, F., Romaniuk, A., and van de Walle, E. (1968) *The Demography of Tropical Africa*, Princeton, NJ: Princeton University Press.

Brown, E. K. A. (1983) 'Patterns of internal migration in Ghana, with special emphasis on the determinants of female migration', unpublished PhD dissertation, University of Pennsylvania.

Brown, R. (ed.) (1950) *African Systems of Kinship and Marriage*, Oxford: Oxford University Press.

Brydon, L. (1985) 'The avatime family and circulation 1900–1977', in Prothero and Chapman (eds), *Third World Countries*, London.

Brydon, L. (1992) 'Ghanaian women in the migration process', in S. Chant (ed.), *Gender and Migration in Developing Countries*, London/New York: Belhaven Press, pp. 91–108.

Burnham P. (1987) 'Changing themes in the analysis of African marriage', in D. Parkin and D. Nyamwaya (eds), *Transformations of African Marriage*, Manchester: Manchester University Press.

Busia, K. A. (1950) *Report on a Social Survey of Sekondi-Takoradi*, London: Crown Agents for the Colonies.

Caldwell, J. C. (1977) 'The economic rationality of high fertility: an investigation illustrated with Nigerian survey data', *Population Studies*, 31(1): 5–26.

Caldwell, J. C. (1980), 'Mass education as a determinant of the timing of fertility decline', *Population and Development Review*, 6(2), June: 225–55.

Caldwell, J. C. (1982) *Theory of Fertility Decline*, London: Academic Press.

Caldwell, J. C. (1989) 'Mass education as a determinant of mortality decline', in J. C. Caldwell and G. Santon (eds), *Selected Readings in the Cultural, Social and Behavioural Determinants of Health*, Canberra: Australian National University.

Caldwell, J. C. (1990) 'Cultural and social factors influencing mortality levels in developing countries', *Annals of the American Academy of Political and Social Sciences*, 510.

Caldwell, J. C. and Caldwell, P. (1987) 'The cultural context of high fertility in sub-Saharan Africa', *Population and Development Review*, 13(3): 409–37.

Caldwell, J. C., Caldwell, P. and Quiggin, P. (1989) 'The social context of AIDS in Sub-Saharan Africa, *Population and Development Review*, 15(2): 185–234.

Caldwell, J. C., Reddy, P. H. and Caldwell, P. (1982) 'Demographic change in rural South India', *Population and Development Review* 8(4): 689–728.

Capron, J. and Kohler, J. M. (1987) 'De quelques caracteristiques de la partique matrimoniale Mossi contemporaine', in C. Oppong et al. (eds), *Marriage, Fertility and Parenthood in West Africa*, Canberra: ANU, pp. 187–223.

Carael M. (1992) 'Women, AIDS and STDs in sub-Saharan Africa: the impact of marriage change', in *Expert Group Meeting on Population and Women*, Gaborone: ESD/P/ICPD.1994/EG.III.

Carael, M., Cleland, J., Deheneffe, J. C. and Adeokun, L. A. (1990) Research on Sexual Behaviour Surveys. Preliminary Findings, IUSSP Committee on Anthropological Demography, seminar on anthropological studies relevant to sexual transmission of HIV, Denmark/Liège: Ording Press.

Chant, S. (1992) 'Conclusion: towards a framework for the analysis of gender-selective migration', in Sylvia Chant (ed.), *Gender and Migration in Developing Countries*, London and New York: Belhaven Press, pp. 197–206.

Chant, S. and Radcliffe, S. A. (1992) 'Migration and development: The Importance of

Gender', in Sylvia Chant (ed.), *Gender and Migration in Developing Countries*, London and New York: Belhaven Press, pp. 1–29.

Chilivumbo, A. (1985) *Migration and Uneven Rural Development in Africa: The Case of Zambia*, Lanham, MD: University Press of America.

Cleland, J. (1989) 'Maternal education and child survival: Further evidence and explanation', in J. C. Caldwell et al., *What We Know About the Health Transition: The Proceedings of an International Workshop*, Canberra: Australian National University, Health Transition Centre.

Cliffe, L. (1978) 'Labour migration and peasant differentiation: Zambian experiences', *Journal of Peasant Studies*, 5(3): 326–46.

Commonwealth Secretariat (1989) *Engendering Adjustment for the 1990s*, London: Marlborough House.

Conde, J. and Diagne, P. S. (1986) 'South–North international migrations: a case study of Malian, Mauritanian, and Senegalese migrants from the Senegal river valley to France', Paris: Development Centre Papers, Organization for Economic Cooperation and Development.

Connell, J., Das Gupta, B., Laishley, R. and Lipton, M. (1976) *Migration from Rural Areas: The Evidence from Village Studies*, Sussex, England: Institute of Development Studies.

Corner, L. (1981) 'Linkages, reciprocity and remittances: the impact of rural outmigration on Malaysian rice villages', in G. W. Jones and H. V. Richter (eds), *Population Mobility and Development: Southeast Asia and the Pacific*, Development Studies Monograph No. 27, Canberra: Australian National University, pp. 117–36.

Coulibaly, S., Gregory, J. and Piche, V. (1980) 'Les migrations voltaïques: importance et ambivalence de la migration voltaïque', Tome I, Centre voltaïque de la recherche scientifique et Institut national de la démographie IDRC, Ottawa, Canada.

Courgeau, D. (1988) *Méthodes de mesure de la mobilité spatiale: migrations internes, mobilité temporaire, navettes*, Paris: Editions de l'Institut national d'études démographiques.

De Jonge, K. (1978) 'Rural development and inequality in Casamance (Southern Senegal)', *Tijdschrift Foor Economische en Sociale Geografie*, 69 (1–2): 68–77.

De Waal, A. (1989) 'Famine mortality: a case study of Darfur, Sudan 1984–5', *Population Studies*, 43(1): 5–24.

Delaunay, D. (1984) *De la captivité à l'exil: histoire et démographie des migrations paysannes dans la Moyenne Vallee du Fleuve Sénégal*, Travaux et Documents de L'ORSTOM, No. 174, ORSTOM, Paris.

Demble, I. and Hugon, P. (1982) *Vivre et survivre dans les villes africaines*, Paris: IEDES Collection Tiers Monde, Presses universitaires de France.

Dengu-Zvobgo, K., Donzwa, B., Gwaunza, E., Kazembe, J., Noube, W. and Stewart, J. (1994) *Inheritance in Zimbabwe: Law, Custom, and Practice*, Harare: WLSA.

Dinan C. (1983) 'Gold diggers and sugar daddies', in C. Oppong (ed.), *Female and Male in West Africa*, London: George Allen & Unwin.

Diop, M. (1989) 'Un exemple de non-insertion urbaine: le cas des migrantes saisonnières de Basse-Casamance à Dakar', in Philippe Antoine and Sidiki Coulibaly (eds), *L'insertion urbaine des migrants en Afrique*, Actes du séminaire CRDI-ORSTOM-URD, 10–14 Février, 1987, Lomé. Paris: Collection Colloques et Séminaires, Editions ORSTOM: pp. 79–92.

Donadje F. (1991) 'Typologie des unions masculines au sud-Benin', in UAPS, *Commissioned Papers, Conference on Women, Family and Population, Volume 1*, Ougadougou: UAPS.

Dovlo, F. E. (1992) 'Problems of the impact of social change on the African family', in N. B. Leidenfrost (ed.), *Families in Transition*, Vienna: International Federation for Home Economics.

Dow, U. and Kidd, P. (1994) *Women, Marriage and Inheritance*, Gaborone: WLSA.

Dubresson, A. (1990) 'Migrations villes et villages de Côte d'Ivoire', in UPAS, *The Role of Migration in African Development: Issues and Policies for the 90s*, Commissioned Papers for The Role of Migration in African Development, Nairobi: Union for African Population Studies, pp. 96–108.

Dupont, V. (1989) 'Insertion différentielle des migrants dans les marches du travail de trois villes moyennes de région de plantation (Togo)', in Philippe Antoine and Sidiki Coulibaly (eds), *L'insertion urbaine des migrants en Afrique*, Actes du Séminaire CRDI-ORSTOM-URD, 10–14 Février, 1987, Lomé. Paris: Collection Colloques et Séminaires, Editions ORSTOM: pp. 105–18.

Dureau, F. (1989) 'Migrations et dynamisation des villes de L'intérieur en Côte d'Ivoire', in Philippe Antoine and Sidiki Coulibaly (eds), *L'insertion urbaine des migrants en Afrique*, Actes du Séminaire CRDI-ORSTOM-URD, 10–14 Février, 1987, Lomé. Paris: Collection Colloques et Séminaires, Editions ORSTOM: pp. 119–34.

Duza, M. B. and Baldwin, C. S. (1979) *Nuptiality and Population Policy*, New York: Population Council.

Duza, M. B. and Conteh, A. (1984) 'Migration to Monrovia: patterns and differentials', Research Monograph Series No. 9, Cairo, Egypt: Cairo Demographic Centre.

Eades, J. (1987) 'Prelude to an exodus: chain migration, trade, and the Yoruba in Ghana', in Jeremy Eades (ed.), *Migrants, Workers and the Social Order*, London/New York: Tavistock Publications, pp. 199–212.

Egil, H. (1974) *Luo Religion and Folklore*, Oslo/Bergen: Universitets forlaget, Munksgaard/Copenhagen: Scandinavian University Books.

Ekejiuba, F. I. (1984) 'Contemporary households and major socio-economic transitions in East Nigeria: towards a reconceptualization of the household', paper presented at the Workshop on Conceptualizing the Household: Issues of Theory, Method and Application, Harvard University, 2–4 November.

Elabor-Idemudia, P. (1991) 'The Impact of Structural Adjustment Programmes on Women and their Households in Bendel and Ogun States, Nigeria', in Gladwin, C. H. (ed.), *Structural Adjustment and African Women Farmers*, Gainesville: University of Florida Press, pp. 128–50.

Elson D. (1987) *The Impact of Structural Adjustment on Women: Concepts and Issues*, London: Conference on the Impact of IMF and World Bank Policies on the People of Africa.

Essone, K. (1990) 'Family and kinship participation in African education', in UNESCO/UNICEF *African Thoughts on the Prospects of Education for All*, UNESCO, Dakar and UNICEF, Abidjan.

Evans-Pritchard, E. E. (1948) *The Divine Kinship of the Shilluk*, Cambridge: Cambridge University Press.

Evans-Pritchard, E. E. (1956) *The Nuer Religion*, Oxford: Oxford University Press.

Ezumah, N. N. (1990) 'Women in development: the role of Igbo rural women in agricultural production', unpublished PhD dissertation, University of Ibadan.

Fall, A. S. (1991) 'Une autre famille? Les réseaux de vosinage en ville', in UAPS, *Spontaneous Contributions to the Conference on Women, Family and Population at Ougadougou, Burkina Faso, April 24–29, 1991*, Union for African Population Studies, Vol. 2, pp. 54–68.

Family Matters (1992) Occasional Papers series, Secretariat, International Year of the Family. Vienna: United Nations.

Fapohunda, E. R. and Todaro, M. P. (1988) 'Family structure and demand for children in Southern Nigeria', *Population and Development Review*, 14(4): 571–94.

Fax, R. (1977) *Kinship and Marriage*, London: Penguin Books.

Findley, Sally and Diallo, Asitan (1988) 'Foster children links between rural populations', in *Proceedings of African Congress on Population*, Vol. 3, Liège: IUSSP/UAPS.

Findley, S. E. (1987) *Rural Development and Migration: Alternative Family Choices in the Philippines*, Boulder, CO: Westview Press.

Findley, S. E. (1989) 'Les migrations féminines dans les villes africaines: leurs motivations et expériences', in Philippe Antoine and Sidiki Coulibaly (eds), *L'insertion urbaine des migrants en Afrique*, Actes du Séminaire CRDI-ORSTOM-URD, 10–14 Février, 1987, Lomé. Paris: Collection Colloques et Séminaires, Editions ORSTOM: pp. 55–70.

Findley, S. E. (1991) 'Confronting the drought: the special role of women and children of rural Mali in the 1983–85 Drought', *POPSAHEL*, CERPOD, Bamako, No. 16.

Findley, S. E. (1992) 'Circulation as a drought coping strategy in rural Mali', in Calvin Goldscheider (ed.), *Population Distribution and Migration in Developing Countries*, Boulder, CO: Westview Press.

Findley, S. E. (1993) 'The Third World city: development policy and issues', in John D. Kasarda and Allan M. Parnell (eds), *Third World Cities: Problems, Policies and Prospects*, Beverly Hills, CA: Sage Publications.

Findley, S. E. and Diallo, A. 'Social appearances and economic realities of female migration in rural Mali', in *Feminization of Internal Migration*, New York: United Nations.

Findley, S. E. and Ouedraogo, D. (1993) 'North versus South: migration choices in the Senegal river valley', presented at the IUSSP International Conference, Montreal, Canada.

Findley, S. E. and Williams, L. (1991) 'Women who go and women who stay: reflections of family migration processes in a changing world', World Employment Program Working Paper, Geneva: International Labour Office.

Findley, S. E., Traore, S., Quedraogo, D. and Diaira, S. (1995) 'Emigration from the Sahel', *International Migration*, 33(3/4): 469–520.

Finnegan, G. A. (1980) 'Employment opportunity and migration among the Mossi of Upper Volta', *Research in Economic Anthropology*, Vol. 3, Greenwich, CT: JAI Press, pp. 291–322.

Foote, K. and Martin, L. G. (eds) (1993) *Family and Development: Summary of an Expert Meeting*, Washington, DC: National Headery Press.

Franqueville, A. (1987) *Une Afrique entre le village et la ville: les migrations dans le Sud du Cameroun*, Collections Mémoires No. 109, Paris: Editions ORSTOM.

Frondeville, A. L. de (1987) 'Une alliance tumultueuse: les commerçantes maliennes du Dakar-Niger et les agents de l'Etat', *Cahiers des Sciences humaines*, 23(1): pp. 89–103.

Gandaho T. (1992) 'Trends in marriage: dissolution and living with husband among currently married women in selected African countries (Senegal, Ghana and Kenya)', London School of Hygiene and Tropical Medicine, unpublished memo.

Gluckman, M. (1943) *Essays on LOZI Land and Royal Property*. Rhodes-Livingstone Papers, No. 10. Livingstone, N. Rhodesia [Zambia]: Rhodes Livingstone Institute.

Goldschmidt-Clermont, L. (1987) *Economic Evaluations of Unpaid Household Work: Africa, Asia, Latin America and Oceania*, Geneva: ILO.

Goldschmidt-Clermont L. (1990) 'Economic measurement of non-market household activities: is it feasible?', *International Labour Review*, 129(3).

Goldschmidt-Clermont L. (1994) 'Assessing women's economic contributions in domestic and related activities', in A. Adepoju and C. Oppong (eds), *Gender, Work and Population in Sub-Saharan Africa*, London: ILO/James Currey.

Goode, W. J. (1963) *World Religion and Family Patterns*, New York: Macmillan.

Goody, J. (1990) 'Futures of the family in rural Africa', in G. McNicoll, and M. Cain (eds), *Rural Development and Population: Institutions and Policy* (Supplement to *Population and Development Review*, 15), New York: Oxford University Press.

Gorman, R. F. (1986) 'Beyond ICARA II: Implementing Refugee-related Development Assistance', *International Migration Review* 20(2): 283–98.

Greenhalgh S. (1990) 'Towards a political economy of fertility', New York: Population Council Working Paper No. 12.

Greenhalgh S. (1991) 'Women in the informal enterprise: Empowerment or exploitation?', New York: Population Council Working Paper No. 33.

Gregory, J. (1989) 'L'insertion des migrantes et des migrants en ville: intérrogations méthodologiques', in Philippe Antoine and Sidiki Coulibaly, (eds) *L'insertion urbaine des migrants en Afrique*, Actes du Séminaire CRDI-ORSTOM-URD, 10–14 Février 1987, Lomé. Paris: Collection Colloques et Séminaires, Editions ORSTOM: pp. 161–72.

Gregory, J. and Piche, V. (1993) 'African Return Migration: Past, Present and Future', *Contemporary Marxism*, 7, Fall: 169–83.

Griffiths, A. (1987) 'Support for women with dependent children: customary, common and statutory law in Botswana', in A. Armstrong and W. Ncube (eds), *Women and Law in Southern Africa*, Harare: University of Zimbabwe Press.

Gubry, P. (1989) 'Rétention de la population et développement en milieu rural: les paysans Bamileke de L'Ouest du Cameroun', XXI EME Congrès international de la Population, New Delhi: UIESP.

Gugler, J. and Flanagan, W. G. (1978) *Urbanization and Social Change in West Africa*, Cambridge: Cambridge University Press.

Guinguido, J. K. Gaye (1990) 'Le phénomène urbain au Bénin: causes, conséquences et rôle des migrations internes dans la croissance de Cotonou', in UAPS, *Spontaneous Contributions to the Conference on The Role of Migration in African Development*, Nairobi, Kenya: Union for African Population Studies, pp. 440–9.

Guinguido, J. K. Gaye, (1992) *La mesure de l'impact des migrations sur l'évolution des ménages: Le cas du Bénin*, Louvain-la-Neuve: Academie-Erasme.

Guyer, J. I. and Peters, P. E. (eds) (1986) *Conceptualizing the Household: Issues of Theory, Method and Application*, New York: American Council of Learned Societies.

Gyepi-Garbrah, B. (1985) *Adolescent Fertility in Sub-Saharan Africa: An Overview*, Boston, MA: Pathfinder Fund.

Hammerslough C. R. (1991) 'Women's groups and contraceptive use in rural Kenya', paper presented at the IUSSP Seminar on the Course of Fertility Transition in Sub-Saharan Africa, Harare (November).

Hans-Egil, H. (1974), *Luo Religion and Folklore*, Oslo/Bergen, Universitets forlaget; Munksgaard and Copenhagen, Scandinavian University Books.

Harbison, S. F. (1981) 'Family structure and family strategy in migration decision making', in Gordon F. DaJong and Robert W. Gardner (eds), *Migration Decision Making: Multidisciplinary Approaches to Microlevel Studies in Developed and Developing Countries*, New York: Pergamon Press, pp. 225–51.

Hart, K. (1973) 'Informal income opportunities and urban employment in Ghana', *Journal of Modern African Studies*, 11: 61–89.

Hart, K. (1987) 'Rural–urban migration in West Africa', in Jeremy Eades (ed.), *Migrants, Workers and the Social Order*, London/New York: Tavistock Publications, pp. 65–81.

Hawthorn, G. (1970) *The Sociology of Fertility*, London: Macmillan.

Henin, R. (1981) *Population, Development and Economic Planning*, PSRI, University of Nairobi.

Henn, J. K. (1983) 'Feeding the cities and feeding the peasants: What role for Africa's women farmers? *World Development* 11(12).

Henn, J. K. (1985) 'Economic ties between peasant and worker: the Beti woman's real labor and the urban wage', in Jean-Claude Burbig (ed.), *Femmes du Cameroon: Meres Pacifiques, Femmes Rebelles*, Paris: ORSTOM/Karthala, pp. 393–400.

Herry, C. (1989) 'Insertion des migrants en milieu urbain: L'exemple de Maradi', in Philippe Antoine and Sidiki Coulibaly, (eds), *L'insertion urbaine des migrants en Afrique*, Actes du Séminaire CRDI-ORSTOM-URD, 10–14 Février 1987, Lomé. Paris: Collection Colloques et Séminaires, Editions ORSTOM: pp. 41–54.

Herry, C. (1991) 'Quelques aspects des relations villes-village', in A. Quesnel and P. Vimards (eds), *Migration, changements sociaux, et développement*, Paris: Collection Colloque et Séminaires, Editions ORSTOM, pp. 231–42.

Herskovits, J. M. (1964) *Economic Transition in Africa*, London: Holt, Rinehart and Winston

Herz, B. (1989) 'Women in development: Kenya's experience', *Finance and Development*, June, pp. 43–5.

Hill, A. and Thiam, A. (1987) 'Marriage, inheritance and fertility management amongst the Malian Fulani', in *The Cultural Roots of African Fertility Regimes*, Proceedings of the Ife Conference, Ile-Ife, Nigeria.

Hirschmann, D. and Vaughan, M., (1984) *Women Farmers of Malawi: Food Production in the Zomba District*, Institute of International Studies, University of California, Research Series, 58.

Hobcraft J. (1992) 'Women's education, child welfare and child survival', paper presented at Expert Group Meeting on Population and Women, Gaborone (June).

Hunt, C. W., (1989) 'Migrant labor and sexually transmitted disease: AIDS in Africa', *Journal of Health and Social Behavior*, 30: 353–73.

Hunter, G. (1962) 'The new societies of tropical Africa', in Sand Pottenberg (ed.), *Culture and Societies of Africa*, New York: Free Press.

ILO (1976) *Employment, Growth and Basic Needs: A One-World Problem*, Report to the World Employment Conference of 1976, Geneva.

ILO (1990) *African Employment Report 1989*, Jobs and Skills Programme for Africa, Addis Ababa: ILO.

ILO (1991) *African Employment Report 1990*, Jobs and Skills Programme for Africa, Addis Ababa: ILO.

Ingstad, B. (1994) 'The grand mother and household viability in Botswana', in A. Adepoju and C. Oppong (eds), *Gender Work and Population in Sub-Saharan Africa*, London: ILO, James Currey and Heinnman.

International Labour Office (1988) 'Report II, rural and urban training in Africa', in *Record of the Seventh African Regional Conference*, Harare.

International Labour Office (1989) 'Report III, cooperatives', in *Record of the Seventh African Regional Conference*, Harare, 1988.

Isiugo-Abanihe, U. C. (1985) 'Child fosterage in West Africa', *Population and Development Review*, 11(1): 53–73.

Isiugo-Abanihe, U. C. (1987) 'High bridewealth and age at marriage in Igboland, in *The Cultural Roots of African Fertility Regimes*, Proceedings of the Ile-Ife Conference.

Isiugo-Abanihe, U. C., Ebigbola, J. A. and Adewuyi, A. A. (1991) 'Urban nuptiality patterns and marital fertility in Nigeria', in *Commissioned Papers, Conference on Women, Family and Population, Volume 1*, Ouagadougou: UAPS.

Ityavyar, D. A. and Ogba, L. O. (1989) 'Violence, Conflict and Health in Africa', *Social Science and Medicine*, 28(7): 649–57.

Izzard, W. J. (1992) *The impact of migration on the roles of women*, Gaborone, Botswana: Government Printers, pp. 654–715.

Jules-Rosette, B. (1985) 'The Women Potters of Lusaka: Urban Migration and Socio-

Economic Adjustment', in Beverly Lindsay (ed.), *African Migration and National Development*, Penn State University Press.

Karlin L. D. (1992) *Obstacles to Women's Entrepreneurship in Africa*, Geneva: ILO, Small Enterprise Development Programme.

Kasonde-N'gandu, S., Bbuku-Chuulu, M., Mbozi, E., Musanya, P., Mwenda, W. and Muyoywe, E (1994) *Inheritance in Zambia: Law and Practice*, Lusaka: WLSA.

Kayongo-Male, D. and Onyango, P. (eds) (1984) *The Sociology of the African Family*, London: Longman.

Kershaw, G. (1975) 'The changing roles of men and women in the Kikuyu family by socio-economic status', *Rural Africana*, 29.

Khasiani, S. A. (1989) 'The impact of refugees in receiving countries in Africa: the cases of refugee women and refugee professionals', in Reginald Appleyard (ed.), *The Impact of International Migration on Developing Countries*, Paris: OECD Publications.

Kikhela, N. (1990) 'Les conditions socio-économiques d'insertion des migrants dans la vie en ville: cas de l'agglomération urbaine de Kinshasa (Zaïre)', in UAPS, *Spontaneous Contributions to the Conference on The Role of Migration in African Development*, Nairobi, Kenya: Union for African Population Studies, pp. 480–92.

Kilbride, P. L. (1986) 'Cultural persistence and socio-economic change among the Abaluya: some modern problems in patterns of child care', *Journal of Eastern African Research and Development*, Vol. 16, Nairobi, Kenya: Gideon S. Were Press, pp. 35–52.

Kilbride, P. L. (1990) *Changing Family Life in East Africa: Women and Children at Risk*, Pennsylvania State University Press (with J. E. Kilbride) (1993 reprinted Nairobi: Gideon Were Press).

Kilbride, P. L. (1992) 'Stigma, role overload and the delocalization of family tradition: problems facing the contemporary Kenyan woman', presented at International Conference, *Ecological and Cultural Change and Human Development in Western Province and Western Kenya*, Golf Hotel, Kakamega, Kenya (with J. Kilbride), August.

Kilbride, P. L. and Janet Capriotti Kilbride (1990) *Changing Family Life in East Africa: Women and Children at Risk*, Pennsylvania State University Press, PA.

Klu, F. E. (1990) 'Urban migration and its linkages in selected urban systems in Liberia: policies, issues and considerations', in UAPS, *Spontaneous Contributions to the Conference on The Role of Migration in African Development*, Nairobi, Kenya: Union for African Population Studies, pp. 505–34.

Kossoudji, S. and Mueller, E. (1983) 'The economic and demographic status of female-headed households in rural Botswana', *Economic Development and Cultural Change*, 31(4): 831–59.

Kothari, D. K. (1982) 'Household structure and migration behaviour in India', paper presented at Population Aaaociation of America, San Diego.

Kumekpor, T. (1972) *Marriage and Family in a Changing Society*. Legon Family Research Papers, No. 3, Legon: Institute of African Studies.

Kurubally, M. A. (1990) 'Labour migration in Lesotho – its implications on the national socio-economic development', in UAPS, *Spontaneous Contributions to the Conference on The Role of Migration in African Development*, Nairobi, Kenya: Union for African Population Studies, pp. 168–80.

Labaran, A. (1986) 'Correlates of agrarian capitalism: land appropriation, concentration and the emergent agricultural structure in the Sokoto region', unpublished MS thesis, Bayero University, Kano.

Lacey, L. (1986) 'Women in the development process: occupational mobility of female migrants in cities in Nigeria', *Journal of Comparative Family Studies*, XVII, (1): pp. 1–18.

Lalou, R. and Piche, V. (1994) Migration et Sida en Afrique de l'Ouest, un état des connaissances, Les Dossiers du CEPED No. 28, Paris.

Lauby, J. and Oded, S. (1989) 'Individual migration as a family strategy: young women in the Philippines', in *Economic Development and Cultural Change*, 38.

Lesthaege, R. J. (ed.) (1989) *Reproduction and Social Organization in Sub-Saharan Africa*, Berkeley, CA: University of California Press.

Lesthaege, R., Kaufman, G. and Meekers, D. (1989) 'The nuptuality regimes in sub-Saharan Africa', in R. Lesthaege (ed.), *Reproduction and Social Organisation in Africa*, Berkeley, CA: University of California Press.

Letuka, P., Matashane, K., Mohale, M., Mamashela, M. and Mbatha, L. (1994) *Inheritance in Lesotho*, Maseru: WLSA.

Lloyd, C. B. (1991) 'The contribution of the world fertility surveys to an understanding of the relationship between women's work and fertility studies', *Family Planning*, 22(3, May/June).

Lloyd, C. B. and Gage-Brandon, A. (1993) 'Women's Role in Maintaining Households: Family Welfare and Sexual Inequality in Ghana', *Population Studies*, 47: 115–31.

Locoh, T. (1988a) 'Structures familiales et changements sociaux', in Dominique Tabutin (ed.), *Population et société en Afrique au Sud du Sahara*, Paris: Editions Harmattans, pp. 441–79.

Locoh, T. (1988b) 'The evolution of the family in Africa', in E. Van de Walle et al. (eds), *The State of African Demography*, Liège: IUSSP.

Locoh, T. (1991) 'Structures familiales d'accueil des migrants et développement des structures familiales multipolaires en Afrique', in Andres Quesnel and Patrice Vimards (eds), *Migration, changements sociaux, et développement*, Paris: Collection Colloque et Séminaires, Editions ORSTOM, pp. 279–96.

Lootvoet, B. (1989) 'Quelques éléments de réflexion sur le financement des activités des artisans et petits commercants en milieu urbain ivoirien', in Philippe Antoine and Sidiki Coulibaly (eds), *L'insertion urbaine des migrants en Afrique*, Actes du Séminaire CRDI-ORSTOM-URD, 10–14 Février 1987, Lomé. Paris: Collection Colloques et Séminaires, Editions ORSTOM: pp. 135–46.

Lule, E. L. (1991) 'Marriage and marital fertility in rural Swaziland', in A. Adepoju (ed.), *Swaziland: Population, Economy, Society*, New York: UNFPA.

Lututala, M. (1990) 'Migrations et développement en Afrique: quelques aspects méthodologiques', in UAPS, *African Population Studies*, No. 4, Union for African Population Studies, pp. 101–20.

Lwoga, C. (1985) 'Seasonal labour migration in Tanzania: the case of Ludewa district', in Guy Standing (ed.), *Labour Circulation and the Labour Process*, London: Croom Helm, pp. 120–54.

Ly, B. (1981) 'African youth between tradition and modernity', in UNESCO *Youth in the 1980s*, Paris: UNESCO Press.

Lynch (1984) *Craftswomen of Kerala*, Women, Work and Development Series, Geneva: ILO.

Mabogunje, A. L. (1990) 'Agrarian responses to outmigration in sub-Saharan Africa', in Geoffrey McNicoll and Mead Cain (eds), *Rural Development and Population: Institutions and Policy* (Supplement to *Population and Development Review* 15), New York: Oxford University Press.

Maboreke, M. (1986) 'Violence against wives: a crime *sui generis*', *Zimbabwe Law Review*, 4(1–2): 88–111.

McDaniel, A. (1990) 'The family and internal migration in Africa: an essay', in UAPS, *Spontaneous Contributions to the Conference on The Role of Migration in African Development*, Nairobi, Kenya: Union for African Population Studies, pp. 450–67.

Macro International (1992) *Demographic Health Survey. A Summary Report for Selected African Countries.*

Mainet, G. (1985) 'Le rôle de la femme dans l'économie urbaine Douala: exemples du Quartier Akwa et de la Zone Nylon', in Jean-Claude Barbier (ed.), *Femmes du Cameroun: mères pacifiques, femmes rebelles*, Paris: Orstom-Karthala, pp. 369–83.

Mair, L. P. (1969) *African Marriage and Social Change.* Oxford: Oxford University Press.

Makannah, T. J. (1990) 'Policy Measures for Stemming Urban in-Migration in Sub-Saharan Africa', in UAPS, *The Role of Migration in African Development: Issues and Policies for the 90s*, Commissioned Papers for The Role of Migration in African Development, Nairobi: Union for African Population Studies, pp. 82–95.

Makinwa, P. K. (1981) *Internal Migration and Rural Development in Nigeria: Lessons from Bendel State*, Ibadan, Nigeria: Heinemann Educational Books Limited.

Makinwa, P. K. (1985) 'The socio-economic contribution of Nigerian women to national development', paper presented at the Seminar on Nigerian Women and National Development, Institute of African Studies, University of Ibadan.

Makinwa-Adebusoye, P. (1988) 'Labour migration and female-headed households', in IUSSP, *Conference on Women's Position and Demographic Change in the Course of Development*, Oslo: International Union for the Scientific Study of Population (Liège).

Makinwa-Adebusoye, P. (1990) 'Female migration in Africa: an overview', in UAPS, *The Role of Migration in African Development: Issues and Policies for the 90s*, Commissioned Papers for The Role of Migration in African Development. Nairobi: Union for African Population Studies, pp. 198–211.

Makinwa-Adebusoye, P. (1991) 'Changes in the costs and benefits of children to their parents: the changing cost of educating children', paper prepared for seminar on the Course of Fertility Transition in Sub-Saharan Africa, Harare, Zimbabwe: 19–22 November.

Makinwa-Adebusoye P. and Olawoye, J. (1992) 'Gender issues in the nexus between population growth, agricultural stagnation and environmental degradation in Nigeria', paper prepared for the World Bank.

Maldonado C. (1989) *The underdogs of the urban economy join forces: Results of an ILO programme in Mali, Rwanda and Togo.*

Malinowski, B. (1929) *The Sexual Life of Savages*, London: London University Press.

Marcoux, R. (1990) 'Structure démographique des ménages en milieu urbain africain: analyse des tendances, étude du cas malien et approches conceptuelles', in UAPS, *Spontaneous Contributions to the Conference on The Role of Migration in African Development*, Nairobi, Kenya: Union for African Population Studies, pp. 199–213.

Marguerat, Y. (1987) 'La place des villes dans les cheminements migratoires', in Philippe Antoine and Sidiki Coulibaly (eds), *L'insertion urbaine des migrants en Afrique*, Actes du Séminaire CRDI-ORSTOM-URD, 10–14 Février, 1987, Lomé. Paris: Collection Colloques et Séminaires, Editions ORSTOM: pp. 173–82.

Marindo-Ranganai, R. (1994) 'Trends in polygynous unions among currently married women in selected African countries: Kenya, Ghana and Senegal', in UNECA, *Third African Population Conference Vol. 3 Conference Papers, Second Part*, Addis Ababa: pp. 145–61.

Marwick (1940) *The Swazi*, London: Frank Cass & Co.

Massey, D. S. (1990) 'Social structure, household strategies, and the cumulative causation of migration', *Population Index*, 56(1): Spring, pp. 3–26.

Mbiti, J. S. (1969) *African Religions and Philosophy*, London, Ibadan, Nairobi, Lusaka: Heinemann Books.

Mboya, P. (1938) *Luo Kitgi Gitimbegi*, Nairobi: East African Publishing House.

Mbugua, W. (1992) 'The dynamics and structure of family formation in Africa', in *The*

Structure and Dynamics of Family Formation in Africa, Dakar: Union for African Population Studies.

Meekers, D. (1992) 'The Process of Marriage in African Societies: A Multiple Indicator Approach', *Population and Development Review*, 18(1): 61–78.

Meintjes, E. F. 'Families in transition – the changing South African situation', in N. B. Leidenfrost (ed.), *Families in Transition*, International Federation for Home Economics.

Mensah-Bonsu H. (1991) 'The law and the family and population policies', in UAPS, *Commissioned Papers, Conference on Women, Family and Population, Volume 1*, Ouagadougou: UAPS.

Mensah-Bonsu, H. (1993) 'The maintenance of child decree – some implications for child welfare and development', unpublished seminar paper.

Mfoulou, Raphael (1989) 'Afrique subsaharienne: tendances migratoires récentes en Afrique noire francophone', in M. Benoit and A. Lamotte (eds), *Actes du Séminare scientifiques sur les tendances migratoires actuelles et l'insertion des migrants dans les pays de la francophone*, Québec: Les Publications du Québec, pp. 73–89.

Mhloyi M. M. (1991) 'Fertility transition in Zimbabwe', paper presented at the IUSSP Seminar on the Course of Fertility Transition in Sub-Saharan Africa, Harare (November).

Mhloyi, M. M. (1994) 'Changing factors affecting fertility decisions in Africa', in UNECA *Third African Population Conference Vol. 3; Conference Papers, Second Part*, Addis Ababa: UNECA, pp. 202–15.

Mijere, N. J. (1990) 'Migration and regional integration: the Case of SADCC', in UAPS, *The Role of Migration in African Development: Issues and Policies for the 90s*, Commissioned Papers for The Role of Migration in African Development, Nairobi: Union for African Population Studies, pp. 257–70.

Mincer, J. (1978) 'Family migration decisions', *Journal of Political Economy*, 86(5): pp. 749–73.

Minvielle, J. P. (1985) *Paysans migrants du Fouta Toro: la Vallée du Sénégal*, Travaux et Documents No. 191, Paris: Editions de l'ORSTOM.

Mitchell, C. J. (1969) 'Structural plurality, urbanization, and labour circulation in southern Rhodesia', in J. A. Jackson (ed.), *Migration*, Cambridge: Cambridge University Press.

Moore, S. (1978) 'Law and social change: the semi-autonomous field as an appropriate field of study', *Law and Society Review*, 7: 719–46.

Morris, P. et al. (1969) *Family and Social Change in an African City*, London: Routledge and Kegan Paul.

Morrison, B. M. (1980) 'Rural household livelihood strategies in a Sri Lankan village', *Journal of Development Studies*, 16(4): 443–62.

Mueller, M. (1977) 'Women and men, power and powerlessness in Lesotho', *Signs*, 3(1): 154–66.

Mukras, M. Sc. and Oucho, J. O. (1985) 'Resource mobilization and the household economy in Kenya', in *Canadian Journal of African Studies*, 19(2): 401–21.

Mukras, M. S. and Oucho, J. (1986), 'Rural-urban migration in Kenya: the case study of Kericho tea estates complex in a regional setting', *Geografisia Annaler*, 66B(2): 123–4.

Mulugeta, H., (1990) 'Emigration and urbanization in Ethiopia', in UAPS, *Spontaneous Contributions to the Conference on The Role of Migration in African Development*, Nairobi, Kenya: Union for African Population Studies, pp. 298–309.

Murray, C. (1981) *Families Divided: The Impact of Migration in Lesotho*, African Studies Series No. 29, Cambridge: Cambridge University Press.

Nelson, E. R. (1976) 'African rural–urban migration economic choice theory and Kinshasa evidence', unpublished PhD dissertation, Yale University.

Nelson, N. (1987) 'Rural–urban child fostering in Kenya: migration, kinship ideology, and class', in Jeremy Eades (ed.), *Migrants, Workers & the Social Order*, London/New York: Tavistock Publications, pp. 181–98.

Nelson, N. (1992) 'The women who have left and those who have stayed behind: rural–urban migration in central and western Kenya', in Sylvia Chant (ed.), *Gender and Migration in Developing Countries*, London/New York: Belhaven Press, pp. 109–38.

Newbury, M. C. (1984) 'Ebutumwa Bw'Emiogo: the tyranny of cassava: a women's tax revolt in eastern Zaire', *Canadian Journal of African Studies*, 18(1): 35–54.

Ngondo, a P. (1992) 'Nuptialité et structure familiale en Afrique au Sud du Sahara', in UAPS, *The Structure and Dynamics of Family Formation in Africa*, Dakar: Union for African Population Sutudies.

Ngongko, W. (1990) 'Labour migration and regional economic cooperation and integration in Africa', in UAPS, *The Role of Migration in African Development: Issues and Policies for the 90s*, Commissioned Papers for The Role of Migration in African Development, Nairobi: Union for African Population Studies, pp. 238–56.

N'Guessan, K. and Zanou, B. (1990) 'Migration et développement agricole en Côte D'Ivoire', in UAPS, *Spontaneous Contributions to the Conference on The Role of Migration in African Development*, Union for African Population Studies, Nairobi, Kenya: 24–28 February, pp. 57–69.

Ngwe, E. (1990) 'Motivations et destinations des migrants ruraux de l'Ouest du Cameroun', in UAPS, *Spontaneous Contributions to the Conference on The Role of Migration in African Development*, Nairobi, Kenya: Union for African Population Studies, pp. 24–42.

Ngwe, E. (1991) 'Marginalisation socio-économique: facteur endogène de l'émigration rurale? Le cas de l'ouest et de l'extrême-nord du Cameroun', in Andres Quesnel and Patrice Vimards (eds), *Migration, changements sociaux, et développement*, Collection Colloque et Séminaires, Paris: Editions ORSTOM, pp. 89–102.

Nigeria, *Demographic and Health Survey (1990)* Lagos: Federal Office of Statistics.

Noube, W. and Stewart, J. (eds) (1995) *Widowhood, Inheritance Laws, Customs and Practices in Southern Africa*, Harare: WLSA.

N'Sangou, A. (1985) 'La contribution des Buyiem Sell-am au développement', in Jean-Claude Barbiere (ed.), *Femmes de Cameroun: mères pacifiques, femmes rebelles*, Paris: Orstom-Karthala, pp. 385–92.

OAU (1981) *Lagos Plan of Action for Economic Development of Africa, 1980–2000*, Addis Ababa: OAU.

OAU (1991) 'Declaration of the Twenty-seventh Ordinary Session of the Assembly of Heads of State and Government on the Employment Crisis in Africa', AHG/DECL.1 (XXVII).

Obbo, C. (1980a) 'Migration,' in *African Women: Their Struggle for Economic Independence*, London: Zed Press, pp. 70–86.

Obbo, C. (1980b) 'Strategies for urban survival', in *African Women: Their Struggle for Economic Independence*, London: Zed Press, pp. 101–21.

Obudho, R. A. (1981) *Urbanization and Development Planning in Kenya*, Nairobi: Kenya Literature Bureau.

Obunga, A. (1987) *Kinship Dependence in an Urban Setting: A Case Study of Buru Buru Estate*, Nairobi: PSRI, University of Nairobi.

Ocholla-Ayayo, A. B. C. (1970) 'Vyvoy Cloveka a Jeho Kulture ve Vychonic Africe', M.Sc. thesis, Prague University.

Ocholla-Ayayo, A. B. C. (1976) *Traditional Ideology and Ethics Among the Southern Luo*, Uppsala: Scandinavian Institute of African Studies (SIAS).

Ocholla-Ayayo, A. B. C. (1980) *The Luo Culture: A Reconstruction of The Material Culture Patterns of an African Traditional Society*, Wiesbaden: Franz Steiner Verlag GMBH.

Ocholla-Ayayo, A. B. C. (1984) 'Socio-cultural dynamics in rural development in Kenya', Tekuza Research Paper Series No. 4, University of Nairobi.

Ocholla-Ayayo, A. B .C. (1985) 'Ethnics, customs and population control in Kenya', Working Paper No. 5, Nairobi: PSRI, University of Nairobi.

Ocholla-Ayayo, A. B. C. (1986) 'Culture and society: its forms of marriage and reproduction moral codes in Kenya', Nairobi: PSRI, University of Nairobi.

Ocholla-Ayayo, A. B. C. (1987) 'Death and burial: an anthropological perspective', in J. B. Ojwang and J. N. K. Mugambi (eds), *The S.M. Otiendo Case: Death and Burial in Modern Kenya*, Nairobi: Nairobi University Press.

Ocholla-Ayayo, A. B. C. (1988a) 'Marriage patterns in Kenya and their inter-relations with fertility', in proceeding of African Population Conference, Dakar: UAPS, Belgium: IUSSP.

Ocholla-Ayayo, A. B. C. (1988b) 'Polygyny and family planning in Kenya', in Khama Rogo (ed.), *A Manual of Clinical Family Planning Practices*, Ministry of Health, Nairobi: Kenya Medical Association.

Ocholla-Ayayo, A. B. C. (1989) 'Urban development without planning: a case study of Migori town in western Kenya', in *City of the Future*, Vol. 1, 7th Era Congress, Rotterdam.

Ocholla-Ayayo, A. B. C. (1990) 'The state of childlessness in African marriage: a Deterring force against family planning efforts', in Elias H. O. Ayiemba (ed.), *Kenya Marriage in Transition*, Population Studies and Research Institute (PSRI), University of Nairobi.

Ocholla-Ayayo, A. B. C. (1991) 'The spirit of a nation: an analysis of policy, ethics and customary rules of conduct for regulating fertility levels in Kenya', Nairobi: Shivikon Publishers.

Ocholla-Ayayo, A. B. C. and Igbozurike, M. (1973) 'Leadership and the masses in Africa south of Sahara: a historical approach to the study of under-development', unpublished seminar paper, S.D. Uppsala University, Doctoral Seminar, October 1973.

Ocholla-Ayayo, A. B. C. and Obunga, A. (1987) 'The impact of kinship ties in the process of urbanization in Kenya', in Proceedings of International Workshop at Uppsala: SIAS, 7–10 Sept. 1987.

Ocholla-Ayayo, A. B. C. and Otticno, J. A. M. (1987) 'Socio-cultural codes of fertility differentials in Kenya', in E. van de Walle and J. A. Ebigbola (eds), *Proceedings of the Ife Conference on True Determinants of African Fertility*, Belgium: IUSSP.

Ocholla-Ayayo, A. B. C. and Ottieno J. A. M. (1988) 'Anthropological techniques for demographic field studies in Kenya', in *Proceedings of African Population Conference, Vol. 3*, Belgium: IUSSP.

Ohadike, P. O. and Teklu, T. (1990) 'Migration and shelter in a suburban African setting', in UAPS, *The Role of Migration in African Development: Issues and Policies for the 90s*, Commissioned Papers for The Role of Migration in African Development, Nairobi: Union for African Population Studies, pp. 156–80.

Okojie, C. E. E. (1984) 'Female migrants in the urban labor market: Benin City, Nigeria', *Canadian Journal of African Studies*, 18(3): 547–62.

Okojie, C. E. E. (1990) 'Migrants in an urban labour activity in Nigeria: trade and commerce in Benin City,' in UAPS, *Spontaneous Contributions to the Conference on The Role of Migration in African Development*, Nairobi, Kenya: Union for African Population Studies, pp. 468–79.

Okoth-Ogendo, H. W. O. (1989) 'The effects of migration on family structures in Sub-Saharan Africa', *International Migration*, XXVII(2) June.

Ominde, S. H., Ocholla-Ayayo, A. B. C. and Oyieng, J. C. (1983) 'Population survey on nutrition/health and family planning of peri-urban population of Kisumu munici-pality', unpublished report, Nairobi: PSRI, University of Nairobi.

Opoku, A. K. (1990) 'Migration and rural development: a case study of Western region of Ghana', in UAPS, *Spontaneous Contributions to the Conference on The Role of Migration in African Development*, Nairobi, Kenya: Union for African Population Studies, pp. 98–114.

Oppong (1973) *Growing up in Dagbon*, Accra: Ghana Publishing Corporation.

Oppong, C. (ed.) (1983) *Female and Male in West Africa*, London: George Allen and Unwin.

Oppong C. (1985) 'Some aspects of anthropological contributions', in G. Farooq and Simmons (eds), *Fertility in Developing Countries: An Economic Perspective on Research and Policy Issues*, London: Macmillan.

Oppong C. (1987) 'Responsible fatherhood and birth planning', in C. Oppong (ed.), *Sex Roles, Population and Development in West Africa*. London: Currey.

Oppong, C. (1988) ' Les femmes africaines: des épouses, des mères et des travailleurs', in Dominique Tabutin (ed.), *Population et société en Afrique au Sud du Sahara*, Paris: Editions Harmattans, pp. 421–40.

Oppong, C. (1991a) 'Relationships between women's work and demographic behaviour: some research evidence in West Africa'. ILO WEP 2–21 Working Paper No. 175 Geneva: ILO.

Oppong, C. (1991b) 'Conjugal and parental roles in African families: old and new models', in UAPS, *Conference on Women, Family and Population* (Ouagadougou, 24–29 April 1991), Dakar: Union for African Population Studies.

Oppong, C. (1992a) 'African family systems in the context of socio-economic change', paper presented at the *Third African Conference*, Dakar, Senegal, 7–10 December 1992, UNECA POP/APC.3/92/Inf.5.

Oppong, C. (1992b) 'Traditional family systems in rural settings in Africa', in E. Berquo and P. Xenos (eds), *Family Systems and Cultural Change*, Oxford: Oxford University Press/Clarendon Press (for IUSSP).

Oppong, C. (1993) 'Socio-economic aspects of sex roles and reproductive health', in Union for African Population Studies, *Conference on Reproductive and Family Health in Africa*, 8–13 November, Dakar.

Oppong, C. (1994) 'African family systems in the context of socio-economic change', in *UNECA Third African Population Conference: Conference Papers*, Addis Ababa.

Oppong, C. and Abu K. (1987) *Seven Roles of Women: impact of education, migration and employment on Ghanaian mothers*, Women, Work and Development Series, No. 13, Geneva: ILO.

Oppong, C. and Bleek W. (1982) 'Economic models and having children: some evidence from Kwahu Ghana', *Africa*, 52(3).

Orubuloye, I. O. (1981) *Fertility and Child-Spacing Practices among Rural Yoruba Women of Nigeria*, Canberra: Australian National University.

Osirike, A. B., (1990) 'Labour migration in rural Nigeria: the state-of-the-art analysis of migrant farmers in Ndokwa local government area of Bendel State', in UAPS, *Spontaneous Contributions to the Conference on The Role of Migration in African Development*, Nairobi, Kenya: Union for African Population Studies.

Osirike, A. B. (1991) 'Migration, dual residence and survival strategy in a depressing rural economy: a study of migrants' families in Bendel State, Nigeria', in UAPS, *Spontaneous Contributions to the Conference on Women, Family and Population at Ougadougou, Burkina Faso, April 24–29, 1991*, Union for African Population Studies, Vol. 2, pp. 227–39

Oucho, J. (1990) 'Migration linkages in Africa: retrospect and prospects', in UAPS,

Conference on The Role of Migration in African Development Issues and Policies for the 90s (Commissioned Papers), Dakar: Union for African Population Studies.

Oucho, J. (1991) 'Migration, family formation and fertility: A potent research area for Africa', Commissioned Papers, Conference on Women, Family and Population, Vol. 1, Dakar: UAPS.

Oucho, J. O. and Gould, W. T. S. (1993) 'Internal migration, urbanization, and population distribution', in Karen A. Foote, Kenneth H. Hill and Linda G. Martin (eds), *Demographic Change in Sub-Saharan Africa*, National Academy Press, Washington, DC: pp. 256–96.

Ouedraogo, D. O. (1989) 'Quelques repères sur l'insertion économique des migrants dans les villes burkinabe', in Philippe Antoine and Sidiki Coulibaly (eds), *L'Insertion urbaine des migrants en Afrique*, Actes du Séminaire CRDI-ORSTOM-URD, 10–14 Février, 1987, Lomé. Paris: Collection colloques et séminaires, Editions ORSTOM: pp. 93–104.

Ouedraogo, D. O. (1990) 'Les mouvements de colonisation agricole dans les pays sahéliens: bilan et perspectives', in UAPS, *Spontaneous Contributions to the Conference on The Role of Migration in African Development*, Nairobi, Kenya: Union for African Population Studies, pp. 181–90.

Ouedraogo, D. O. (1992a) 'Migrations, réfugiés et vie de famille en Afrique', *Nations Unies Conseil économique et social, Commission économique pour l'Afrique, Troisième Conférence africaine sur la population*, Réunion des Experts, Dakar, Sénégal, 7–10 Décembre, pp. 1–24.

Ouedraogo, D. O. (1992b) 'Transferts de population et changements de rôles de la femme au Sahel', *Cahiers québecois de démographie*, 21(1): 151–66.

Page, H. (1988) 'Fertility and family planning in Africa', in E. Van de Walle et al. (eds), *The State of Africain Demography*, Liège: IUSSP.

Page, H. J. (1989) 'Child rearing versus child-bearing: co-residence of mother and child in Sub-Saharan Africa', in R. Lesthaeghe (ed.), *Reproduction and Social Organization in Africa*, Berkeley, CA: University of California Press.

Palmer, I. (1991) *Gender and Population in the Adjustment of African Economies: Planning for Change* (Women, Work and Development No. 19), Geneva: ILO.

Pebley, Anne and Mbugua, Wariara (1989) 'Polygyny and fertility in sub-Saharan Africa', in R. Lesthaege et al. (eds), *Reproduction and Social Organisation*, Berkeley, CA: University of California Press.

Phillips, A. (1953) *Survey of African Marriage and Family Life*, London: Oxford University Press for International African Institute.

Piche, V., Gregory, J. and Coulibaly, S. (1980) 'Vers une explication des courants migratoires voltaïques', in *Labour, Capital and Society*, 13(1): 76–103.

Pilon, M. and Pontie, G. (1991) 'Développement inégal et mobilité: le cas des Moba-Gurma du Nord Togo', in Andres Quesnel and Patrice Vimards (eds), *Migration, changements sociaux, et développement*, Paris: Collection colloque et Séminaires, Editions ORSTOM, pp. 103–25.

Popkin, B. and R. M. Doan (1990) 'Women's roles, time allocation and health', in J. C. Caldwell et al. (eds), *What We Know About the Health Transition: The Proceedings of an International Workshop, Volume II*, Canberra: Canberra Australian National University, Health Transition Centre.

Population Reference Bureau (1992) *Adolescent Women in Sub-Saharan Africa: A Chart-Book on Marriage and Child-Bearing*, Washington, DC: Population Reference Bureau.

Population Reference Bureau (1992) *Adolescent Women in Sub-Saharan Africa*, Washington, DC.

Postel E. (1992) 'The value of women, women's autonomy, population and policy trends', paper presented at Expert Group Meeting on Population and Women, Gaborone (June).

Pottier, Johanne (1988) *Migrants No More: Settlement and Survival in Mambwe Villages Zambia*, Bloomington, IN: Indiana University Press.

Poulter, S. (1979) *Legal Dualism in Lesotho*, Roma: Morija.

Radcliffe-Brown, A. R. and Daryll Forde (eds) (1950) *African Systems of Kinship and Marriage*, London: Oxford University Press for International African Institute.

Rees J. R. (ed.) (1959) *Africa: Social Change and Mental Health*, New York: The Free Press.

Rempel, H. and Lobdell, R. A. (1978) 'The role of urban-to-rural remittance in rural development', *Journal of Development Studies*, 14(3): 324–41.

République du Mali, Direction Nationale de la Statistique et de l'Informatique (1990) *Recensement général de la population et de l'habitat: résultats définitifs ensemble du pays*, Bamako: DNSI, Bureau de Recensement.

Rindfuss, R. R. and Van den Heuvel, Audrey (1990) 'Cohabitation: precursor to marriage or an alternative to being single?', *Population and Development Review*, 16(4): 703–26.

Roberts, S. (1972) *Restatement of Tswana Family Law*, London: Sweet and Maxwell.

Rogge, J. R. (1988) 'Africa's refugees: causes, solutions, and consequences', unpublished paper presented at the African Population Conference, Dakar, 7–12 November.

Rogge, J. R. and Akol, J. O. (1989) 'Repatriation: its role in resolving Africa's refugee dilemma', *International Migration Review*, 23(2): 184–200.

Rondeau, C. (1989) ' Les restauratrices de la nuit à Bamako, Mali', *Labour, Capital and Society*, 22(2): 262–87.

Rose, L. (1988) 'A woman is like a field', in J. Davidson (ed.), *Agriculture, Women and Land: The African Experience*, Boulder, CO and London: Westview.

Ruel, S. (1995) 'The scourge of land mines: UN factiles hidden peace time killers', *United Nations*, New York: Focus.

Russell, M. (1989) 'Kinship, homestead and the custody of Swazi children', Report to UNICEF, Mbabane.

Russell, S. S. (1993) 'International migration', in Karen A. Foote, Kenneth H. Hill and Linda G. Martin (eds), *Demographic Change in Sub-Saharan Africa*, Washington, DC: National Academy Press, pp. 297–349.

Rwezaura, B. (1992) 'From native law and custom to customary law: changing political uses of customary law in modern Africa', unpublished monograph.

Sadik, N. (1989) *The State of World Population 1989*, New York: UNFPA.

Sadik, N. (1991) *The State of World Population*, New York: United Nations Population Fund.

Safilios-Rothschild, C. (1986) *Socio-economic Indicators of Women's Status in Developing Countries, 1970–1980*. New York: The Population Council.

Saito, K. A. and Weidemann, C. J. (1990) *Agricultural Extension For Women Farmers in Africa* (World Bank Discussion Paper), Washington, DC: World Bank.

Sawadogo, R. C. (1990) 'La prise de décisions dans les migrations rurales: étude du statut du décideur dans les actes principaux du F'ait Migratoire', in UAPS, *Spontaneous Contributions to the Conference on The Role of Migration in African Development*, Nairobi, Kenya: Union for African Population Studies, pp. 79–97.

Sawadogo, R. C. (1992) 'Famille africaine d'hier et de demain: quelle compréhension pour quelles interrogations?', in UPAS, *The Structure and Dynamics of Family Formation in Africa*, Dakar: Union for African Population Studies.

Schapera, I. (1941) *Married Life in an African Tribe*, New York: Sheridan House.

Schapera, I. (1959) *A Handbook of Tswana Law and Custom*, London: Oxford University Press.

Schultheis, M. J. (1989) 'A symposium: Refugees in Africa – the Dynamics of Displacement and Repatriation', *African Studies Review*, 32(1): 1–69.

Scott, C. and Blacker, J. G. C. (1974) *Manual of Demographic Sample Surveys in Africa*, UNECA/UNESCO E/CN.14/CAS.7/17/Rev.2.

Seasay, I. M. (1990) 'Migration and urban growth in Sierra Leone: issues and policy options for the 1990s', in UAPS, *Spontaneous Contributions to the Conference on The Role of Migration in African Development*, Nairobi, Kenya: Union for African Population Studies, pp. 280–97.

Sembajwe, I. (1990) ' Effects of emigration to South Africa on Lesotho's demography and economy', in UAPS, *Spontaneous Contributions to the Conference on The Role of Migration in African Development*, Nairobi, Kenya: Union for African Population Studies, pp. 154–67.

Singelmann, J. (1991) 'Global assessment of levels and trends of female internal migration, 1960–1980', *United Nations Expert Group Meeting on the Feminization of Internal Migration*, Aguascalientes, Mexico, 22–25 October, pp. 1–34.

Smelser, N. J. (1967), *Sociology: An Introduction*, New York: Wiley International.

Smelser, N. J. (1970) *Industrialization and Society*, Paris: UNESCO Press.

Smith, M. G. (1965) 'The Hausa of northern Nigeria', in James L., Gibbs, Jr. (ed.), *Peoples of Africa*, New York: Holt, Rinehart and Winston.

Southall, A. W. (ed.) (1961) *Social Change in Modern Africa*, London: Oxford University Press.

Southall, A. W. and P. C. W. Gutkind, (1956) *Townsmen in the Making*, London: Macmillan Co.

Sow, B. (1990) 'Emigration du père et mortalité infanto-juvénile au Sénégal Oriental', in UAPS, *Spontaneous Contributions to the Conference on The Role of Migration in African Development*, Nairobi, Kenya: Union for African Population Studies, pp. 428–39.

Ssekamatte-Ssebuliba, J. B. (1992) 'Determinants of infant and child mortality in Uganda', unpublished PhD dissertation, Brown University, Providence, RI.

St. Pierre, M. H., Gregory, J. and Simmons, A. (1986) 'Structure démographique des ménages et comportement migratoire en Haute-Volta (Burkina Faso)', in D. Gauvreau, J. Gregory, M. Kempeneers and V. Piche (eds), *Démographie et sous-développement dans le Tiers-Monde*, Montreal: McGill University Press, pp. 111–42.

Standing, G. (ed.) (1985) *Labour Circulation and the Labour Process*, ILO-WEP study, London: Croom Helm.

Stark, O. (1984) 'Rural-to-urban migration in LDCs: a relative deprivation approach', *Economic Development and Cultural Change*, 32(3): 475–86.

Stichter, S. (1985) *Migrant Laborers*, Cambridge: Cambridge University Press.

Sudarkasa, N. et al. (1977) 'Women and migration in contemporary West Africa', in Wellesley Editorial Committee, *Women and National Development: The Complexities of Change*, Chicago: University of Chicago Press.

Sy, M. (1991) 'Migrations féminines selon les ethnies au Sénégal', in UAPS, *Spontaneous Contributions to the Conference on Women, Family and Population at Ougadougou, Burkina Faso, April 24–29, 1991*, Union for African Population Studies, Vol 2, March, pp. 285–304.

Tienda, M. and Booth, K. (1988) 'Migration, gender and social change: a review and reformulation', Population Research Center/NORC, paper prepared for *IUSSP Conference on Women's Position and Demographic Change in the Course of Development*, Oslo, Norway, pp. 1–31.

Toto, J. P. (1990) 'Brazzaville de 1974 à 1984: dix ans de migration et de croissance démographique', in UAPS, *Spontaneous Contributions to the Conference on The Role of*

Migration in African Development, Nairobi, Kenya: Union for African Population Studies, pp. 310–20.

Toure, A. (1985) *Les petits métiers à Abidjan: l'imagination au secours de la conjoncture*, Paris: Karthala.

Traore, S. (1991) 'Stratégie migratoire et structures des ménages dans la Vallée du Fleuve Sénégal', in UAPS, *Spontaneous Contributions to the Conference on Women, Family and Population at Ougadougou, Burkina Faso*, Union for African Population Studies, Vol. 2, pp. 117–30.

Trincaz, P. (1989) 'L'importance de la famille dans les processus d'insertion urbaine des Serer du Bassin arachidier', in Philippe Antoine and Sidiki Coulibaly (eds), *L'insertion urbaine des migrants en Afrique*, Actes du Séminaire CRDI-ORSTOM-URD, 10–14 Février, 1987, Lomé. Paris: Collection colloques et séminaires, Editions ORSTOM: pp. 33–40.

UAPS (1992) *The Structure and Dynamics of Family Formation in Africa*, Dakar.

Uchudi Masudi, L. (1990) 'Migrations internes et développement économique au Zaïre: un casse tête en terme d'aménagement du territoire', in UAPS, *Spontaneous Contributions to the Conference on The Role of Migration in African Development*, Nairobi, Kenya: Union for African Population Studies, pp. 43–56.

Ukaegbu, A. O. (1981) 'Marriage habits and fertility of women in tropical Africa: a socio-cultural prespective', in J. Dupaquier et al., *Marriage and Re-marriage in Populations of the Past*, New York: Academic Press, pp. 127–37.

UN (1965) *Universal Declaration of Human Rights*, Article 21, New York: UN.

UN (1985) 'Estimates and Projections of Urban, Rural and City Populations, 1950–2025: The 1982 Assessment,' New York: United Nations, Department of International Economic and Social Affairs, ST/ESA/SER.R/SB.

UN (1987) *The Family: National Family Policies: Their Relationship to the Role of the Family in the Development Process* (Vienna: Centre for Social Development and Humanitarian Affairs), New York: UN.

UN (1988) *First Marriage: Patterns and Determinants*, New York: UN.

UN (1989) *Adolescent Reproductive Behaviour Evidence from Developing Countries*, Vol. II, New York: UN.

UN (1990) *Patterns of First Marriage: Timing and Prevalence*, New York: UN.

UN (1991a) *1994 International Year of the Family*, New York: UN.

UN (1991b) 'Building the smallest democracy at the heart of society', Vienna: UN.

UN (1992) *Family Matters* (Occasional Papers Series), Vienna: Secretariat, International Year of the Family.

UNDP (1991) *Human Development Report 1991*, Oxford/New York: Oxford University Press.

UNDP (1992) *Human Development Report 1992*, Oxford/New York: Oxford University Press.

UNDP (1993) *Human Development Report 1993*, Oxford/New York: Oxford University Press.

UNDP (1994) *Human Development Report 1994*, Oxford/New York: Oxford University Press.

UNECA (1984) *Kilimanjaro Plan of Action for African Population and Self-Reliant Development*, Arusha, Tanzania, 9–13 January (Report of the Second African Population Conference).

UNECA (1992a) *Dakar/Ngor Declaration of Population Family and Sustainable Development*, Third African Population Conference, Dakar, Senegal, (7–12 September).

UNECA (1992b) *Study on Social Security System and National Development*, ECA/OAU, Sixth meeting of the conference of African Ministers for Social Affairs, Addis Ababa, Ethiopia, 18–23 May.

UNECA (1993) *Economic and Social Conditions in Africa 1990/91*, Addis Ababa, Statistical Annexes, Table 2, A-8.

UNECA (1994a) *Implementation of the Kilimanjaro Programme of Action and Dakar/Ngor Declaration on Population, Family and Sustainable Development*, paper submitted to the Eighth Session of the joint conference of African Planners, Statisticians and Demographers, 21–26 March, Addis Ababa, Ethiopia.

UNECA (1994b) 'Economic Report on Africa 1994', *The Social Situation*, document ECA/CM. 202.

UNECA (1994c) *Review of Economic and Social Conditions in Africa*, paper submitted to the Eighth Session of the Joint Conference of African Planners, Statisticians, and Demographers, 21–26 March, 1994, Addis Ababa, Ethiopia.

UNESCO (1956) *Social Implications of Industrialization and Urbanization in Africa South of Sahara*, Paris: UNESCO Press.

UNESCO (1981) 'Youth: their behaviour and their hopes' (synthesis report presented at the General Conference of UNESCO at its twenty-first session'), in *Youth in the 1980s*, Paris: The UNESCO Press.

UNFPA (1991) *Incorporating Women into Population and Development: Knowing Why and Knowing How*, New York: United Nations.

UNICEF (1992) *The State of the World's Children*, New York: Oxford University Press.

Uwaka, C. T. and Uwaegbute, A. C. (1982) 'The role and contribution of rural women to agricultural development in eastern Nigeria', *Journal of Education and Development*, 2(2): 447–61.

Vaa, M. (1989) 'Self-employed urban women: case studies from Bamako', *Journal of the Union for African Population Studies*, Vol. 2, Dakar: UAPS.

Vaa, M. (1991) 'Work, livelihoods and family responsibilities in urban poverty', in Kristi Anne Stolen and Mariken Vaa (eds), *Gender and Change in Developing Countries*, Oslo: Norwegian University Press, pp. 121–46.

Vaa, M., Findley, S. E. and Diallo, A. (1989) 'The gift economy: a study of women migrants' survival strategies in a low-income Bamako neighborhood', *Labour, Capital and Society*, 22(2): 234–60.

Van den Berghl (ed.) (1965) *Africa, Social Problems and Change and Conflict*, San Francisco, CA:.

Vimard, P. (1991) 'Migration et dynamique familiale: ethique du lien social ou logique de fragmentation?', in Andres Quesnel and Patrice Vimards (eds), *Migration, changements sociaux et développement*, Paris: Collection Colloque et séminaires, Editions ORSTOM, pp. 203–13.

Vimard, Patrice and Guillaume, Agnes (1991) 'Mobilités familiales et spatiales des enfants en Côte d'Ivoire', in *Migrations, Changements sociaux et développement*, Paris: Orstrom Editions, pp. 203–13.

Wagner, G. (1939) *The Changing Family among the Bantu Kavirondo*, Oxford: Oxford University Press.

Wagner, G. (1949) *The Bantu of Southern Kavirondo*, London: Oxford University Press.

Wagner, G. (1954) 'The Abaluyia of Kavirondo (Kenya)', in D. Forde (ed.), *African World: Ideas and Social Values of African Peoples*, London: Oxford University Press.

Watkins, S. C. (1991) 'More lessons from the past: women's formal networks and fertility decline', paper presented at the IUSSP Seminar on the Course of Fertility Transition in Sub-Saharan Africa, Harare (November).

Weber, M. (1949) *The Methodology of the Social Sciences*, Glencoe: The Free Press.

Weisner, T. S. (1976) 'The structure of sociability: urban migration and urban-rural ties in Kenya', *Urban Anthropology*, 5(2): 199–223.

Weist, R. E. (1973) 'Wage labor migration and the household in a Mexican town', *Journal of Anthropological Research*, 29(3): 180–209.

Welsh, Dagnino and Sachs (1987) 'Transforming family law: new directions in Mozambique', in A. Armstrong (ed.), *Women and Law in Southern Africa*, Harare: Zimbabwe Publishing House.

WHO (1990) *AIDS and Family Planning*, Geneva: WHO.

Wirth, Louis (1938) 'Urbanism as a way of life', *American Journal of Sociology*, 44(18), July.

WLSA-Zimbabwe (1994) *Inheritance Laws: Customs and Practices in Zimbabwe*, Harare: WLSA.

Wood, C. H., (1981) 'Structural changes and household strategies: a conceptual framework for the study of rural migration', *Human Organization*, 40(4): 338–44.

Woodman, G. (1985) 'How state courts create customary law in Ghana and Nigeria', paper presented to the Commission on Folk Law and Legal Pluralism, Ottawa.

World Bank (1988) *Report of the Task Force on Food Security in Africa*, Washington, DC: World Bank.

Yamuah, M. (1990) 'Migration to Banjul and Kombo Saint Mary', in UAPS, *Spontaneous Contributions to the Conference on The Role of Migration in African Development*, Nairobi, Kenya: Union for African Population Studies, pp. 235–46.

Yapi, D. A. (1989) 'La périlleuse insertion des migrants à Abidjan: l'etat et les migrants face à la question du logement', in Philippe Antoine and Sidiki Coulibaly (eds), *L'insertion urbaine des migrants en Afrique*, Actes du Séminaire CRDI-ORSTOM-URD, 10–14 Février, 1987, Lomé. Paris: Collection colloques et séminaires, Editions ORSTOM: pp. 147–60.

Yeye, D. A. (1991) 'Stratégie de survie de la famille au Bénin durant la situation de crise de 1987 à 1989', in UAPS, *Spontaneous Contributions to the Conference on Women, Family and Population at Ougadougou, Burkina Faso*, Union for African Population Studies, Vol. 2, pp. 305–16.

Youssef, N. and Hetner, C. (1984) 'Rural households headed by women, a priority concern for development', *WEP Working Paper* 31. Geneva: ILO.

Zachariah, K. C. and Conde, J. (1981) *Migration in West Africa: Demographic Aspects* (Joint World Bank-OECD Study), Oxford: Oxford University Press.

Zambia (1992), *Demographic and Health Survey*, Lusaka: Central Statistics Office.

Zlotnik, H. (1993) 'South-to-North migration since 1960: the view from the South', in IUSSP, *Proceedings of the International Union for the Scientific Study of Population*, Vol. 2, Montreal, 24 Aug.–1 Sept., Liège, Belgium: pp. 3–14.

Index